Private Power
for the
Public Good

A History of the Carnegie Foundation
for the Advancement of Teaching

Ellen Condliffe Lagemann

With a new Foreword by Lee S. Shulman
President, The Carnegie Foundation
for the Advancement of Teaching

College Entrance Examination Board

New York

First printing, 1983
Wesleyan Paperback, 1988
College Board Paperback, 1999

Copies of this book may be ordered at $20 per copy from College Board Publications,
Box 886, New York, NY 10101-0886, (800) 323-7155.

Library of Congress Catalog Card Number: 98-074940
International Standard Book Number: 0-87447-634-8

Printed in the United States of America.

For Nicky

Contents

List of Illustrations   x

Foreword to the College Board Edition   xi

Preface   xvii

PART I   *Visions of Community*

1. Andrew Carnegie and the Gospel of Wealth   3

    Goodness and Richness: A Double-Bind   5
    The Education of a Philanthropist   7
    "Wealth"   14

2. Henry Smith Pritchett and the Gospel
   of Efficiency   21

    The Education of a Scientist   23
    The Politics of "Professional" Science   26
    Reforming a College   29
    The Gospel of Efficiency   32

3. Founding the Foundation   37

    *The Administrative Structure of the
    Carnegie Foundation*   38
    A Break with Tradition   41
    The Personal Politics of Social Change   44
    A Pension Fund and a "Great Agency"   53

PART II   *Technologies of Influence*

4. Surveying the Professions   59

    *The Circumstances in Medicine at the Time of the
    Flexner Report*   61

Abraham Flexner and the Flexner Report   66
The Outcomes of the Flexner Report   71
The Carnegie Foundation and Legal Education   75
*The Circumstances in Law at the Time of the
Carnegie Foundation Surveys*   76
The Reed Report   79
Engineering Education   84
*The Professional Preparation of Teachers for
American Public Schools*   86
*Education in Vermont and the American Association
of University Professors*   89

5. Systematizing Educational Measurements   94
The Growth of the High School   96
The College Board and the SAT®   99
The Pennsylvania Study   101
A General Examination Board   108
Establishing the Educational Testing Service   115

6. Renewing the Foundation   122
*Growth and Change in American Higher Education
in the 1950s and 1960s*   124
An Emerging "Public"   126
A New Collaboration   129
The Carnegie Commission on Higher Education   136
Quality and Equality   138
*The Carnegie Council on Policy Studies
in Higher Education*   143
Appraisals of the Carnegie Council   145
*A Renewed, Reestablished, and Reorganized
Foundation*   150

PART III   *The Great Society*

7. Corporate vs. State Responsibility: Henry Pritchett
and "The Social Philosophy of Pensions"   159

The Financial Problems of Carnegie Pensions   160
The "Moral" Problems of Carnegie Pensions   161
The Challenge of Social Insurance   165
The Comprehensive Plan: TIAA   168
Liberty and Efficiency Through Voluntary Associations   173

8. Central vs. Local Control: The Carnegie Foundation
   and Its Critics   179
   Josiah Royce and "Provincialism"   180
   Herbert Croly and "The New Nationalism"   183
   Other Proponents of "Local Self-Interest"   185
   Pritchett's Legacy   189

Bibliographic Note   195

Notes   207

Index   239

Illustrations

(between pages 56 and 57)

Andrew Carnegie in 1863
Andrew Carnegie at Skibo Castle
Henry S. Pritchett as a boy
Andrew Carnegie and Henry S. Pritchett
The Board of Trustees of the Carnegie Foundation
for the Advancement of Teaching, 1912
Andrew Carnegie, about 1915
Henry S. Pritchett, about 1905
Abraham Flexner
William S. Learned
Clark Kerr
The Carnegie Commission on Higher Education, 1973
Publications of the Carnegie Commission and Carnegie Council
Alan Pifer
Caricature of Andrew Carnegie

Foreword

The 1906 congressional charter of the Carnegie Foundation for the Advancement of Teaching expresses its mission as: "...to do and perform all things necessary to encourage, uphold, and dignify the profession of teaching and the condition of higher education...." At that time, providing retirement pensions for college teachers was seen as the most direct way for the foundation to "dignify the profession of teaching." In the present decade, this mission is pursued through a policy agenda aimed at elevating teaching to a position of greater standing within higher education and the broadly construed educational enterprise. How did Mr. Carnegie's foundation evolve from a pension fund to a major policy and research center? What impact has it had on the countenance of American education, and what have been the persistent tensions that have confronted its leaders? What can we, nearly a century after its founding, learn from the experiences of this foundation that can further our understanding of the continuing challenges of defining wise, prudent, and equitable educational policy in a democratic society?

My own engagement with these questions occurred quite unexpectedly. At a National Academy of Education dinner in the spring of 1996, I was seated next to my good friend Ellen Lagemann. I mentioned that I had been nominated for the presidency of the Carnegie Foundation for the Advancement of Teaching, an organization about which I knew little except for the eminence of Ernest Boyer, its late president, who had died several months earlier. Because I thought it unlikely that anything would come of the nomination, I began to change the subject. I did not anticipate the vigor of Ellen's reaction. She appeared surprised that I would even consider becoming a candidate for the foundation presidency. In addition to the fact that I had assiduously avoided administrative entanglements throughout my career, Ellen insisted that my own educational dispositions and those of the foundation were somewhat different. She avowed that the Carnegie Foundation had historically, under the leadership of its first president, Henry Pritchett, its first eminent senior scholar, Abraham Flexner, and their early successors, represented a consistent preference for elite expertise over representative democracy, for standardization over local variation, for policy over practice, and for private over public concerns. These, she reminded me, were out of step with most of my own inclinations. I asked Ellen how she knew so much about this institution. "I wrote a history of the Carnegie Foundation for the Advancement of Teaching," she said. "I had better send you a copy before you do something rash."

A week later, an inscribed copy of *Private Power for the Public Good* arrived, and I read it in one sitting. It was a remarkable story, rendered even more interesting by the frequency with which the history of this small institution intersected with major events in the history of American education. Lagemann described how Andrew Carnegie's original concept of a foundation to provide pensions for chronically underpaid college faculty members had evolved almost immediately into a "great agency" of policy research and political persuasion. The foundation's accomplishments had been legion. Because it was not a philanthropic foundation, with activities centered on grant-making, but an operating foundation that conducted and published its own studies, this was a foundation whose work involved investigation and persuasion, not strategic gifts. From the Flexner Report, which was associated with revolutionary changes in American medical education, to the creation of the Educational Testing Service and Clark Kerr's vision of federal student loans for higher education, the foundation engaged itself with many of the most controversial education issues of the time. By 1918, Pritchett had relieved the foundation of its original mission as a provider of pensions by creating an independent agency called the Teachers Insurance Annuity Association (TIAA).

Lagemann judged that the foundation's policies had typically supported the quest for efficiency and the privileges of professional expertise. I understood the basis for her judgments, always offered in a temperate and evenhanded manner, even when I occasionally disagreed with her interpretations. For example, where she saw Pritchett and Dewey on opposing sides regarding the centrality of science and professional expertise in education, I more often saw them in agreement. And I had been, through both my research and my rhetoric, one of the earliest supporters of the National Board for Professional Teaching Standards, hardly evidence for an inclination to oppose standards, science, and a preference for elite expertise.

After writing *Private Power for the Public Good*, Lagemann wrote a history of the Carnegie Corporation of New York, *The Politics of Knowledge*. In the latter, many of the same themes recurred, as she explored the manner in which philanthropy provided opportunities for private wealth to guide, influence, and direct public policy.

The Carnegie Foundation for the Advancement of Teaching, having essentially gone broke from underestimating the expenses of its early pension commitments, was effectively absorbed by its younger and wealthier sibling, the Carnegie Corporation of New York. Two of the corporation's presidents, John Gardner and Alan Pifer, served concurrently as president of both the foundation and the corporation. Lagemann's account of the foundation's history ends with its renewal as an independent agency in 1979. In that year, upon completion of the last reports of Kerr's Carnegie Council, Ernest Boyer was selected to become the seventh president of the foundation and to guide its rebirth as an independent institution. First in Washington, and subsequently in Princeton, the foundation under Boyer's leadership published a series of influential reports, broadening its agenda from a primary focus on higher education to including education from early childhood through graduate and professional school, and from formal to informal and corporate education.

To Ellen Lagemann's surprise (though with her blessing!), I accepted the foundation's presidency in 1997. The foundation is now located in northern California and has built a new program that rests firmly on its legacies, while offering a critical view of many of its most admired accomplishments. When I accepted the job, I told the board that its new agenda might entail seeking to redress the unintended consequences of some of the foundation's most significant early successes. For example, the Flexner Report had introduced a concept of scientific medicine that might have inadvertently directed attention from enhancing the health of patients and their families to treating diseases and to a concept of professional expertise that gave short shrift to professional integrity. Multiple-choice testing had made assessment more equitable and evenhanded but may have reduced its capacity to evaluate deeper understandings and dispositions. Ironically, that very form of testing aimed at equity was later to be accused of exacerbating the adverse impact of testing on minorities and women. And Clark Kerr's Carnegie Classification, with its serious attention to specifying the distinctive features of research and doctoral institutions of higher education, may have contributed to an overheated emphasis on research over teaching at universities in the United States, especially through its definitions of Research I and Research II universities.

The reason for a new printing of this book is not the need to chronicle the accomplishments and the tensions surrounding one of the nation's oldest foundations. For this is a book in which the saga of the Carnegie Foundation gives this outstanding historian of education the opportunity to examine some of the most persistent policy issues in our society. Moreover, the issues about which Lagemann writes have not gone away. In the late 1990s we are again confronted with the question of standards and assessments, with efficiency and excellence, with centralized versus more local control of education. Education in the professions remains a great challenge. Never have questions of accountability for all institutions of education been more politically salient.

Near the end of the book, Lagemann sums up her observations:

There are inescapable tensions between views of community as national and as local; between efforts to assert "the public interest" and "local self-interest"; between the needs that can be fulfilled by "private power" and by public participation in power; between the specialized knowledge of experts and the less trained and perhaps less codified insights of non-experts; between excellence as "*the* best" and excellence as diverse "bests." (p. 192)

This book has provided the foundation's eighth president with an invaluable chronicle of the institution's development. My colleagues and I have no desire to replicate our past; we would be fools to ignore it. Indeed, our new program places heavy emphasis on the "profession of the teacher" and the centrality of the teaching role in educational organizations. We have created advanced study centers for teachers from both K–12 and postsecondary institutions. These centers aim to advance the work of teaching as a legitimate form of scholarship. We are initiating a long-term comparative program of research on teaching and learning in the education of professionals. We are subjecting the doctorate to careful analysis, especially from the perspective of its function (or dysfunction) in preparing future generations of university and college teachers. We are examining the ways in which the intellectual and vocational missions of higher education contribute to, or compete with, higher education's responsibility to prepare its students morally, ethically, and as citizens in a democracy.

Although much has changed since 1906, our mission remains the same. With the help of Lagemann's astute analysis, we hope to do all things necessary to encourage, uphold, and dignify the profession of teaching.

LEE S. SHULMAN
Menlo Park, California
December 1998

Preface

This book is a history of the Carnegie Foundation for the Advancement of Teaching. Established in 1905 as a pension fund for college professors, the Carnegie Foundation is one of the philanthropic trusts created by the steel magnate Andrew Carnegie. One year after it was organized, it obtained a Congressional charter that allowed it not only "to provide retiring pensions, without regard to race, sex, creed, or color, for the teachers of universities, colleges and technical schools" in the United States and Canada, but also "in general, to do and perform all things necessary to encourage, uphold, and dignify the profession of the teacher and the cause of higher education." This charter enabled the Foundation to become a sponsor of educational surveys and policy reviews, many of which have had important outcomes for the organization of American education.

Through its studies, the Carnegie Foundation defined paradigms of professional education that are still prevalent and in so doing helped to extend formally trained and certified competence as a basis for social status in the United States. In the same way, the Foundation promoted the use of standardized testing, through that support helping to increase reliance on "objectively" demonstrable academic ability and achievement as a basis for the apportionment of educational opportunity. Finally, and again through the publication of studies, the Foundation delineated purposes and administrative procedures for different levels and types of academic institutions and thereby helped to foster systematization in American education. Abraham Flexner's famous study of medical education was sponsored by the Carnegie Foundation. The Educational Testing Service of Princeton, New Jersey, grew out of the

Foundation's activities. The Basic Educational Opportunity Grants established by Congress in 1972 were proposed in a report of the Carnegie Commission on Higher Education, which was organized and supported by the Foundation. And the Teachers Insurance and Annuity Association was established by the Carnegie Foundation to assume and extend the benefits originally offered under its pension plan.

In themselves developments such as these are worth considering, and they are described in this book. But the purpose of the book is not simply to chronicle the causes and activities in which the Carnegie Foundation has participated. It is rather to consider the history of this Foundation, its organization and major programs over roughly seventy-five years, in relation to the larger social issues of the twentieth century. Hence, the book is centrally concerned with the growth of science and the implications that has had for democratic politics, as systematically organized special knowledge has fostered belief in expertise and reliance upon experts as policy makers. It is also concerned with problems of social diversity, especially as those have been related to questions of educational organization. One cannot look at the history of the Carnegie Foundation without considering relationships between education and social stratification. Finally, and most important, it attempts to raise the continuing problems of community that are so apparent in the United States. It deals with conflicts between different groups, different interests, and different social goals, and in that way is a book about politics.

The Carnegie Foundation always has been deeply engaged in the politics of knowledge. Its efforts to develop and institutionalize programs of educational reform have involved attempts to persuade people to its point of view, through the careful presentation and dissemination of information, the securing of authoritative endorsements, and the establishment of group alliances. Foundation efforts have always met with similar efforts on the part of critics and opponents to persuade people to alternate points of view. Questions of social-group power have therefore been at issue along with questions about the power—the validity and value—of different ideas and proposals throughout the history of this foundation.

Also evident are some of the dilemmas associated with the traditional philanthropic claim that "private power" can be "for the public good." Because questions of politics have been so important in the activities of this foundation, as they doubtless also have been in the activities of other foundations, its history illuminates three familiar but crucial points: first, that "the public good" is a theoretical concept that becomes elusive when one begins to consider the actual variety of group interests that have existed and still exist in the United States; second, that in actuality if not in theory, any form of purposive social action, including foundation philanthropy, must represent the interests of some groups better than others and must advance some social priorities at the expense of others; and third, that in the distance between the theoretical concept of "the public good" and the actuality of group interests lie the problems of community and the problems of public policy making in a large and diverse modern democratic society.

This book advances no new suggestions as to how these problems can be overcome, although in emphasizing conflict rather than achievement and in stressing the problems of community that can be seen in the history of the Carnegie Foundation it argues implicitly throughout and explicitly at the end that the needs of a nationally integrated society are better served when different and conflicting interests are recognized and acknowledged than when they are ignored, let alone denied. Such recognition cannot resolve the problems of diversity and participation that are the central problems of community in the United States. But such recognition can at least help to sustain self-conscious awareness of the difficulties of democratic governance in a society where differences in interest exist; and such self-conscious awareness is necessary if tolerance for difference is to survive and if the process of policy making rather than merely the substance of any given policy is ever to become the means for strengthening society through the sense and experience of "community."

This book, then, is a close study of one foundation that attempts to raise and emphasize old but still vital political problems. Its thesis is that the notion of "private power for the public good" is problematical at best. The critical, but hopefully balanced, perspective it seeks does not derive from a belief that private philanthropic foundations and other publicly accountable centers of "private power" are either illegitimate or without significant value in a democracy. One can raise serious and important questions about the legitimacy of the very notion of "private power," but those questions are not the ones that are most relevant here. The key questions in this instance are more specific. They have to do with the dilemmas of private power as those can be seen in the history of one institution; they have to do with which groups, interests, and priorities the Carnegie Foundation has been most sensitive to and how the interpretation of "private power for the public good" implicit in that originated from turn-of-the-century social thought and circumstance.

The Carnegie Foundation was organized during the era in American history when small, isolated local communities were beginning to lose some of their separateness and distinctiveness, as population growth, industrialization, and technological inventions lessened geographic distance and encouraged the emergence of a more closely interconnected national society. These changes, combined with a growing concern with community and a heightened faith in science and in its powers when applied to social problems, led some people to hope that the conflicts and inefficiencies of politics could be transcended and national progress insured by elite ("the best men") determination of public policy. This hope was institutionalized in the Carnegie Foundation, largely through the efforts of its first president, Henry Smith Pritchett.

A very able if dogmatic man, Pritchett set the course of the Carnegie Foundation. He was directly supported in his work by a prominent board of trustees, most of them college presidents, who tended to share his point of view; and he was indirectly supported by the values and beliefs that originated in that aspect of "Progressivism" that was more elitist than populist in effect—as well as, at times, in intent. Pritchett's successors at the Carnegie Foundation have not shared all of his beliefs or opinions, and they have not acted in the same ways that he did. Inevitably, however, they have been wittingly and unwittingly constrained and empowered by the traditions and the basic institutional design Pritchett established.

As many contemporary problems cannot be understood without appreciating their origins, so the problems of the Carnegie Foundation's interpretation of how "private power" could be used "for the public good" cannot be understood without full knowledge of the aspirations and assumptions that Pritchett brought to and built into the Foundation. Because I have found many of those aspirations and assumptions comprehensible yet dismaying, I also have found many aspects of the Foundation's history troubling. This study seeks to avoid an overemphasis on personal judgments, attempting wherever possible to allow the circumstances of a situation and the participants involved to speak for themselves. Most assuredly, however, personal biases have shaped the book, are evident in the book, and at times are explicitly stated. Those, too, need a word of explanation.

I was invited to write this book and also a second book about the history of the Carnegie Corporation of New York by Alan Pifer, who was at the time president of both foundations. Pifer had long been interested in the history of philanthropy and wanted a historian to study where and how the activities of these two

Carnegie trusts fit into the larger scheme of things. I was interested in the project for a number of reasons. I had just finished a
biographical study of the education of five women social reformers (*A Generation of Women: Education in the Lives of Progressive
Reformers*, Harvard University Press, 1979) and wanted a change
of genre. Institutional histories promised that. In addition, I had
(and continue to have) many unanswered questions about "progressive" social reform. Research into the history of foundation
philanthropy seemed a reasonable way to pursue some of those
questions. Finally, because education has been a central concern of
both the Carnegie Foundation and Carnegie Corporation, studying their activities was likely to enable me to extend my primary
interest in the history and contemporary problems of American
education. For all of these reasons, Pifer and I agreed that I would
undertake the project. More specifically, we agreed that my work
would be supported by the Carnegie Corporation, with a small additional grant from the Carnegie Foundation; that I would have
full access to Corporation and Foundation papers; and that neither
organization would be involved in the substantive and interpreta-
tive questions that would arise in connection with my research
and writing.

Nevertheless, because I have been supported by the Carnegie
Corporation and the Carnegie Foundation and have had extended
conversations with a number of Carnegie Corporation officers and
staff members (especially those who were, like Pifer, once affiliated with the Foundation), my work may reflect a somewhat greater
interest in and sense of the difficulties associated with foundation
administration than might otherwise have been the case. And yet,
if that has been a factor in setting the focus of this book, my perspective has been shaped primarily by my earlier work in women's
history and in education.

Women's history originated from the realization that traditional history was a partial history. Mostly written by men and

largely concerned with the accomplishments of men, traditional history was based on categories of analysis and source materials that did not reveal the differences between men and women and that did not bring to light the concerns and activities that were most important to women as women. Like scholars working in black history and ethnic histories, therefore, scholars working in women's history have rejected the "we" implicit in so many traditional, largely male-defined accounts. In writing women's history one learns to be sensitive to who is speaking for whom, when people speak for and about each other's interests. That lesson, along with the belief that one way to extend the value of women's history is to apply the kinds of questions it has helped to frame to aspects of the past that would not fall within the traditional boundaries of women's history, has influenced my interests in and view of the history of the Carnegie Foundation.

Beyond that, reading in the philosophy of education, particularly in the writings of John Dewey and Jane Addams, has heightened my sense of the importance of questions of participation in the processes through which bases for association are defined. Dewey and Addams were contemporaries of Henry Pritchett, and their writings suggest that they would have acknowledged the importance and difficulties involved in what Pritchett was trying to do at the Carnegie Foundation, while dissenting from his belief that expertise was a sure and sufficient means to promote the public good. There are many grounds on which one may criticize Dewey and Addams, but if one were to draw a single major distinction between progressive social thinkers, Dewey and Addams would fall among the thinkers who were most concerned with the processes of community definition and Pritchett would fall among those who were most concerned with the "efficiencies" of actual institutional designs for community. I have tended to find thinkers in the first group more congenial. Needless to say, we must move beyond thinkers in both groups, beyond "progressive" formulations of social problems, but questions of participation and community process must remain compelling, and they have provided the themes that organize the book as well as the basis for its interpretation.

Finally, two preferences about the writing of history are implicit in the choices I have made. Some people believe that history is most interesting and useful as a direct means for commenting on contemporary problems; others, that it is most valid as a more indirect means to that end. If the special task of history is to provide perspectives on the present—the kind of detachment from the immediate that may enable one to see the present more fully—I tend to think the second approach is more effective. Based on that assumption, this book deals at greater length and in more detail with the early years of the Carnegie Foundation's history than with the later, and seeks to emphasize lines of development from the past to the present. It engages less directly with some contemporary issues than others might believe it should. But it does this purposefully, in order to allow similarities and dissimilarities between past and present to suggest the potential for future conflicts and problems and to demonstrate that the significance of "progress" only becomes apparent with time.

Many of the concepts used in this book, among them power, authority, community, bureaucracy, and professionalism, have been defined differently by different people. This book has been informed by discussions of these concepts, although precise and explicit definitions do not appear. Sometimes it is helpful to introduce such definitions into a historical work, but in this instance that practice seemed to detract from the main interest. The meaning I have assigned to these concepts should be clear from the discussions in the text, and where my thinking has been directly influenced by a specific work, that is indicated in the notes or discussed in the bibliographic note following the text.

A great number of people have helped me write this book. At

the Carnegie Corporation I have profited especially from conversations with Alan Pifer, David Robinson, Barbara Finberg, Sara Engelhardt, Alden Dunham, and Fritz Mosher. Florence Anderson, longtime secretary of the Corporation and Foundation, knows by heart the main lines and the details of the history of both institutions. She has been wonderfully patient and helpful in unearthing documents and has saved me from many errors of fact. No doubt, all of these people would disagree with parts or all of my interpretation. But they have been consistently generous in responding to requests for information and scrupulous in refraining from efforts to shape my views.

Outside of the Corporation, I have benefited from interviews, telephone conversations, and correspondence with Ernest Boyer (now President of the Carnegie Foundation), Margaret Gordon, Clark Kerr, Lewis Mayhew, David Riesman, Ralph Tyler, and Martin Trow. John Smart and Mary Stuart shared their studies of the Carnegie Commission. Mary Ann Dzuback helped me find many fugitive sources and has shared my interests as they have emerged. Marvin Lazerson offered especially incisive criticisms of an early draft of the book. Lawrence Cremin has listened to endless rehearsals of my ideas, both in the classes we teach together and the many conversations we have had. He has encouraged my thinking and writing and has been a very good friend. Jeannette Hopkins accepted the book for publication and then insistently asked me what it was really about. Her questions helped me restructure the study, and her editing has improved it throughout. To all of these people I am very grateful.

The book is dedicated to my son, Nicky. Without his willingness to share me with "Uncle Andrew," and without my husband's affection, support, and helpfulness, it could not have been written. I owe them more than a preface can acknowledge.

E. C. L.

PART I

Visions of Community

Americans have always been concerned with defining and creating communities. As John Higham once observed, "American history has been in considerable measure a struggle between rival ways of getting together."[1] Throughout the twentieth century, philanthropic foundations have been important participants in this struggle. It is in relation to problems of community that one must consider the history of the Carnegie Foundation for the Advancement of Teaching.

At the time this foundation and other early philanthropic trusts were organized, questions of community were of urgent concern to many Americans.[2] During the early years of the century, economic growth and reorganization, technological advances, population expansion, increasing social diversity, and new ideas derived from and associated with science began to transform a nation of "island communities" into what Graham Wallas first called "The Great Society."[3] Foundation philanthropy was a response to this transformation. It was rooted in a long tradition of philanthropic efforts to establish the values, shape the beliefs, and define the behaviors that would join people to one another, but it represented an effort to bring greater deliberateness and a more national orientation to the definition and fulfillment of common needs and interests.

In the case of the Carnegie Foundation, views of community were important from the first. They were apparent in the thought of the two men who collaborated in founding the Foundation, the steel baron and philanthropist Andrew Carnegie and the scientist and educator Henry Smith Pritchett. Born in 1835, Carnegie was essentially a man of the nineteenth century, whereas Pritchett, who was born twenty-two years later in 1857, was more a twentieth-century man. Carnegie saw philanthropy as a rather simple distributive mechanism that should be used to promote individual enlightenment; Pritchett saw it as a means for promoting social "efficiency" through institutional reform. Carnegie's perspective reflected an individualistic view of the sources of progress. He believed that the extension of greater opportunities for individual self-development would be sufficient to promote community well-being. Pritchett did not disagree with Carnegie's insistence upon the importance of self-development or with his belief in the social value of individualism. But Pritchett's hopes for philanthropy were based on his more acute perception of a new need for national integration and his greater interest in finding explicit "scientific" principles for the development of institutional systems.

For all the differences between them, though, Carnegie and Pritchett were alike in their belief that growth and change had created a situation in which purposive efforts to strengthen and extend social bonds would be required. More important, perhaps, they agreed that the trusteeship of personal wealth could meet this need by helping to ensure greater prosperity and better lives for all people. They concurred in the age-old premise upon which private philanthropy has been based: they were convinced that "private power" could be "for the public good."[4]

Not all people subscribed to the assumptions about "getting together" that were implicit in the conviction Carnegie and Pritchett shared. Whether and how "a few" could and should attempt to define and advance the good of "the many" was in dispute long before the Carnegie Foundation was established. At least since Rousseau tried to explicate the differences between "the general will" and "the will of all," people have worried about questions that are essential to the premises upon which private philanthropy has been predicated.[5]

Obviously, then, considering rival ways of "getting together" is essential to a study of the Carnegie Foundation. Views of community shaped the Foundation's policies as well as public reactions to those policies. Different views of community and strategies for community organization were in contest even as Carnegie and Pritchett initially launched the Foundation.

– 1 –
Andrew Carnegie and the Gospel of Wealth

Andrew Carnegie was born in a small cottage in Dunfermline, Scotland, fourteen miles northwest of Edinburgh. In 1848, six months before his thirteenth birthday, he immigrated to Pittsburgh, Pennsylvania, with his family. Soon after he went to work as a bobbin boy in a cotton factory, moving on from there to become a telegraph operator, a supervisor on the Pennsylvania Railroad, and then, for thirty years, a steel entrepreneur in business for himself. When he retired in 1901, he had amassed so large a fortune that J. P. Morgan was moved to remark upon assuming control of the steel companies Carnegie had built: "Mr. Carnegie, I want to congratulate you on being the richest man in the world!"[1]

Carnegie did not remain "the richest man in the world" for very long; by the time he died in 1919, he had given most of his fortune away. He had donated vast sums to build libraries. He had furnished innumerable churches with funds for the purchase of pipe organs. He had created a scholarship fund for university students in Scotland. He had been a benefactor of Negro education in the United States. And he had established a number of institutions that still bear his name—notably, the Carnegie Institute of Pittsburgh, the Carnegie Institution of Washington, the Carnegie Foundation for the Advancement of Teaching, the Carnegie Endowment for International Peace, and the Carnegie Corporation of New York.[2]

Short, wiry, and energetic, Carnegie was a man of abundant contradictions. He thrived on action and was always busy, planning, negotiating, and visiting his works, and yet, for all the bustle, he may have been happiest when left alone with a volume of Shakespeare or with a telescope. He was "a tremendous personality," the writer Richard Watson Gilder once said, "dramatic, wilful, generous, whimsical, at times almost cruel in pressing his own conviction upon others, and then again tender, affectionate, emotional, always imaginative, unusual and wide-visioned in his views...inconsistent in many ways."[3] One observer described him as the most complex of all the "robber-barons."[4] Carnegie could lobby for high protective tariffs in the United States, while urging free trade policies for Great Britain. He could talk of "the brotherhood of man," while closing a plant to secure reductions in wages. He could support Henry Clay Frick's handling of the 1892 Homestead Strike, which led to violence and bloodshed, and claim later that "nothing I have ever had to meet in all my life, before or since, wounded me so deeply....It was so unnecessary."[5] And, most striking of all, he could work tirelessly to accumulate a fortune and work just as tirelessly to dispose of it before he died.

One of Carnegie's associates said he was "the most consistently happy man" he had ever known, and that may well have been true.[6] Yet, although many who knew him best never realized it, he found life perplexing—filled, on the one hand, with joy, triumph, and comfort, and, on the other, with despair and painful self-doubt. A rich man who wanted to be a good man, Carnegie was not at all sure that he could be both. He shared with many others before him the sometimes conflicting values of a puritan and a Yankee, of a populist and a capitalist, of a man who wished for brotherhood with all men while acting the part of paternalistic leader. He believed in individualism and also in equality. He was concerned with strengthening the bonds of community as well as with preserving for the individual the right to live according to personal talent and conscience.

Philanthropy, which combined both concerns, was Carnegie's answer and release from the ethical questions that deeply troubled him. In philanthropy he believed, or at least hoped, he had found a way to ensure that the "surplus wealth" of the few would be used for the benefit of the many; economic advance would become a means for restoring the kind of community harmony that he associated somewhat wistfully with an earlier day. A hardheaded, individualistic businessman who was also something of a romantic communitarian, Carnegie looked to philanthropy to speed the advent of the "ideal State."

GOODNESS AND RICHNESS: A DOUBLE-BIND

Carnegie came of a poor but proud Scottish family. His father, William Carnegie, was a Chartist leader. His maternal grandfather, Thomas Morrison, and a maternal uncle, Thomas Morrison, Jr., were well-known Scottish radicals who missed no opportunity to attack the English monarchy and the established church and to advance the cause of working-class rights. Another uncle, George Lauder, whom Carnegie especially loved, was a living link to local historical and cultural heroes, Robert Bruce, Rob Roy, and Robert Burns. Carnegie wrote, "As a child, I could have slain king, duke, or lord, and considered their death a service to the state."[7] But his life led in another direction, to friendship with men like Lord Rosebery, whose politician father Carnegie's grandfather had constantly pilloried in letters to the press, to the employment of scores of laborers, and to the making of a fortune such as the world had rarely, if ever, seen.

In coming to the United States, the Carnegie family had been seeking prosperity. William Carnegie had been a handloom weaver in Dunfermline, and with the spread of factory production, he had been increasingly unable to make a living. To follow relatives to the United States was a natural step. Even Andrew Carnegie's Scottish uncles thought of the American Republic as the embodiment of true democracy and working-class opportunity, and, far more important, Margaret Carnegie, Andrew's strong and determined mother, believed that on the other side of the Atlantic her boys would have what they did not have at home—a chance through hard work and sober living to acquire the decencies and comforts they obviously deserved. The Protestant work ethic was, therefore, as much a part of Andrew Carnegie's inheritance as radical politics was, and the values of that ethic, not only thrift and endeavor, but also respect for earned rewards, sparked his ambitions, sustained his driving energies, and allowed him to take pleasure in the fulfillment of his mother's expectations and hopes.

A tension between goodness and richness, between egalitarian political sympathies and individualistic economic pursuits, was thus inherent in the values Carnegie acquired as a child. Those values encouraged him, on the one hand, to strive for worldly success, and, on the other, when he had made a fortune, left him feeling tainted, afraid that he might be the pariah of his clan. Sitting alone in a room in the St. Nicholas Hotel in New York City one night in the winter of 1868, Carnegie compiled a self-appraisal in which he made these feelings clear. After carefully calculating his financial assets and investments, he wrote:

Thirty three and an income of $50,000 per annum. By this time two years I can so arrange all my business as to secure at least 50,000 per annum. Beyond this never earn—make no effort to increase fortune, but spend the surplus each year for benevolent [sic] purposes. Cast aside business forever except for others.

Settle in Oxford & get a thorough education making the acquaintance of literary men—this will take three years active work—pay especial attention to speaking in public.

Settle then in London & purchase a controlling interest in some newspaper or live review & give the general management of it attention, taking a part in public matters especially those connected with education & improvement of the poorer classes.

Man must have an idol—The amassing of wealth is one of the worst species of idolitary [*sic*]. No idol more debasing than the worship of money. Whatever I engage in I must push inordinately therefor should I be careful to choose that life which will be the most elevating in its character. To continue much longer overwhelmed by business cares and with most of my thoughts wholly upon the way to make more money in the shortest time, must degrade me beyond hope of permanent recovery.

I will resign business at Thirty five, but during the ensuing two years, I wish to spend the afternoons in securing instruction, and in reading systematically.[8]

As things turned out, of course, Carnegie did not renounce the "idolatrous" pursuit he both loved and hated until he was sixty-six, and, by the time he did retire from business, he no longer saw that step as a retreat—a means to "recovery." In the talk, readings, lectures, and camaraderie of the salon world of New York City, as well as in private contemplation and perusal of classic and contemporary authors, Carnegie found ideas that enabled him to feel righteous in his richness and at peace in his world. As a result of his own synthesis of ideas that were formative for many Americans, he came to believe that the individual's pursuit of private profit was a public benefit that could promote the good of all.

THE EDUCATION OF A PHILANTHROPIST

Soon after resigning from his job with the Pennsylvania Railroad and moving to New York City in 1867, Carnegie met a striking and rather charismatic woman, Anne Charlotte Lynch Botta. Botta was the wife of a New York University professor of Italian whose Murray Hill home was a gathering place for a diverse but lively crowd: among others, Margaret Fuller, Edgar Allan Poe, Horace Greeley, Julia Ward Howe, Andrew D. White, first president of Cornell, William Cullen Bryant, and, after 1867, Andrew Carnegie. Ralph Waldo Emerson made the Botta household "his usual New York stopping place," calling it "the house of expanding doors."[9] One of Botta's "chief characteristics," Carnegie said in a biographical sketch of her, "was that of recognizing and encouraging unknown men and women, and giving them opportunities to benefit, not only from her own stores of wisdom, and from her charming manners and conversation, but from the remarkable class she drew around her."[10] Carnegie had found a mentor whose sponsorship and friendship helped him to find the intellectual resources he needed to align his life with his hopes for human progress and his wish to do good in the world.

Through Botta, Carnegie gained membership in the Nineteenth Century Club, a salon-like group of quasi-religious seekers, in which, according to Carnegie, "able men and women discussed the leading topics of the day in due form, addressing the audience one after another." Carnegie's first talk was on "The Aristocracy of the Dollar," and that talk, along with several subsequent ones, provided "excellent training," he claimed, "for one had to read and study for each appearance."[11] In itself such training may have been valuable to Carnegie, but his membership in the Nineteenth Century Club was most important because it was here that he seems first to have encountered the writings of the English philosopher and Social Darwinist Herbert Spencer.

Carnegie quickly avowed his discipleship to Spencer, while unwittingly misinterpreting many of Spencer's central principles. In favoring philanthropy, Carnegie contradicted all of the extreme laissez-faire premises associated with Spencer's own arguments concerning "the survival of the fit." In a sense, nevertheless, Carnegie took him to heart, and, as he accurately and repeatedly attested, Spencer played an important role in the development of his thought. Of his first reading of Spencer, Carnegie said in his *Autobiography*: "Reaching the pages which explain how man has absorbed such mental foods as were favorable to him, retaining what was salutory, rejecting what was deleterious, I remember that light came as in a flood and all was clear. Not only had I got rid of theology and the supernatural, but I had found the truth of evolution. 'All is well since all grows better' became my motto, my true source of comfort. Man was not created with an instinct for his own degradation, but from the lower he had risen to the higher forms. Nor is there any conceivable end to his march to perfection. His face is turned to the light; he stands in the sun and looks upward."[12] Carnegie found in Spencer, not a doctrine to guide him, but "a truth" to enlighten him, "a truth" that could prove that his acquisitive "instinct" need not be debasing.

To have discovered a philosopher whose ideas could provide assurance that his business acumen was not a sign of ignoble character brought Carnegie enormous relief. As he told a gathering of theology students at St. Andrew's University in Scotland in a 1902 talk, "A Confession of Religious Faith," the works of Herbert Spencer and Charles Darwin had been "revelations" to him. "Here was the truth which reconciled all things...the alembic which harmonized hitherto conflicting ideas and brought order out of chaos."[13] After discovering the theory of evolution, Carnegie could continue in business more able to believe that as a rich man he could also be good.

In Spencer, Carnegie found a thinker who restored him to hopefulness after his despairing personal accounting of 1868, and, through conversations with Botta and other members of her circle, he also found or was affirmed in a religious outlook that would help to sustain his renewed optimism about life. Botta was an admirer of the Unitarianism of William Ellery Channing and of the Transcendentalism of Ralph Waldo Emerson. Although she did not belong to a church, according to a friend, "she was an evangelical moralist in conduct...[who] would go to hear everybody preach."[14] Following her lead, Carnegie also became an "evangelical moralist," conveying his views in frequent public speeches and in the numerous travelogues, essays, and biographies he produced beginning in the 1880s. Willing to listen to and learn from adherents of any religious persuasion and able to find "truth" in all of the world's sacred philosophies, Carnegie came, in addition, to resemble Botta in his ecumenical perspective. And finally, again like Botta, he arrived at the conviction that true divinity lay within the soul or the conscience of the individual, religion therefore being a matter of personal enlightenment, or the awakening, disciplining, and then the following in conduct of the noble thoughts ("instincts") one found within.

Carnegie carefully explained in his *Autobiography* that there had not been "one orthodox Presbyterian" in his family. His father and many other relatives had "found refuge for a time in the doctrines of Swedenborg"; his mother had been "a great reader, always, Channing the Unitarian was...her special delight."[15] Carnegie's relatives had apparently substituted for the harsh doctrines of Calvin the more accepting, hopeful, beneficent, and personal faith of men like Swedenborg and Channing, who saw good rather than evil in the promptings and inner voices of the individual's soul. With Botta's help, and under the indirect influence of Emerson, Carnegie found a faith that was much like theirs.

Carnegie never systematically described his religious beliefs, and they were most likely eclectic and unsystematic in any case. But he did indicate the essence of his faith in his talk to the theology students at St. Andrew's University in 1902. He told them:

...feelings of awe, reverence, and resignation, which are essentially religious...lift us into the immensities far above all that is mean and squalid, the petty cares and troubles, the anxieties and disappointments of human existence. It is in the serene atmosphere of the gods, in communion with their noblest thoughts, that we resolve to strive to attain the highest standard of conduct; that we forget and forgive injuries, mostly fanciful as our injuries are,—see how petty all our troubles are, how great our belongings; that we long to be of service to others and realize that in communion with the gods man himself becomes god-like in all the trials of life.

. . . .

The relative position given to doctrines as well as the doctrines themselves differentiate theological creeds and systems of religion. It is a growing belief with me that in the not distant future increasing importance will be attached to one truth until it overshadows all others and proves the center around which the religious sentiments will finally gather—the declaration of Christ, 'The Kingdom of Heaven is within you.'...The best test of fitness for a heavenly life hereafter and the strongest assurance of one, is...such a life here upon earth....Unless in some degree the Kingdom of Heaven is within him here, man hopes in vain for heaven beyond.

And he closed with a summation of the life to which he hoped his faith would lead him:

The ideal man, as I have sometimes tried to imagine him, is he, who although hoping for everlasting existence with those he loves, yet concentrates his thoughts and efforts upon the duties of this life in which he has been placed, strictly obeys the judge within, doing right, avoiding wrong, neither for hope of reward nor fear of punishment, here or hereafter, but solely because his conscience tells him it is right or wrong—virtue being its own ample reward. He remembers Abou-Ben-Adhem and believes with Franklin that the worship most acceptable to God is service to man, and acts accordingly; hails science which has revealed an illimitable, indestructible and constantly expanding universe under the reign of law, and also the divine law of his being which leads man ever steadily upward, thus assuring him that all is well, since all grows better.[16]

The beliefs Carnegie acquired and developed through acquaintance with Anne Botta and her friends did not diminish his wish to be like the vigorous men he had so admired in his youth. They convinced him of two points: first, that his pursuit of wealth had not been idolatrous, but evidence of man's natural and continuing search for a better way of life; and second, that if his prosperity, as opposed to his father's poverty, was evidence of man's evolution to a "higher form," then, his "instincts" were not degrading, but a resource that had been given to him in order that he could better serve. Because he sincerely believed that all men should take their own private conscience as their one and only guide, Carnegie was more inclined to proclaim his convictions than he was to explain them. But the ideas he encountered and transformed and distilled, in his own way and according to his own subjective needs, were vital intermediaries through which he found a way to connect his life to those of the family ideals to which he had feared he had been disloyal. Spencer, Channing, and Emerson, among others, made it possible for Andrew Carnegie to turn his dour self-appraisal of 1868 into a confident self-justification, expressed most forcefully in an 1889 essay on "Wealth."

Before turning to that essay, however, one needs to consider two last and far less specific influences in the shaping of Carnegie's views. First, even while entranced with Anne Botta and her coterie, Carnegie was steadily involved in his business, and his business practices had an influence on his thought. His success as an industrialist was based largely on technological advances in the production of steel and on the application to steel manufacturing of administrative methods derived from the railroads. These innovations enabled Carnegie to reduce production costs and to increase output; the result, given a fairly steady and high demand for steel, was high and growing profits. Nevertheless, as Alfred D. Chandler, Jr., has pointed out, Carnegie's business was essentially entrepreneurial in its organization, with Carnegie himself making most of the critical management decisions. It was built around the division of the production process into functional departments or units that could then be coordinated to achieve overall increases in efficiency, and was in that sense "modern," although it did not join the process of production to distribution through management, and was in that way still "small" in the scale of integration it represented.[17]

This organizational structure demonstrates that Carnegie's business was heavily dependent upon the skill of individuals—his own, as well as that of the engineers who designed his plants and production processes and that of the few trusted lieutenants upon whom he relied to oversee the daily plant routines. His belief in the efficacy of the individual and his insistent reliance or claims to reliance on his own personal views were a logical outgrowth, not only of his intellectual encounters with writers and thinkers, but also of the practical business experience that enabled him to see meaning in what those writers and thinkers said and believed.

Carnegie's business practices also influenced his views, especially his views of his own responsibilities as a man of wealth, in another less direct, more subtle, and perhaps more important way. As a result of the actions of men like Carnegie, the American economy was transformed during his lifetime. It began to develop larger and more specialized units of production and ever more hierarchically organized corporate structures. These changes brought enormous wealth to those at the top and, according to a contemporary estimate, helped to raise the nation's annual per capita income from $308 in 1850 to $1036 in 1890, but they also lessened the independence and capacity of many working people to live as free individuals; and this led, in turn, to labor conflict as well as to a more general concern with the consequences of economic consolidation and the accumulation of wealth in the hands of economic consolidators.[18]

This concern was evident in many ways. In 1890, for the first time, the federal census calculated the distribution of the nation's wealth, finding that 91 percent of American families held 29 percent of the wealth, and that the remaining 71 percent of the nation's wealth was held by 9 percent of American families.[19] At the end of the century, as Daniel T. Rodgers has noted in his study of the work ethic, the once buoyantly self-confident rags-to-riches literature began to exhibit "a kind of nervous tic…a need to rebut the suspicion that the immensely increased scale of business had closed off opportunities."[20] Two of the most popular books of the period dealt, however differently, with these matters: Henry George's *Progress and Poverty* offered a panacea for inequality, crime, corruption, and other evils through a "single tax" and Edward Bellamy's *Looking Backward* offered a utopian vision of the rebirth of an egalitarian community along quasi-socialistic lines. Even as optimistic a man as the statistician Carroll D. Wright, who believed that economic change had been of benefit to all, claimed that "the assertion that the rich are growing richer and the poor poorer has for some reason taken more complete possession of the popular mind than any other single one."[21] On the basis of this kind of evidence, Morton Keller has suggested that "the consequences of economic change were as central a concern of thoughtful Americans in the late nineteenth century as slavery and the character of the Union had been in the mid-century decades."[22] If Carnegie's worries about his wealth were reinforced by these concerns, the solution he saw in philanthropy was certainly shaped by them. His essay on "Wealth," while a significant personal statement, was also a classic description of the central issues of the day.

"WEALTH"

"Wealth" first appeared in the *North American Review* and was immediately and widely reprinted, often under the title "The Gospel of Wealth." It began with a simple assertion: "The problem of our age is the proper administration of wealth, that the ties of brotherhood may still bind together the rich and the poor in harmonious relationship."[23] Using language and avowing an ideal that resonated with the values of many of his contemporaries,

Carnegie went on to develop an argument that rested on three assumptions.

The first assumption had to do with economic inequality, which Carnegie now claimed to regard as an inevitable, necessary, and not entirely unfortunate outcome of social progress. According to the views he expressed in "Wealth," he believed that discrepancies in economic status had initially arisen "when the capable, industrious workman said to his incompetent and lazy fellow, 'If thou dost not sow, thou shalt not reap'" (p. 5). Thus asserting a right to the rewards of their own labor, "able men" had been motivated to apply "the inventions of this scientific age" to advance society's material development (pp. 4 and 2). It might be appealing to believe, said Carnegie, "that man should labor, not for himself alone, but in and for a brotherhood of his fellows"; however, the facts of the matter rendered that "noble ideal" impractical in the real and present world, incentives having produced invention, invention having produced progress, and progress having led, not only to economic distinctions among people, but also to a universally higher standard of living (p. 6).

To-day the world obtains commodities of excellent quality at prices which even the preceding generation have deemed incredible...The poor enjoy what the rich could not before afford. What were the luxuries have become the necessaries of life. The laborer has now more comfort than the farmer had a few generations ago. The farmer has more luxuries than the landlord had, and is more richly clad and better housed. The landlord has books and pictures rarer and appointments more artistic than the king could then obtain (pp. 2–3).

Closely related to Carnegie's insistence that all would continue to benefit from the maintenance of an economic system that allowed the free-play of individual self-interest was a different, but not contradictory claim. That claim, which once again expressed a familiar and popular consensus of opinion, was that, however improved already, society could and should be still further improved.

As described in "Wealth," progress, like all things, had had a "price." With economic development, "rigid castes are formed," Carnegie stated, "and, as usual, mutual ignorance breeds mutual distrust" (p. 3). That there was a need to reduce the social and political divisions that were the "price" of industrialization was, thus, the second doctrine the essay proclaimed.

Finally, coming to his central point, Carnegie advocated that the millionaire become a steward, his special version of "duty" being:

> to set an example of modest, unostentatious living, shunning display or extravagence; to provide moderately for the legitimate wants of those dependent upon him; and after doing so, to consider all surplus revenues which come to him simply as trust funds, which he is called upon to administer, and strictly bound as a matter of duty to administer in the manner which, in his judgement, is best calculated to produce the most beneficial results for the community (p. 13).

By investing, not in themselves and their progeny, but in programs and institutions that would "provide part of the means by which those who desire to improve may do so," the wealthy could help to recreate the ties of social kinship that had characterized an earlier age (p. 15).

Almsgiving would not do that, Carnegie argued. Almsgiving, in supporting "the slothful, the drunken, the unworthy," deflected resources that could otherwise be used to assist in the development of the poor but ambitious, who might be the "able"; it did little to promote intergenerational mobility as an antidote to the dangers of "caste"; and in supporting the worthless, it might perpetuate dependency. If "the millions of the rich were thrown into the sea," Carnegie insisted, it would perhaps assist mankind as a whole more than "indiscriminate charity" (p.14). Because stewardship, by contrast, promised the fulfillment, not of individual need, but of the communal need to encourage the development of the best, stewardship might, in time, remove the barriers that heretofore had prevented the emergence of "an ideal State" (p. 11). The importance of stewardship was, therefore, the third postulate of this moral philosophy for the very rich.

On the suggestion of the editor of the *North American Review* Carnegie embroidered the essay with suggestions for projects to illustrate the kind of benevolence the philanthropist might choose. These included a number of traditional ideas, for example, support for university buildings, and a few that would become Carnegie's special stock in trade, particularly support for library buildings, which he considered one of the most important "ladders upon which the aspiring can rise" (p. 16). The latter indicate, as his actual giving did also, that Carnegie tended to support institutions and projects that bore a striking resemblance to the sources to which he attributed his own education and individual "genius." Thus, having found useful information and pleasure in reading, he supported the building of libraries as a means for encouraging the buying and reading of books; having found in poetry, art, drama, and music the "awe, reverence, and resignation" that were for him "the religious sentiments" necessary to the resolve "to strive to attain the highest standard of conduct," he supported cultural centers and gave enormous sums for the purchase of church pipe organs in order to make the sources of personal enlightenment more generally available; having found as a result of science "the truth of evolution," which was not only a revelation, he claimed, but a great source of personal comfort, he hoped through support for the scientific research of "exceptional" men to promote man's search for "truth"; and, having found instruction in the lives of admirable men and women, he hoped through pensions such as those the Carnegie Foundation would give to professors to honor and call attention to people who had exemplified the virtues of selfless service.[24]

Gifts for these purposes as well as the suggestions for philanthropy that Carnegie included in "Wealth" clearly show that he equated progress with individual excellence and achievement. His view of community was a view of busy, independent people held together by taken-for-granted loyalty to common values. Carnegie did not have any concept of "the group."

Much pleased with his essay on "Wealth," Carnegie believed he had justified the individual's right, even responsibility, first, to accumulate as much money as possible, and, then, to distribute that money as wisely as possible. He believed he had shown that by allowing the individual to pursue his or her talent, all would gain from invention and economic growth; and that by asking those who had demonstrated the greatest talent to become trustees for their "poorer brethren," all would also gain as a result of their superior capacity to discern ways to help others to rise. Commenting on the essay, he said:

Acting in accordance with this advice, it becomes the duty of the millionaire to increase his revenues. The struggle for more is completely freed from selfish or ambitious taint and becomes a noble pursuit. Then he labors not for self, but for others; not to hoard, but to spend. The more he makes, the more the public gets. His whole life is changed from the moment that he resolves to become a disciple of the gospel of wealth, and henceforth he labors to acquire that he may wisely administer for others' good. His daily labor is a daily virtue. [25]

Not all of Carnegie's contemporaries agreed with his appraisal. William Jewett Tucker, the Andover theologian who became president of Dartmouth College, was one sharp critic of the essay. It was, he said, an apologia for an unjust social order; in avoiding the crucial distributive, as opposed to redistributive, issues with which people were becoming concerned, Carnegie had presented a "necessarian [sic] view of extreme riches" that would not promote justice and would promote "patronage." According to Tucker: "Within proper limits, the public is advantaged by the gifts of the rich, but if the method becomes the accepted method, to be expected and relied upon, the decline of public self-respect has begun. There is a public public spirit to be cherished as well as a private public spirit."[26] Tucker preferred greater structural change than Carnegie would have favored, given his belief in individual accomplishment and "genius" as the source for social progress.

Most commentators seemed to think that Carnegie's essay was at least a true expression of conscience and laudable for the generosity of spirit it revealed. Here was a new corporate captain, reputedly already one of the world's wealthiest men, confessing that he, too, was concerned with the need for reform. What is more, while avowing awareness of increasing rigidity and disharmony in modern society, he had expressed confidence in progress.[27]

"The Gospel of Wealth" was an affirmation of old traditional American values. Not only did "the man of wealth," according to Carnegie, have a duty to practice diligence in his calling, which included service to others, but his "poorer brethren," while, in the end, responsible for their own lot, could be helped to help themselves rise, through the increased benevolence new concentrations of wealth would allow. As Peter Cooper and Ezra Cornell and, more recently, Leland Stanford had shown, Carnegie said with admiration, they could be helped most if helped indirectly, through the provision of facilities for education; and they should be helped only if hard work, temperance, and worthiness had shown that they would be an asset to the community. In asserting that philanthropy could provide "ladders" to the poor, and in that way recreate the brotherly spirit of the eighteenth and early nineteenth century shop, where, Carnegie apparently assumed, the able apprentice could inherit his master's spot, he had asserted the continuing validity of an old postmilliennialist dream. Industrialism may have had its "price," but with virtue and through the stewardship of wealth, the world would still, in time, be redeemed as "the ideal State."

Believing that "all is well, since all grows better," Carnegie turned from describing "The Gospel of Wealth" to its practice, hoping through deed and example, even more than through precept, to promote enlightenment and to prove that there was indeed beneficence in a not always pretty world.

Henry Smith Pritchett and the Gospel of Efficiency

Henry Smith Pritchett was one of the men Andrew Carnegie turned to for assistance in administering his wealth.[1] An astronomer by training, Pritchett was president of the Massachusetts Institute of Technology (MIT) at the time he and Carnegie first met. Greatly interested in the 1901 announcement of Carnegie's gift of ten million dollars to endow a center for scientific research (it became the Carnegie Institution of Washington), he wrote to Carnegie, and a close relationship grew up between the two men. It was on Pritchett's suggestion and with his help that Carnegie established the pension fund for college professors that became the Carnegie Foundation for the Advancement of Teaching.

Chosen to serve as the Foundation's first president in 1905, Pritchett, beginning what amounted to a second career, turned the Foundation into a forceful and effective proponent of systematization in American education, and through education, in American life. As an advocate of organization and efficiency, Pritchett was especially concerned with establishing the university as both a consolidated and a consolidating center of knowledge-related activities. His signal contribution to the changes in culture and social structure that occurred in the United States in the early twentieth century was to direct some of Carnegie's wealth and the power that came with it to the organization of

American education along more modern, national, scientific, and bureaucratic lines.

Thorstein Veblen's phrase "Captain of Erudition" describes Pritchett well. He was tall, handsome, lean, and dignified in bearing. In many ways, he embodied the traits of a late Victorian gentleman. His rhetoric, embroidered with facts and statistics, was often stirring and earnestly moral. His opinions derived from principle and were tenaciously argued and adhered to. Very different in outward manner from Carnegie, who appeared to be so consistently happy, optimistic, genial, and jolly, Pritchett impressed those who knew him as purposeful, serious, and highly self-disciplined. Writing to Abraham Flexner, who published a biography of Pritchett four years after Pritchett's death in 1939, one associate said:

His figure was compact, his clothes were well-cut, his beard neatly trimmed, and even in old age he looked as if his body were close-knit and hard. His steady blue eyes...were observing eyes...I don't believe anyone would have called him a "hail-fellow-well-met," but he was certainly a companionable person. I have heard that his assistants in the Carnegie institutions were a little in awe of him and that he never encouraged or indulged in familiarities. Very likely. He was not easy-going with himself, and he had had too much executive experience to want to encourage the notion that he might be easy-going with others, and too fair minded to take liberties which he wouldn't want others to reciprocate. Besides, I believe that underneath all the social facility which his rich worldly experience had given him, he cherished an unusual reserve....He never became excited and his conversation always led to something worthwhile. I don't think small talk and gossip interested him in the slightest, but he dealt with any subject that did interest him in a simple and fresh way."[2]

As precise and focused in his thought as in his appearance, Pritchett had the kind of mind that could synthesize vast amounts of detailed information and then produce clear and simple charts and diagrams to illustrate a principle or plan. Carnegie was a divergent, eclectic, self-educated thinker; Pritchett was the reverse.

His scientific training was evident in the way he approached problems and sought to resolve them. His "faith" in science as a means to "truth" was essential to all aspects of his point of view.

THE EDUCATION OF A SCIENTIST

Born on the Missouri frontier in 1857, Pritchett had no formal schooling until he reached the age of ten. Like many families in the border states, his family was divided by the Civil War and suffered greatly during the war. He saw one of his uncles leave for service with the Confederate army and saw him brought home dead a week later by his Unionist brother, Henry's father. Confederate marauders threatened his father's life, forcing him to leave Missouri and his teaching job for sanctuary in the East. Henry stood with his mother while their house was repeatedly ransacked, sometimes by young men his mother recognized as favorite pupils of his father. And he rode with whichever soldiers, Confederate or Union, would allow him to tag along on their forays, until his own saddle, bridle, horse, and knife were stolen.

After the Civil War, Pritchett studied with his father, who was also a school principal, a Methodist minister, and, by avocation, an astronomer. Pritchett apparently wanted to be a lawyer, as prominent frontier leaders often were, but his father urged him to be an astronomer, and, bowing to his father's wishes, he left Missouri at the age of eighteen to study at the Naval Observatory in Washington, D.C.

In Washington, Pritchett lived and studied in apprentice-like fashion with his father's friend Asapha Hall. Hall was a prominent astronomer, who had discovered the satellites of Mars. He was the Observatory's director. Pritchett worked also with William Harkness, John R. Eastman, and Simon Newcomb, whom he assisted in charting the rotations of the moon. In 1878, he was appointed assistant astronomer in the Naval Observatory, thereby gaining professional recognition and a professional affiliation with one of the nation's leading centers of astronomical research.

At this time, Pritchett was also asked to become a founding member of Washington's elite Cosmos Club, whose purpose was "to bring into the social intercourse of scientific men in Washington the opportunity for personal contact, for good talk, for the forming of friendships...which unites the love of study and of books with the fellowship of Men."[3] Its members were prominent scientists and scholars, many of them associated with the newly founded Johns Hopkins University. These then saw their club as different from and better than the "sophisticated" New York clubs (Pritchett said: "There was a suspicion among us simple folk in Washington that the things done in clubs in New York might not be entirely suitable for scientific men"); and also more proper than Washington's more political, Congressional Club (Pritchett said: "It was strongly suspected that the members of the Congressional Club were given not only to the consumption of strong waters, but that they also played games that ought not to be played by dignified scient.fic gentlemen").[4] Membership in this club gave Pritchett a sense of having joined the elect. "I have a notion that when all go to Heaven," he once remarked, "and of course all members of the Cosmos Club will be there—we shall find Heaven made up of little clubs of good fellows."[5] In some ways this "Heaven" was like the upper strata of the social organization he later wished to develop in the United States. The small and unusual community Pritchett found in the Cosmos Club led him to identify with colleagues whose example and ideals would be hard to reconcile with the research opportunities of the small-town world to which he would return.

At this time, it was still relatively rare to be able to engage in scientific research as an integral part of one's daily occupation. The founding of Johns Hopkins University in 1876 had marked a real and symbolically significant step toward the association of teaching and research in academic life, but few professorial positions combined the two pursuits. To engage in the study of science as a sideline after work, as Pritchett's father did, was often all that even a would-be research scientist could afford to do.[6]

In 1880, when Pritchett returned to Missouri to take over the observatory his father had developed in connection with his school, he, too, had to divide his time, research becoming secondary. He was appointed to the faculty of Washington University in St. Louis and taught mathematics and astronomy there for sixteen years, for fourteen also serving as the director of the university's observatory. The contrast between his work at the Naval Observatory and in this growing, but still provincial, Midwestern city was stark. His principal work was the teaching of relatively elementary mathematics; his opportunities for research were limited to the few occasions when he could leave St. Louis, as he did in 1882 to observe the transit of Venus in New Zealand and again in 1889 to observe a total eclipse of the sun in California.

According to the Flexner biography, the observatory Pritchett directed was "limited to a transit instrument for determining time, located in a little shack....It was inadequate for the accurate work which he was eager to carry on."[7] Pritchett used this equipment to fulfill the kind of immediately utilitarian scientific function that new, more theoretical, inquiry-oriented conceptions of scientific utility were coming to replace. He made the observatory the local source of standard time. This accomplishment impressed a proud St. Louis author, who claimed that "the Washington Observatory in connection with the university is one of the most important in the world. It gives time...to thousands of public, railroad and other clocks, regulating the official time and correcting it to actual time over a larger area than any other observatory in the world, with the single exception of that of Greenwich, near London, England."[8] But to Pritchett, as to Flexner also, this observatory seemed far less grand. In 1894, several years after the death of his wife, Pritchett left St. Louis for Germany.

At the University in Munich, Pritchett's education as a professional scientist was back on track. Perhaps for the first time, he encountered "the new astronomy" of astrophysics. Within a year, he completed the doctorate with highest honors. He also traveled throughout Europe and found in the clubs of the German universities a variant of the Cosmos Club— "not only an agency for the cultivation of GEMÜTHLICHKEIT," but also "what the Methodists call a means of grace."[9] Reluctantly, he returned to Washington University in 1895, to "teach the Freshman year" but fortunately he did not stay long.[10] In 1897, he was asked to become superintendent of the U.S. Coast and Geodetic Survey.

THE POLITICS OF "PROFESSIONAL" SCIENCE

At the Coast Survey, Pritchett's work had to do with the development of charts, maps, and other official descriptive instruments and measures. It required the kind of knowledge of precise calculation and measurement he was already noted for. In addition, the job put him at the center of a conflict between professional and political claims to authority over government science, and summoned up his political skills, establishing his firm reputation as an administrator.

For reasons George H. Daniels and others have explored in detail, the autonomy of scientists was at the time under considerable question. American science had developed rapidly after the Civil War, partly because the public had been able to accept scientists' claims concerning the utilitarian value of their work. Those claims had helped to increase post-War federal appropriations for science via direct grants to government bureaus and indirect grants to land grant colleges. They also had encouraged the transferral of more and more authority for scientific policy decisions from the executive to the bureau level. Not surprisingly, however, as science became more specialized, theoretical, oriented toward collegially defined problems and standards, and removed from the realm of lay comprehension and public involvement, research activities began to be questioned. Politicians and scientists disputed who would evaluate the scientific work that was done under public auspices and with public monies.[11]

Although the Coast Survey had once been in the hands of such illustrious scientists as Alexander Dallas Bache, Benjamin Peirce, and Thomas C. Mendenhall, this conflict between science and government had touched the Survey. Pritchett's immediate predecessor, a political appointee, had tried to fire three distinguished Survey scientists. The clamor that resulted within the scientific community had been considerable; indeed, it had led to his removal from office. Pritchett's appointment was seen as a triumph for scientific autonomy and for the professional community with which he was affiliated. He entered a situation in which he was asked to defend and advance the cause of science and the professional claims of scientists by interpreting the value of science and of scientific professionalism to people outside the scientific domain.

Pritchett's effectiveness in securing independent status for the Office of Weights and Measures indicates that he was successful in the effort. What had been little more than a paper agency run out of the Survey's offices was transformed into the National Bureau of Standards. Describing the politics surrounding Congressional approval of the Bureau in *Science,* Pritchett downplayed his own role in the matter but praised the achievement. The Bureau's organization included a visiting committee that would report on its "efficiency and needs." Pritchett could therefore assure both scientists and politicians that "I shall be greatly disappointed if this does not have a wholesome effect on the bureau itself, and on the relations of the bureau with Congress and with the department. It is scarcely possible that a Secretary of the Treasury [to whom the bureau chief reported] will dismiss from office a competent head of the bureau who is supported courageously by this committee, nor will he appoint to the office of director a man whom they consider incompetent and unsuitable." Beyond that, the Bureau's establishment, he pointed out, was a triumph of scientist-politician cooperation. It grew out of work done by the University of Chicago scientist Samuel S. Stratton and by Secretary of the Treasury Lyman J. Gage and his assistant Frank A. Vanderlip. According to the Senate testimony of Secretary Gage, which Pritchett quoted with approval, the Bureau represented governmental recognition of the need to counter a "looseness in our methods" and a "looseness in our ideas" by asserting "the binding sanction of accuracy in every relation of life."[12] Apparently Pritchett had turned a politician into a defender of science and its vital import to national development.

Pritchett's work at the Coast Survey led to his appointment as president of MIT in 1900. The skill he had displayed in Washington as an interpreter of scientific concerns was no doubt a large factor in his selection—MIT needed money and one of Pritchett's jobs as president was to lobby the Massachusetts legislature for support.

Pritchett never discussed the matter directly, but his inclination to continue in the role of interpreter for science, and to leave research, no doubt sprang, in part, from a discrepancy between the "ideal" and the "real": between the practice of science as Pritchett had known it in Washington and had heard of it through conversations with his Johns Hopkins, Cosmos Club friends, and the practice of science as he had had to pursue it for so many years. He had seen the kind of German university his colleagues raved about and shared their enthusiasm for it; and he knew first-hand how different American colleges were. According to an 1882 survey conducted by Thomas C. Mendenhall, fewer than 30 of the approximately 400 American colleges and universities then in existence offered laboratory instruction of any kind.[13]

As Pritchett admitted in 1926, "the old astronomy" he had been trained in was also becoming more of a hobby for "the amateur astronomer" than a field of research for the "professional" researcher.[14] "The old astronomy" of measurement and location had been useful in mapping the visible world. But it was not useful in gauging the volume and mass and the chemical composition of stars and planets, and as that possibility arose with the development of astrophysics, that became the center of professional interest in astronomy. As Pritchett may well have realized for the first time in Germany, his technical expertise was being declassed. He could contribute more to the profession as an interpreter for science than he could as a researcher or a practitioner.

REFORMING A COLLEGE

As he obliquely suggested in his inaugural address, Pritchett went to MIT in order to change MIT. His first speech there was entitled "The Educated Man and the State." Its message was summed up in the following charge:

Until we bring into our college life and into our college training such influences as will strengthen the character as well as the intellect, until the time shall come that the educated man shall by reason of his training be not only more able than his untrained neighbor, but also more patriotic, more courageous, better informed concerning the service of the State, and more ready to take up its service,—until such a spirit is a part of our system of higher education, that system will not have served the ends which education should serve in a free State and for a free people.[15]

Pritchett was suggesting that educational reform was a necessity if the United States was to have a cadre of highly trained and public-spirited leaders. His interest in educational reform derived from a concern for leadership, combined with the belief that "the scholarly influences in the colleges are, on the whole, relatively less...than in the college of fifty years ago." The college, he thought, had become like a "business organization," with advertising, recruitment and placement services, and "athleticism" running rampant. "In no other institution have the commercial tendencies of our national life been more strongly reflected than in our college-universities," he said; and these commercial tendencies "develop the college side of the composite American universities rather than the research side."[16]

Referring to an "evil" (commercialism) that had great symbolic meaning within turn-of-the-century vernacular culture, Pritchett built a strong argument for an ideal that was still only well-cherished within the scientific community. The encouragement of the "scholarly influences" to support "the research side" of universities was presented not as a professional interest but as a public need. Described in this way, Pritchett's interest in training leaders and in promoting scientific research was appealing. Some might have said that these goals were important, but neither the only, nor necessarily the most important, goals for American colleges. They would have favored greater diversity in higher education than Pritchett did. However that may be, as an interpreter for science, Pritchett was a single-minded advocate for the research university that he saw as "the home of the true scientific spirit," and he was able to style his arguments for reform to appeal to audiences that did not yet fully understand or appreciate the aspirations he shared with his scientific colleagues.[17] His rousing speeches were persuasive to those who heard them at MIT and elsewhere, at least until his rhetoric was translated into an actual campaign for the restructuring of MIT. Then local college loyalties created a backlash of resistance.

Soon after his arrival in Boston, Pritchett met Harvard's president, Charles W. Eliot. The two men quickly became close friends and remained so until Eliot's death. Eliot proposed to Pritchett a favorite plan of his, to combine MIT and the Lawrence School of Science at Harvard. The suggestion fit in with Pritchett's interest in strengthening the humanities side of MIT's dual curriculum, which had always included the humanities as well as the theoretical and applied sciences. Furthermore, since the merger would make new funds available to MIT, and in terms of principle it seemed sound, the plan was appealing. As Pritchett explained to the alumni of MIT, the "Men of Technology," he believed that a merger would enhance the quality of scientific education. The history of American education proved, he argued, that "the lowering of standards comes not from co-operation and alliance between institutions but from competition between them."[18] Because it promised to raise the caliber of the scientific training in Boston and throughout the Northeast, the merger seemed to Pritchett to be educationally and administratively wise.

The alumni and faculty did not see it this way. They considered Pritchett's willingness even to suggest this merger as akin to treason. They had an interest, as Pritchett did not, in the maintenance of MIT's institutional autonomy and integrity. Its traditions and its close connection with the city of Boston should not be surrendered, they thought, in a take-over by the growing, more nationally oriented colossus in Cambridge. After long and bitter negotiations, the plan was defeated in 1905. Soon after, Pritchett left MIT. The repudiation of his reform plans led him to believe that he could accomplish more for his cause from outside the college than from within. He had expected to be president of the Carnegie Foundation while also serving as president of MIT, but as it turned out his second career was entirely devoted to making the Carnegie Foundation an effective advocate for the principles for which he had failed to gain favor at MIT.

THE GOSPEL OF EFFICIENCY

As president of the Carnegie Foundation, Pritchett would work to achieve the kind of national organization through educational systematization he first discussed in 1900. In speeches at MIT, and at the Foundation, he outlined his social vision. Many of his talks during this period stressed the point he praised in Lyman Gage's testimony about the National Bureau of Standards. In an address to a college audience in 1902, he said, for example:

The close of our Civil War found us still in the pioneer state of national development. There was abundant room for men to live the pioneer life, if they so desired. Pioneer methods still held in our farming, in our mining, in our manufactures, and even in our conceptions of education and life....But the economic change which has taken place in the period since the war has taken us out of the pioneer stage. Population has poured in upon us from all the nations of the world, and, although our vast area is not yet settled to a density comparable with that of Europe, nevertheless economic conditions are here approaching those of the old world, and it becomes more and more necessary that every human being should become an effective, economic unit.[19]

Foreshadowing later descriptions of the characteristics of a "mature," "modern," or even "postindustrial" economy, Pritchett linked changing circumstances to the need to develop high levels of professional and technical competence through formal school training. At a 1901 meeting of the New England Cotton Manufacturers' Association, he said:

the conditions of modern life are such, the facilities of communication are so great and play such a part in success, the relations of men are so complex and upon so large a scale, that the time is near when those who are to direct great organizations, who are to control and develop manufactures, who are to trade between nations—in a word, the Captains of Commerce—must look upon their calling as a profession, not a business; and for this profession there is a training to be had in the schools which will not only save time for the individual, but which will develop a broader, a more efficient and a higher type of man.[20]

He discussed the same point again a year later in an address on "The Place of Industrial and Technical Training in Popular Education." Arguing in this instance that "Massachusetts with nearly twice the average schooling per individual" produced "twice the amount of wealth per individual as compared with the nation's average," he urged support for vocational education as what some would today call an investment in "human capital."[21] Even for women, about whom he very rarely spoke, Pritchett believed vocational training could be valuable. With such education, women would be better able to fill the need the economy had for them in "the 'semi-professional' vocations, such as those of the teacher, of the librarian, of the secretary, and of the many professions which depend upon the application of science...such, for instance, as the better ordering of the household, the furnishing of good food under sanitary conditions and at reasonable prices, and the adaptation of clothing to the varied conditions of our life and of our climate."[22]

Pritchett's speeches tended to apply to education the kinds of assumptions that were evident in the natural resource conservation movement that was emerging at this time. The similarity was hardly a coincidence. The conservation movement was supported by many of the natural scientists active in the work Pritchett had supervised at the Coast Survey. He shared with them much in the way of experience and vision; indeed, he shared with them an ideology Samuel P. Hays has called "the gospel of efficiency." The significance of the conservation movement, Hays has written:

stemmed from the role it played in the transformation of a decentralized, nontechnical, loosely organized society, where waste and inefficiency ran rampant, into a highly organized, technical, and centrally planned and directed social organization which could meet a complex world with efficiency and purpose. This spirit of efficiency appeared in many realms of American life, in the professional engineering societies, among forward-looking industrial management leaders, and in municipal government reform, as well as in the resource management concepts of Theodore Roosevelt. The possibility of applying scientific and technical principles to resource development...imbued all in the conservation movement with a kindred spirit. These goals required public management....They also required new administrative methods, utilizing to the fullest extent the latest scientific knowledge and expert, disinterested personnel. This was the gospel of efficiency—efficiency which could be realized only through planning, foresight, and conscious purpose. [23]

Like other evangels of this gospel, Pritchett believed that the nation could no longer afford the wasteful, selfish, individualistic behavior that had been acceptable on the frontier. His interest in the planned articulation of people—human resources—through the systematization of education derived in part from his awareness of the phenomenal growth of the United States in the decades after the Civil War. He had seen this growth in St. Louis, whose population almost doubled in the ten years between the 1860 and 1870 censuses. More important than this, however, Pritchett's vision of prosperity and order through the development and organization of education derived from his confidence in science as a means to progress in every sphere of national life. It was his faith in science that oriented his approach to the problems of growth.

Pritchett defined the "scientific method" as "open-mindedness" and "intellectual sincerity." It was, he repeatedly argued, the one sure means to "the truth."[24] In a speech he delivered at the University of California in 1910, he said: "The great function of science is not in the inventions which the physical sciences have contributed, not even in the mastery over disease and suffering which its study has developed. The great service of science to humanity is to search out the laws of the universe and to point men to the consequences of their disobedience; to deliver men from fear and to bring mankind into a larger and clearer faith,—a faith in the truth as the outcome of brave and honest thinking." [25] Pritchett was a secular but still a very religious man in his attitudes and philosophy. His "faith" was science, his church, the university; and, with the new power to know the natural order that science provided, he believed a new possibility existed for achieving human harmony. His interest in educational planning and standardizing derived as much from his faith in science as a means for discovering "the laws" that should govern the world, as it did from his clearly related wish to foster science through the development of institutions that would allow scientists to undertake the sort of research studies he himself had seldom been able to do.

As president of the Carnegie Foundation, Pritchett identified himself usually as an educator rather than as a scientist. But he was always an interpreter for the community from which he came. In science and in "its home ... the university" he saw a new means for training men for "service," service to the "truth," which he believed to be "the property of no party, of no creed, of no source of authority."[26] With such men as its leaders he hoped the United States could enter the modern world. The "individualistic conception of human progress," which was, of course, the conception of progress Andrew Carnegie held, was no longer sufficient, Pritchett argued, in an era when "the effective grouping together of great numbers of individuals" was both possible and necessary. What the world needed, instead, he urged was a conception of progress based on the development of great leaders. To help build "The Great Society" Pritchett believed:

The call of the world...is for leaders—...for leaders who think; for men and women who...can teach other[s]...to organize upon a cultural basis in which the machinery of organization shall not absorb the spirit it is meant to serve; in which corporations shall have souls, in which parties shall not lose sight of principles, in which organized groups shall not be merely on the basis of self-interest; in which philosophy and religion and science and industry and material progress shall all be threads in the fabric of human culture....For such leadership...humanity looks to its universities.[27]

– 3 –

Founding the Foundation

At four o'clock in the afternoon of November 15, 1905, twenty-five men gathered in the living room of Andrew Carnegie's Fifth Avenue mansion in New York City. Their purpose was to initiate the business of the Carnegie Foundation for the Advancement of Teaching, originally a ten million dollar trust Carnegie had established to provide pensions for college and university professors in Canada and the United States. Most of the twenty-five were college presidents from the nation's more established and prestigious, privately endowed institutions of higher education. Among them were Charles W. Eliot of Harvard, Nicholas Murray Butler of Columbia, Arthur T. Hadley of Yale, David Starr Jordan of Stanford, Jacob Gould Schurman of Cornell, and Woodrow Wilson of Princeton.[1] Unanimously they elected Henry Smith Pritchett to serve as the Foundation's chief executive.

Pritchett was the logical candidate for the job. He was favored by Carnegie, who had relied on his suggestions and advice in designing the trust, and he was also favored by the trustees. In fact, it was on the urging of Nicholas Murray Butler and William Rainey Harper of the University of Chicago (who was not able to attend the Foundation's first meeting) that Pritchett decided to consider the job in the first place.[2] With trustee cooperation he hoped he could make this new pension fund into what he described to Carnegie as "one of the Great Agencies not only in dignifying the teachers calling but also in standardizing American education."[3]

THE ADMINISTRATIVE STRUCTURE OF THE CARNEGIE FOUNDATION

Two aspects of the Foundation's original governance structure stood behind Pritchett's hopes for the Fund. First, it had a board of trustees composed of men, virtually all of whom shared Pritchett's interest in collegiate reform. Some have been recognized as university builders: Eliot, Butler, Harper, and Jordan, especially. Others are less well-known today, but were important reformers at this time. Edwin B. Craighead, president of Tulane University, is an example. Like Pritchett, he had been born in Missouri, educated there and in both Leipzig and Paris, and in a variety of important educational positions had been effective in raising the standards of college study. At Tulane his main concern was modernizing the medical school that was associated with the university, by linking it to a hospital and gaining financial support for its laboratories.[4] With the possible exceptions of Carnegie's nephew and his financial secretary, all members of the Carnegie Foundation's original Board were likely to support Pritchett in fulfilling the hope he had expressed before agreeing to become president of the Foundation—that it "might count for a large influence in the educational problems."[5] The only noncollege president in addition to Carnegie's nephew and financial secretary was Frank A. Vanderlip, who had been Lyman Gage's assistant at the Treasury when Pritchett was at the Coast Survey.

Charles W. Eliot was elected chairman of the Board at the same meeting that chose Pritchett as president. Eliot and Pritchett saw eye to eye on almost everything. The collaboration they had established in connection with the plan to merge MIT and the Lawrence School of Science at Harvard continued at the Carnegie

Foundation, beginning even before their "skillful handling" of the first meeting of the trustees.[6]

Pritchett's sense that the Carnegie Pension Fund could be important also arose from the fact that its pensions were to be distributed selectively. According to the "letter of gift" sent to the men Carnegie appointed as initial trustees, pensions were to go to professors in nonsectarian universities, colleges, and technical schools that were not under state control; they were to be distributed "under such conditions" as the trustees chose to "adopt from time to time."[7] What this meant, as became obvious at the trustees' first meeting, was that this board could and would engage in institutional standard setting as a means for reforming and distinguishing among the motley array of schools and colleges that had grown up all over the United States.

Immediately after the election of officers, the trustees received a memorandum that Pritchett helped to author. It said that "the most important question with which the Board has to deal, if it is to do its business with institutions rather than deal directly with individuals, is that of determining what educational standard shall be set up: in other words, what is a 'college' in the sense in which this Board will construe it?"[8] The answer to that question, as set forth in the Foundation's *1st Annual Report*, was that "an institution to be ranked as a college" had to meet at least the following requirements: in addition to being nonsectarian and free of state control, it had to have no fewer than six full-time professors "giving their entire time to college and university work"; it had to offer a four year course of study in the liberal arts and sciences; and it had to require for admission "not less than the usual four years of academic or high school preparation."[9]

Nothing about this last requirement or any of the other standards the Foundation subsequently adopted was "usual." Of the more than six hundred institutions of higher education listed with the U.S. Bureau of Education at this time, only fifty-two made it onto the Foundation's original "accepted list."" From the very first, selectivity was the goal. The Foundation was organized to strengthen those colleges in which the "scholarly influences" were such that they might become, if they were not already, the kind of "true universities" in which science might flourish. Since a college could be added to the Fund's "accepted list" of institutions whenever it was certified by the Foundation as meeting the standards of a "college," it was also organized, as the *1st Annual Report* indicated, so that its "influence may result not simply in the raising of certain assumed standards, but in the bringing in of reasonable unity in our arrangement of educational institutions."[11] Favoring the kinds of colleges its trustees represented, which were feeling something of a pinch from the growing state universities (one of the two major categories of nonaccepted colleges, denominational colleges being the other) the Foundation was designed to give the nation's older, private, primarily Eastern colleges a boost in what was, in essence, a highly competitive and unregulated industry.

As early as May of 1906, when Pritchett described "Mr. Carnegie's Gift to the Teachers" for the *Outlook,* he had sufficient confidence in the potential of this trust to note that "from the standpoint of the administration of trust funds, and particularly of educational trusts, this board of trustees presents two characteristics of unusual interest." First, it was managed by "a body of experts in education, drawn from all parts of the United States and Canada"; second, it was "a central agency in educational administration, which represents not a locality or a single institution, but which aims to take into account the educational needs of all sections." For these reasons, Pritchett prophesied, and prophesied correctly, "the scope of the Carnegie Foundation for the Advancement of Teaching as a centralizing and standardizing influence in American education promises to outweigh in importance the primary purpose of the fund [i.e. pensioning], great as that primary purpose is."[12] In the Carnegie Foundation he had already institutionalized "the gospel of efficiency."

A BREAK WITH TRADITION

The development of centralization and expert administration were important to Pritchett, but they were not goals Carnegie had sought as a philanthropist. One of Carnegie's personal secretaries made this point very directly in 1914 in connection with an incident having to do with the Carnegie Corporation, a grant-making foundation established in 1911 with most of Carnegie's wealth to promote "the advancement and diffusion of knowledge and understanding among the people of the United States."[13] In addition to being president of the Carnegie Foundation, Pritchett was a trustee of the Corporation, and in that capacity hired the economist Alvin Johnson to survey the libraries established with Carnegie funds. Johnson's study documented what Pritchett had suspected: many libraries and few common standards for library operations. It also suggested, among other things, that the Corporation establish some mechanism for overseeing future Carnegie library operations. When presented to the Corporation's small group of trustees, James Bertram, formerly Carnegie's personal secretary and now secretary of the Corporation, exploded (Carnegie himself was not present). He charged that Johnson's recommendation absolutely contradicted "Mr. Carnegie's intentions. He wanted to give libraries to communities," Bertram stated, "and leave the communities absolutely free to manage them any way they might see fit. He abominated centralized, bureaucratic control. That is exactly what you want to introduce."[14]

James Bertram was entirely correct, and his perception of the transformation that was slowly taking place in the Carnegie Corporation's program was foreshadowed by the organizational design Pritchett advised Carnegie to establish for the Carnegie Foundation. The two features Pritchett saw as most promising for the Foundation's capacity to promote educational reform, the composition of its board of trustees and the selective distribution of its pensions, diverged from established patterns of Carnegie giving and ran counter to several of Carnegie's best known and most deeply held convictions.

As he indicated on many occasions, Carnegie wanted to make educational opportunities more widely available. He was especially interested in supporting small, local colleges, and tended to refuse requests from the kinds of institutions that would, in fact, be assisted by this new pension plan. Even when approached by close and cherished friends whom he wanted to help, Carnegie was often obdurate in this preference. He told William Gladstone that he would not give money for the Bodleian library at Oxford because it only helped scholars; he told Daniel Coit Gilman, whom he had chosen to be the first president of the Carnegie Institution of Washington, that he would not give library money to Johns Hopkins, since "great universities get large bequests and millions are bestowed upon them...[while] small institutions are struggling, educating young men for a trifle a year"; and planning for the CFAT got started when he told Henry Pritchett that he would not provide a pension fund for MIT.[15]

It is possible, of course, that Carnegie did not realize that the exclusion of state-supported and denominational colleges would mean that funds would not reach many of the small, local colleges he tended to favor. But he certainly knew that the trustees he had appointed, and appointed as representatives of their institutions, came from large, relatively well-endowed colleges, the very colleges that he often said were not within his "field." Very possibly he simply thought of the pensions as assistance to teachers, whom he considered noble wherever they taught, and failed to grasp that the means by which the pensions were distributed could in itself be an instrument to ends other than simple administrative efficiency.

Although it may seem entirely natural for Carnegie to have appointed a board of trustees made up of "experts in education," that step also ran counter to his tradition and convictions as a philanthropist. The trustees Carnegie had chosen to oversee previously established institutions such as the Carnegie Institute of Pittsburgh and the Carnegie Institution of Washington had included men drawn from a variety of occupations. Often, trustees had been friends of Carnegie's; sometimes they had been men he did not know but admired; and, on occasion, they had been occupants of public offices Carnegie wanted to have represented on the board. In no instance had they been chosen because they were "experts." In describing the kinds of trustees he wanted for the cultural center he established in 1895 in Pittsburgh, Carnegie had said: "The last men I should appoint to manage a business are experts. The expert mind is too narrow...I wish to trust my fund to a committee dominated by able men of affairs, who have within reach the expert element with which they can confer. Besides this, I wish a large number of officials directly from the people in the committee, as I am satisfied that unless the institution be kept in touch with the masses, and therefore popular, it cannot be widely useful."[16]

Even though the Carnegie Foundation had purposes different from the Pittsburgh arts center, it is nevertheless difficult to reconcile the distrust for experts that Carnegie expressed on that occasion and others with the make-up of the Foundation's board. Perhaps Carnegie thought of these college presidents as men of wide, rather than "narrow," "expert" vision. It was Pritchett, after all, and not Carnegie himself, who used that term to describe them. Perhaps he assumed, as Pritchett himself said, that these men were representatives of the teachers the Foundation would serve and for that reason would keep it "popular." Certainly, he liked to be surrounded by college presidents, and that also may have skewed his view. Whatever his reasons, Carnegie most likely did not realize either that the appointment of a board of college presidents would in itself lend public credence to the claim that here, indeed, was a "Great Agency," or that it would foster suspiciousness in the minds of the teachers the Foundation was meant to "dignify," college presidents often having been seen by professors as neither representatives for, nor sympathizers with their professional academic interests.

Even before he became president of the Carnegie Foundation, Pritchett had gained a decisive position in the designing of this trust. He had helped Carnegie choose the Foundation's trustees, in the process convincing Carnegie not to appoint himself to the Board as he had at first intended to do; and he had also convinced Carnegie that pensions should be given primarily on the basis of a professor's institutional affiliation. Pritchett's role as a Carnegie advisor grew out of his role as a spokesman for science and educational reform. Pritchett recognized the potential power inherent in accumulated private wealth and had a clear sense of how such power could be used to promote the kind of social organization he believed the United States needed. For this reason, he had begun to cultivate Carnegie's trust, respect, reliance, and affection as far back as 1901. His personal relationship with Carnegie was no less carefully crafted than the administrative design of the Foundation he led.

THE PERSONAL POLITICS OF SOCIAL CHANGE

Planning for the Carnegie Institution of Washington served as the initial medium for Pritchett's suit. Although Carnegie had not yet firmly set the precise purposes of the Institution, his endowment for a science center was announced to the press in December of 1901. In consequence, a lively debate ensued on the most useful ways to use this large gift for scientific research. With other members of the scientific community, Pritchett joined in this debate. He responded to James McKeen Carrell's invitation to set forth his ideas for the Institution in the columns of *Science* and he wrote directly to Carnegie, offering congratulations and further suggestions.[17]

When an article entitled "America's Inferior Position in the Scientific World" appeared in the January, 1902, number of the *North American Review,* Pritchett quickly called the article to Carnegie's attention, claiming it "curious" that the article suggested an institution so much like the one Carnegie had in mind.[18] That was not entirely accurate, of course. The article recommended the establishment of an independent research institute in the nation's capital, and it was not yet clear that Carnegie's endowment would be spent to establish this kind of center. Nevertheless, Pritchett's comment was prophetic and may have been intended to be compellingly so. Pritchett thought the endowment should be used to create an American equivalent of the Royal Institute in London. At least one historian has suggested that this article, which was written by a free-lance writer whose specialty was science, may have been quietly but purposefully commissioned and then, not by happenstance, published in Carnegie's favorite journal in order to influence his views.[19] After reading the article Carnegie reordered his still unpublished priorities for the Institution, and, in light of Pritchett's favorable comments on the article, began to think of him as an interesting and intelligent friend.[20]

In the months that followed Pritchett's first exchange with Carnegie, he continued his efforts to make himself known to the man he came to call "the Laird." Extended personal correspondence enabled him to press his suit. His letters to Carnegie varied in substance, but they were all much the same in style. Each pre-

sented its writer as a dispassionate admirer, as a colleague independently dedicated to the causes Carnegie favored, and as a man
who wished to be a respectful but personal friend. They volun-
teered favorable comments on Carnegie's speeches and published
writings; they asked for Carnegie's advice and invited his assessment of Pritchett's own endeavors; and wherever possible they
pointed out the interests, experiences, and aspirations the two
men had in common. Thus, in sending Carnegie a copy of some
sermons he had given to MIT students, Pritchett suggested that
their underlying premises pointed "in the direction of some of
your own work"; and in praising a speech Carnegie had made at a
library opening, he confessed that, like Carnegie, he too was the
"product of a small public library."[21] As was particularly obvious
in the letter that alluded to the commonalities in their education,
Pritchett's representations to Carnegie tended to emphasize points
of compatibility and to deemphasize points of difference. They
were carefully crafted to create bonds of identity and a sense of camaraderie—the kind of personal relationship that would enhance
Pritchett's chances for shaping the uses to which Carnegie would
assign his wealth.

In the spring of 1904, both men were invited to a White
House luncheon given by Theodore Roosevelt and, according to
Pritchett, they just "happened" to sit together and to have "considerable conversation" on the train going back to New York. The
following summer, when Pritchett was in Europe, he was invited
to Carnegie's summer home in Scotland where, he said, the
Carnegie Foundation was born in the "walks and talks" he and
Carnegie had together.[22] Pritchett's emphasis on coincidence and
luck in his retrospective descriptions of his encounters with
Carnegie and his apparent casualness when a chance for meetings
just "happened" to occur may have been not a little disingenuous.

Like the "curious" *North American Review* article and like the article he wrote for *Science* about the establishment of the National

Bureau of Standards, this posture indicates how skillful Pritchett could be in disassociating himself from plans that he favored and worked tirelessly for. By maintaining a semblance of objective disinterest, Pritchett enhanced his image as a selfless public servant, and with that his effectiveness as an advocate for the principles and causes in which he believed. No less than selfish "commercialism," personal ambition and subjective interest were objects of suspicion to many people at this time. In fact, Pritchett was opposed by other scientists as a candidate to succeed Daniel Coit Gilman as president of the Carnegie Institution of Washington because his interest in the position was too widely known.[23] In this era of high faith in scientific truth and of growing professionalism, Pritchett's effectiveness as a partisan depended in no small measure on the success with which he could divest himself of all vestiges of personalism. Because he did not overtly seek this new position, Pritchett was able to become an increasingly close Carnegie advisor.

As he became established in a position of trust and power, Pritchett began to place before Carnegie carefully phrased suggestions for new projects that seemed compatible with Carnegie's own philanthropic goals. Writing to Carnegie on December 21, 1904, Pritchett ventured the following "Christmas thought": "that there is no one distinctive thing you could do that would be so far-reaching in its effects on education in our country as the establishment of...a retirement fund in one of our large institutions; and I should hope that the Institute of Technology might be considered in making up your mind."[24]

This "Christmas thought" had been carefully contemplated. In his 1903 president's report at MIT, Pritchett had discussed MIT's need for such a fund.[25] And by 1904 his concern with gaining an endowment for pensions was quite keen. The plan to merge MIT and Harvard's Lawrence School of Science that he and Charles Eliot had proposed was in trouble with the MIT alumni and faculty by this time. If he could rusticate old, powerful, and well-respected faculty members in a dignified way, as through the granting of a pension, he would be able to remove some of the negative voices raised against an alliance he strongly supported.

To Pritchett's dismay, Carnegie did not acquiesce in his suggestion. Rather, he countered with an expression of interest in a more general pension fund.[26] By 1904, pensioning was an increasingly accepted and common way of expressing corporate responsibility and Carnegie himself enjoyed giving pensions.[27] One of his first acts as a philanthropist had been to establish pensions for the men at Carnegie Steel, and before the arrival of Pritchett's request, on the suggestion of Andrew D. White (the former president of Cornell), his old friend from the days of Anne Botta's salon, he had added Mrs. Ezra Cornell to the private pension list he maintained. "Where can money be better used than in providing for a dear old lady left destitute in old age," he wrote to White with characteristic ebullience. "This is better than Library Building and equal to The Hague Temple. I think [it] beats even that."[28] The chance to assist the widow of a man Carnegie looked up to as one of the first practitioners of the "Gospel of Wealth" may have brought special pleasure, but pensioning always gave him considerable satisfaction. As a trustee of Cornell University, Carnegie had also discovered that professors with several decades of experience earned no more than office clerks at Carnegie Steel and had been shocked by that fact.[29] For all these reasons and because a pension fund would fit in well with his belief in promoting enlightenment by rewarding and calling attention to individuals who were exemplars of nobility and service, he met Pritchett's proposal with a counter suggestion. He asked him to investigate the possibility of creating a more general pension scheme.

Still in search of the money he needed for MIT, Pritchett made inquiries among his friends on how he might arrange a meeting with John D. Rockefeller, Jr.[30] But, in the meantime, unwilling to give up the position of trust he had so carefully cultivated with Carnegie, he also set out to help Carnegie develop a general pension plan, while seeking indirectly but effectively to improve upon the "old man's" idea.[31]

Pritchett introduced Carnegie to Frank A. Vanderlip, who was now vice-president of the City Bank and who was presented to Carnegie as "a very interesting and high-minded man."[32] This move was natural, sensible, and shrewd. Vanderlip had become one of Pritchett's closest friends. They had first met during Pritchett's time at the Coast Survey, and by 1905, a friendship born of a close work-related acquaintance and compatible interests and ideals had ripened into an almost fraternal relationship. Vanderlip took care of Pritchett's finances and sat on the MIT board of trustees. Pritchett stayed at his home on his frequent visits to New York City and Vanderlip also offered the services of his office at the City Bank.[33]

Pritchett could expect that Vanderlip would impress Carnegie. A self-educated man from the middle-west, Vanderlip, like Carnegie, had risen meteorically to wealth and power through hard work, the favors of his superiors, and successful financial investments. Of Vanderlip's own acknowledgment, so earnest of purpose and so fascinated by his work that he never learned to play, he also gave evidence of being a man of "character." He was admired by many men of Carnegie's acquaintance—J. P. Morgan, George F. Baker, and James Stillman were grooming the City Bank's vice-president to inherit their dominion in the financial world. If Carnegie investigated, he would learn that Vanderlip was one of the already knighted young wizards of Wall Street.[34]

Pritchett could also assume that Vanderlip could be relied upon to style his advice so that Carnegie would be led to a sensible plan. As their cooperation in establishing the National Bureau of Standards had demonstrated, Pritchett and Vanderlip were in close agreement on matters of national development. Like Pritchett, Vanderlip was an admirer of all things German. And, also like Pritchett, he believed that Germany's cultural and industrial development were largely the result of her educational system. The social and economic benefits the United States would derive from a similarly comprehensive, coordinated, and clearly stratified system of schooling were abundantly evident to both men.[35] In Vanderlip, Pritchett had a financial expert in whom both he and Carnegie, for different reasons, could trust.

Having recruited an ally, Pritchett could be candid. On February 6, 1905, he wrote to Vanderlip to explain that Carnegie had asked him to collect "the data for forming an approximate estimate of what sum would be required in order to establish a pension system covering the principal representative institutions of higher learning in the country." He described how he would calculate such a figure and urged Vanderlip, who was about to call on Carnegie, to "bear in mind this talk of mine with Mr. Carnegie in what he says to you. He had in his mind, I think, rather the insurance system than the pension system: in other words he had a plan for furnishing insurance at a little more than cost, possibly in co-operation with some insurance company. This, I think, is impossible, but the pension plan might be worked out."[36] Discrepancies in terminology notwithstanding (what Pritchett called "insurance" probably being what Carnegie called a "pension"), one point is clear. Andrew Carnegie's initial conception of a pension fund involved a contributory scheme.[37]

A contributory retirement fund would have appealed to Carnegie's general inclination for gifts that provided partial rather than full support, for gifts that were an incentive to self-help. Further, by mandating that whatever capital Carnegie invested in the plan be matched by other sources, a contributory retirement fund could reach a larger number of beneficiaries than a non-contributory plan could do. As Carnegie no doubt hoped, a contributory plan might have brought recognition and at least some assistance to many of the teachers in the small, local, "struggling" colleges he so admired. As Pritchett had anticipated, Vanderlip's calculations appear to have been decisive in convincing Carnegie to drop what Pritchett had called the "insurance" idea in favor of the kind of pension plan that was established. Pritchett's assertion that Vanderlip "hypnotized the old man" may have been exaggerated, but it was not entirely off the mark.[38] Carnegie expressed his indebtedness to Vanderlip, and Vanderlip helped to write the undated memo that was placed before Carnegie sometime before April of 1905.[39]

That memo described two plans: Plan A for pensions without insurance and Plan B for pensions with insurance.[40] Neither embodied what seems to have been Carnegie's initial concept of pensions as old age insurance requiring an employee contribution. Nevertheless, with two carefully drawn and detailed plans in front of him, Carnegie decided to act. Eager to move—at the time the library business was slowing down to one gift a day and no other project was in the works—and pleased with the idea of a dramatic announcement immediately following his departure for Europe, Carnegie chose Plan A, "an organization that would work." Whether he did so with reservations is impossible to determine; that he was swiftly and effectively prevailed upon to deed ten million dollars to a board of trustees Pritchett recommended to administer a plan whose full implications he did not thoroughly understand at the time, seems, in retrospect, undeniable. By the time Carnegie left New York for the summer of 1905, a "letter of gift" describing his newest philanthropy had been drafted, mailed, and released to the press. The key features of the Foundation's administrative structure had been set.[41]

None of this should suggest that Carnegie was hoodwinked. He was no man's dupe. After the Foundation was in operation, he often reminded Pritchett that "I don't think you should disguise the fact that [the Foundation] is first and foremost a pension fund. The closer union it may bring about is incidental, though important."[42] Yet he also believed that "next to the relief afforded to the teachers of mankind by the Fund comes the good work it is doing in raising the standards of education," and more forthrightly expressed this belief to Charles W. Eliot, who served as a mediator when Carnegie's and Pritchett's hopes for the Foundation seemed most at odds.[43] Obviously, then, though Carnegie did not fully agree with Pritchett's strategy, he too thought the Foundation would be a significant force in promoting community well-being.

Beyond that, Pritchett did not always triumph in putting his priorities before Carnegie's. In at least two ways, Carnegie turned the tables. In March of 1908, when he realized that state universities also wanted to be considered for eligibility in the pension fund, Carnegie increased the Foundation's endowment from ten million dollars to fifteen million dollars so that professors in these colleges could be included.[44] Furthermore, having encouraged Pritchett to believe that he might triple or quadruple the Foundation's endowment on his death, Carnegie foreclosed that possibility in 1911 when he deeded all of his remaining wealth to the separate foundation, the Carnegie Corporation of New York.[45]

Pritchett was dismayed when this happened. At the time, he and Carnegie had a major disagreement over what Carnegie did and did not owe the Foundation by way of future endowments, and Pritchett suggested in pique that "I am quite ready...to drop out quietly and let someone take up the work who might express his friendship for you more fortunately."[46] The dispute that began in this way continued in recurrent disagreements over Corporation obligations to the Foundation, although Pritchett and Carnegie managed to smooth over their personal tiff. Carnegie wanted Pritchett as president of the Foundation, and the Corporation's 1913 gift of one and a quarter million dollars to endow the work of a "Division of Educational Enquiry" may have been a conciliatory gesture on his part. Although this was hardly the sum Pritchett had anticipated or needed to carry forward the work in which he was by then engaged, he was probably too deeply involved by this time to have made good on his threat. To have left would have been to abandon the considerable progress he already had made in shaping Carnegie's philanthropy according to his view of communal needs. And where, in any case, was he now to go? To have moved on yet again probably would have been more difficult than it had been earlier.

A PENSION FUND AND A "GREAT AGENCY"

In the end, then, conflicts between Carnegie and Pritchett resulted in a draw. Their collaboration was not easy. It was based on assumptions and practices that had prevailed in the very different worlds from which each man had come. In the nineteenth century world of entrepreneurial business, Carnegie had made a fortune by identifying talented individuals and by allowing them considerable freedom of action. He had once said of himself: "I am neither mechanic nor engineer, nor am I scientific. The fact is I don't amount to anything in any industrial department. I seem to have had a knack of utilizing those that do know better than myself."[47] Having decided that Pritchett was "one of the men who can do things," he may have practiced his "knack" again.[48] At the least he gave Pritchett substantial scope, if not as much as Pritchett wished. And since Pritchett did establish a pension fund, Carnegie believed that his duty as a philanthropist had been fulfilled. Furthermore, when it became obvious that the Foundation's income would not be sufficient to meet even the demands of a selective pension distribution scheme, Pritchett set up the Teachers Insurance and Annuity Association of America (TIAA). Organized to be essentially occupation-wide and based on a contributory plan, TIAA was much like the plan Carnegie seems to have wanted in the first place. Although he was very old and tired when TIAA was launched in 1917, Carnegie constantly inquired about its progress. He seems to have realized that TIAA would more closely embody his original idea.[49]

Pritchett, for his part, also acted as he had been trained to do. Unlike personal secretaries such as James Bertram, whom he often referred to as "clerks," Pritchett believed he had an obligation to reconcile Carnegie's stated wishes with what he thought to be the actual needs of American education. And, since his perception of those needs diverged considerably from Carnegie's, Pritchett used all of his knowledge and skill, as well as all of the support he could garner from his large network of acquaintances, to fulfill objectives other than those Carnegie envisioned.

Pritchett found Carnegie's ideas no less "impossible" than other men of scientific background did. During the early years of the Carnegie Institution of Washington, no one had seen a realistic way to fulfill Carnegie's insistent wish that, however the Institution was organized, it should find and support the "exceptional man" wherever he might be. Carnegie apparently hoped that by establishing the Institution, its officers would continue the quest he was most interested in as a philanthropist—identifying and encouraging "genius." But the officers of the Carnegie Institution could not do that, nor would they. Not its trustees, but its administrators, were scientists, and like Pritchett they had been trained to the increasingly professional ideals of the American scientific community. Inevitably, therefore, despite many discussions concerning how the Institution could fulfill Carnegie's wishes for it, it had rewarded and supported the work of people who could be identified through the credentialling and promotional processes that were coming to serve as guidelines by which scientists recognized ability and accomplishment.[50]

Carnegie's hopes for progress were "old-fashioned" by the turn of the century. They derived from a belief in the individual and in the power of individual enlightenment and individual action that was less widely held than it once had been. Pritchett's hopes for progress were far more up-to-date. They were "modern." They reflected a faith in science and derived from a belief in the power of coordinated and efficient group action that was becoming increasingly pervasive throughout American society. They were predicated on the assumption that experts should design the future course of national development. The Foundation these two men established together was a hybrid of their views—a pension fund that also would be "one of the Great Agencies...in standardizing American education."[51] In a sense, it was an "island community" of like-minded, socially similar "experts in education." But it was an "island community" that was already linked to many other communities. It would play a significant role in shaping the values and the institutions of "The Great Society."

Andrew Carnegie in 1863 at the age of 27

(Courtesy of the Carnegie Corporation of New York)

Andrew Carnegie at Skibo Castle, which he
built in 1898

Henry S. Pritchett as a boy.
Pritchett became the first
president of the Carnegie
Foundation

Andrew Carnegie (left) and Henry S. Pritchett (right),
enlarged from Board portrait
(*Courtesy of the Carnegie Foundation for the Advancement of Teaching*)

The Board of Trustees of the Carnegie Foundation for the Advancement
of Teaching, 1912
(*Courtesy of the Carnegie Foundation for the Advancement of Teaching*)

One of the last pictures of Andrew Carnegie,
taken about 1915
(*CORBIS/Bettmann*)

Henry S. Pritchett around the time
(1905) he became first president of
the Carnegie Foundation for the
Advancement of Teaching

(*Courtesy of The MIT Museum and
Historical Collections*)

Abraham Flexner, author of *Medical
Education in the United States and Canada*

*(Courtesy of the Carnegie Corporation
of New York)*

William S. Learned, long-time
Carnegie Foundation staff member
and organizer of the
Pennsylvania Study

*(Courtesy of the Carnegie Foundation
for the Advancement of Teaching)*

Clark Kerr, chairman
of the Carnegie
Commission on
Higher Education and
of the Carnegie Council
for Policy Studies in
Higher Education

(Courtesy of Clark Kerr)

The Carnegie Commission on Higher Education, 1973. (Left to right) Row 1:
Ralph Besse, David Riesman, Katharine McBride, Clark Kerr, Patricia Roberts
Harris, Nathan Pusey; Row 2: William Friday, Stanley J. Heywood, Clifton W.
Phalen, Norton Simon, William Scranton; Row 3: Kenneth Keniston, Kenneth
Tollett, Carl Kaysen, Joseph Cosand, David D. Henry;
Row 4: James A. Perkins, Theodore Hesburgh, C.S.C.

(Courtesy of Clark Kerr)

Some of the publications of the
Carnegie Commission and
Carnegie Council

(Courtesy of John Phillips,
Chronicle of Higher Education)

Alan Pifer, sixth president of the
Carnegie Foundation
for the Advancement of Teaching

*(Courtesy of the Carnegie Corporation
of New York)*

Caricature of Andrew Carnegie, *Harper's Weekly,* May 24, 1913
(*Courtesy of the Carnegie Endowment for International Peace*)

PART II

Technologies of Influence

"The Engineer," Henry Pritchett once said, "is a solver of practical problems. To fit him for this he needs technical knowledge and usually a formal technical training; but the real test of his ability as an engineer is found in the success with which he attacks engineering problems."[1] And what was an engineering problem? Pritchett did not answer that question in this particular speech, although his assertion on another occasion—that "the problem of organization is the problem of the civilized world to-day, and particularly of our own country"—generally describes his sense of the answer. The engineer was an organizer: "no longer a mere specialist...he is...the executive officer, the manager, the agent, the director ."[2] The engineer would find efficient ways to solve practical problems.

Not only Pritchett, but those who followed him as president of the Carnegie Foundation have been engineers in this very broad sense. Their problem has always been to organize the Foundation so it could help to organize American education according to changing perceptions of social need. In the early years of the twentieth century, the Foundation became involved in the development of standards for professional education. One result was the noted Flexner report on medical education. Beginning at that time, and continuing through the 1920s, 1930s, and 1940s, the Foundation became a proponent of "scientific" standards for measuring educational achievement, first by units" and then by tests. More recently, it became an advocate for planned growth in postsecondary education, primarily through its sponsorship of the Carnegie Commission on Higher Education and the Carnegie Council on Policy Studies in Higher Education.

In all that it has done, the Carnegie Foundation has tried to marshall its resources so that it could develop what Clark Kerr, who was chairman of both the Carnegie Commission and the Carnegie Council, called "blueprints for action."[3] Its studies have always been purposeful—technologies of influences. It has been through these studies that the Carnegie Foundation has tried to serve as the "Great Agency" Henry Pritchett envisioned as a necessary counterweight to the centrifugal tendencies of American education and American society.

– 4 –

Surveying the Professions

In 1910 the Carnegie Foundation published its most famous report, Abraham Flexner's *Medical Education in the United States and
Canada*. Long thought to have originated the reorganization of
medical training that occurred in the United States during the
early decades of the twentieth century, this report more recently
has been shown to have supported and accelerated a trend it did
not itself begin. What the Flexner report did initiate, however,
was the Carnegie Foundation's professionalizing campaign—its
effort to define and institutionalize nationally uniform, science-
based, training paradigms that would serve as prerequisites for entrance into the professions.

Obviously this campaign was an integral part of the Foundation's more general effort to standardize American education, and
derived from its concern with developing the university as one of
the new institutional hubs of American society, a focal point for a
more national and functionally defined social organization. The
Foundation's concern was, of course, shared by many "progressive"
elements in American society. Most of the leaders of the medical
profession, a number of the leaders of the legal profession, and
some members of the engineering and teaching professions,
among others, also looked to the university to develop, transmit,
and certify the special knowledge that would augment and sustain
the authority and autonomy they wished to claim. These people
became the Foundation's allies in its professionalizing campaign.

With and through the alliances it could build with these other proponents of professionalism, the Foundation was also able to seek recognition for its own related and entirely compatible claims. Its professionalizing campaign supported the assertion that the Carnegie Foundation was not only a pension fund, but also and more important a central agency of educational administration, which would play a role in defining the spheres, the functions, and the relationships among the variety of institutions involved with higher education. By sponsoring surveys that had nothing whatsoever to do with pensioning, it was possible to educate the public to Henry Pritchett's and the trustees' view of the Foundation's most important purpose.

Legally, such surveys were allowed by the power that had been vested in the Foundation when its original 1905 New York State charter was replaced in March of 1906 with a Congressional charter. The charter change had been urged by Pritchett. The first charter had set forth as the Foundation's objectives a variety of activities having to do with pensioning and had also allowed bequests to promote "the cause of science and education." But the Foundation did not have the resources necessary for such bequests. Its actual capacity to do more than pensioning was therefore limited. For this reason, the second charter, which doubtless appealed to Carnegie because of the fuller—Congressional—recognition it gave to his benevolence, was worded in a less specific way. It allowed the Foundation, in addition to pensioning, to "do and perform all things necessary to encourage, uphold, and dignify the profession of the teacher and the cause of higher education" in the United States and Canada.[1]

Technically feasible for this reason, the Carnegie Foundation professionalizing campaign was initially made possible by professional association interest in the possibility of independent evaluations of professional schools. This was made clear in the "Plan for an Examination of the Status of Professional Education" approved by the Foundation's trustees prior to the commissioning of the Flexner report. Written by Pritchett, this plan stated that "an unsatisfactory situation" was known to exist in the training of American professionals. Low standards, it explained, "permit the unfit and often times the unworthy to enter" even the most elevated callings. But the time for reform was at hand. Carnegie studies, Pritchett had ascertained, would be welcomed by the professional associations, and, because "conditions" were then "fluid," would have a significant "chance to influence in the right direction." As this memorandum concluded, the potential benefit of surveys of professional training to the "cause of education" indicated that it would be "one of the most fruitful projects the foundation could undertake."[2] Circumstances within the professions, particularly within the medical profession, made it possible for the Carnegie Foundation to become the kind of "Great Agency" Pritchett hoped it would be.

THE CIRCUMSTANCES IN MEDICINE AT THE TIME OF THE FLEXNER REPORT

By 1908, when the Flexner report was started, many American doctors were eager to raise the requirements for entrance to their field. There had been an increasing supply of doctors: in 1900 there were approximately 25,000 medical students registered in 154 medical schools, compared to approximately 15,000 students in 118 schools ten years earlier.[3] There were also increasing numbers of trained nurses, midwives, and other potentially competitive health practitioners. Higher educational prerequisites for medical practice were of considerable professional interest because they might help curb what was thought to be an excessively competitive market situation worsened by a proliferation of the other, also professionalizing, groups of health practitioners (nurses especially) that might divide the medical field by function, and thereby limit the physician's domain.[4]

Supporting this concern with income, control, and status was the belief that new patterns of training would result in better medical service. Entrance restrictions to the profession through education were considered in both the profession's and the public's interest. By the turn of the century physician dissatisfaction with old forms of medical training was increasingly common. The transmission of known techniques and therapies via an apprenticeship, preceded in most cases by no more than elementary school study and supplemented in some cases by attendance at the lectures offered in small, proprietary colleges established, owned, and staffed by local practitioners, had seemed adequate before the rise of scientific medicine. But scientific medicine, which was a demonstrably more effective medicine for the diagnosis and cure of disease, could not be taught in this way.[5]

American doctors had discovered the inadequacy of American medical education through their study in Germany, where approximately 15,000 American medical personnel, about one-half of the nation's leading physicians, received advanced training between 1870 and the First World War. In Germany they had been exposed to exciting innovations in medical techniques and theories as well as to a research orientation and an emphasis on specialization still unknown in the United States. Many of these doctors found the opportunities that awaited them back in the United States disappointing and constraining.[6] Their experience was not unlike Henry Pritchett's after his return from Germany to Washington University to "teach the Freshman year."

William Henry Welch, the pathologist who became the first head of the Johns Hopkins Medical School, on his return to New York from Germany in 1878, found he could not teach medicine within an existing medical college as he wished and was best able to do, and as he thought necessary to transmit the techniques and information he had learned. His immediate solution to the problem was unusually creative. In silent partnership with two other doctors recently back from Germany, William S. Halsted and T. Mitchell Prudden, Welch established what Donald Fleming has described as "a kind of medical faculty of their own, cutting across institutional lines, silently eluding the seniority system...of the medical professors, and giving beneath the surface and in the interstices of the formal instruction an almost Germanic tutelage— a shadow medical college of the city of New York uniting the best resources of all the schools."[7] Welch was an unusual man, with a special ability to surmount constraints. He subsequently achieved fame and influence.

Reform had become, by the 1880s and 1890s, a personal and professional necessity for a self-conscious and increasingly powerful cadre of American doctors like Welch. Even the specialization that so often followed from advanced study abroad, which was most immediately evident in the rapid formation of specialized professional societies (sixteen of the eighteen original members of the American Physiological Society founded in 1887 had studied in Germany, and German-trained doctors were disproportionately represented in the ten other special groups formed before 1890), argued for the revamping of medical training along research-based disciplinary lines.[8]

Inspired by admiration for German medicine and by a desire to emulate the educational paradigm on which it was based, interest in reform was furthered by the opening of the Johns Hopkins Medical School in 1893. Joined to both a university and a hospital, and made possible by a large endowment, Hopkins replicated the scientifically oriented and inquiry-based pedagogy of German medical training. It drew visitors from all over the country. Its remarkable faculty sent out remarkable students to staff what were emerging as the key juncture points of the profession: the most prestigious medical schools, the most important committees of the professional associations, and the leading professional journals.

Whether one knew of Hopkins through actual familiarity with the experiment in Baltimore or through acquaintance with Hopkins' graduates, "Welch's rabbits," the favorable consensus of opinion surrounding the new medical school showed even those who had no European training that the didactic classroom lectures of the average proprietary school were old fashioned and second-rate.[9] In consequence, by 1908, a trend toward standardizing the Hopkins model through proprietary school mergers, the establishment of medical school connections with hospitals and universities, and the far more controversial establishment of full-time clinical professorships, all were underway.[10]

Growing professional concern with institutionalizing a new paradigm for medical training had led to the formation in 1904 of an organized lobby—the American Medical Association's (AMA) Council on Medical Education. The Council was composed primarily of doctors associated with the more modern and prestigious medical schools. Its purpose was to coordinate, facilitate, and accelerate the efforts of professional groups interested in reform, for example, the National Confederation of State Medical and Licensing Boards and the Association of American Medical Colleges. To achieve this end, the Council had set an "ideal standard" for medical schools: entrance requirements equivalent to university entrance requirements; a medical curriculum including one year of basic science, two years of laboratory science, and two years of clinical science; and a culminating year of internship at the end; and on the basis of this standard it had begun to inspect medical schools and to rate them as acceptable, doubtful, or unacceptable (Class A, B, or C). The Council operated very much like the Carnegie Foundation in determining which institutions would be eligible for its pension fund. Despite these measures, however, the doctors associated with the Council, particularly its president Arthur Dean Bevan of Rush Medical College in Chicago, were dissatisfied with the profession's movement toward reform. They believed that if the "ideal standard" could be raised and the rating a medical school received after inspection could be published, change would be fostered even more effectively and faster.[11]

The Council on Medical Education, although largely self-sustaining, was an arm of the AMA, and presumably for that reason, Bevan was unable to get the Council to adopt the procedures he favored. The AMA, which represented "regular" physicians, had been established in 1847, at a time of great rivalry between medical sects (regular, homeopathic, hydropathic, chronothermal, botanic, and other physicians). It did not establish itself as a closely integrated, national group until the early twentieth century. Only at that time, as a result of an administrative reorganization that linked the national association to state, county, and local medical societies, did the AMA begin to assume its modern form, although even then it did not encompass the entire medical profession. In 1900 it had had approximately 8,400 members and by 1910 it had 70,000 members. Approximately one half of the country's physicians and surgeons belonged.[12]

Many AMA members were associated with medical schools that could not yet meet the Council's "ideal standard." To have raised that standard even further and to have published medical school ratings might well have caused sufficient upset to injure emerging Association and professional unity. Furthermore, since Council ratings were seen as biased in favor of the more modernized schools from which the Council members tended to be drawn, more forceful action would likely have been misinterpreted and discredited. Therefore, as Council president Arthur Bevan explained many years later, it "occurred to some members of the Council that, if we could obtain the publication and approval of our work by the Carnegie Foundation for the Advancement of Teaching, it would assist materially in securing the results we were attempting to bring about."[13]

Council president Arthur Bevan apparently approached Henry Pritchett, and Pritchett then urged his fellow trustees, some of whom were reluctant to venture too boldly beyond Andrew Carnegie's known intentions for the Foundation, to read the new charter as "broad enough to include the study of education at every point where it may affect the higher institutions."[14] The discovery that doctors believed that "if the light can be turned on by an outside agency rather than by those in the profession, it will do great good" led the Foundation to sponsor a report that was designed to make it appear as a prime sponsor of a medical school transformation that was already well underway.[15]

ABRAHAM FLEXNER AND THE

FLEXNER REPORT

In the fall of 1908, Abraham Flexner returned to New York from two years of study in Berlin. He was forty-two years old, unemployed and in need of money, ambitious and, as he put it later, eager to make "a layman's contribution to education."[16] Flexner apparently did not want to return to his original calling—he had been a schoolmaster in Lexington, Kentucky—and he did not want to teach in an American college. While in Germany, he had been writing a book, *The American College,* that was severely critical of American higher education and strongly supportive of university ideals. He had made careful note of a newspaper announcement of the Carnegie Foundation's establishment, and throughout his book he referred to Pritchett's early annual reports. Flexner wanted to work at the Carnegie Foundation; and, having secured an introduction to Pritchett from Ira Remsen, the president of Johns Hopkins (where Flexner had gone to college) and a Foundation trustee, he met Pritchett just after the Foundation had decided to sponsor professional school studies. Pritchett looked at the proofs of Flexner's new book and hired him to conduct the first study, the medical report that was to be the Carnegie Foundation's Bulletin Number Four.[17]

In the biography Flexner later wrote of Pritchett he said that when asked to undertake the study he had responded:

"I am not a physician; aren't you confusing me with my brother Simon at the Rockefeller Institute for Medical Research [who was a prominent pathologist]?"

"No," rejoined Pritchett. "I know your brother well. What I have in mind is not a medical study, but an educational one. Medical schools are schools and must be judged as such. For that, a very sketchy notion of the main functions of the various departments suffices. That you or any other intelligent layman can readily acquire. Such a study as I have in mind takes that for granted. Henceforth, these institutions must be viewed from the standpoint of education. Are they so equipped and conducted as to be able to train students to be efficient physicians, surgeons, and so on?"[18]

Flexner's fortuitous arrival in Pritchett's office allowed him to secure just the kind of author he needed. Beyond Flexner's full agreement with professional values, the fact that he was not a doctor and that he had been an educator would give the Council what it wanted— "the weight of an independent report of a disinterested body"—and the Foundation what it wanted—the establishment of educators as the arbiters of all training matters, even those that concerned the strongest and best organized of all the professions.[19]

Pritchett took Flexner along to a December, 1908, meeting with members of the Council on Medical Education. According to the minutes of that meeting, it was there agreed "that while the Foundation would be guided very largely by the Council's investigations, to avoid claims of partiality, no more mention should be made in the report of the Council than any other source of information."[20] Then Flexner set off to read about medical education in Germany, to study the Council's medical school reports and ratings, to confer with faculty members at the Johns Hopkins Medical School, and, finally, often accompanied by N. P. Colwell, the secretary of the Council, to visit all of the 155 medical schools in existence in North America at the time.

These visits were brief. Flexner wrote later: "In half an hour or less I could sample the credentials of students filed in the dean's office....A few inquiries made clear whether the faculty was composed of local doctors, not already 'professors' in some other local medical school, or the extent to which efforts had been made to obtain teachers properly trained elsewhere. A single question elicited the income of a medical school....A stroll through the laboratories disclosed the presence or absence of apparatus, museum specimens, library, and students; and a 'whiff' told the inside story regarding the manner in which anatomy was cultivated." [21] Following several visits, Flexner would return to New York, write up his data, mail a copy of his findings to the schools' deans, and then set out again. Within a year the report was finished. It was a truly brilliant exposé and program for reform.

The report was divided into two sections. The first described the historical and contemporary situation in medicine and presented the case for reform. Its argument may be schematically summarized as follows:

—The American medical school is now well along in the second century of its history. It began, and for many years continued to exist, as a supplement to the apprenticeship system..." [22]

—With the foundation early in the nineteenth century at Baltimore of a proprietary school, the so-called medical department of the so-called University of Maryland, a harmful precedent was established. Before that a college of medicine had been a branch growing out of the living university trunk. [23]

—Quite aside from the history, achievements, or present merits of any particular independent medical school, the creation of the (proprietary school) type was the fertile source of unforeseen harm to medical education and to medical practice. Since that day medical colleges have multiplied without restraint... [24]

—In the wave of commercial exploitation which swept the entire profession...the original university departments were practically torn from their moorings. The medical schools of Harvard, Yale, Pennsylvania, became, as they expanded, virtually independent of the institutions with which they were legally united...For years they managed their own affairs along proprietary lines.[25]

—Johns Hopkins Medical School...was the first medical school in America of genuine university type, with something approaching adequate endowment, well-equipped laboratories conducted by modern teachers, devoting themselves unreservedly to medical investigation and instruction, and with its own hospital, in which the training of physicians and the healing of the sick harmoniously combine to the infinite advantage of both. It has finally cleared up the problem of standards and ideals.[26]

—We may safely conclude that our methods of carrying on medical education have resulted in enormous over-production at a low level, and that, whatever the justification in the past, the present situation...can be more effectively met by a reduced output of well-trained men than by further inflation with an inferior product.[27]

—If the sick are to reap the full benefit of recent progress in medicine, a more uniformly arduous and expensive medical education is demanded.[28]

Flexner then moved on to describe what such an education should consist of. It had to be preceded by a minimum of two years of college work in science. It should include during the first two years fundamental laboratory instruction in the basic medical sciences "arranged and organized with a distinct practical purpose in view." It should emphasize during the last two years more advanced hospital-based training in clinical practice, the point being to learn "by doing."[29]

Finally, before presenting in a separate section the results of his medical school visiting, Flexner turned to the all important question of "reconstruction." He described exactly what a reformed national system of medical education should look like. It was to be based on several key principles: for example, the production of enough new physicians to provide one doctor for every 1500 people and the placement of medical schools in cities (usually no more than one per city) so that they could affiliate with the universities that would be best able to develop them. It was to be regional in organization. This is what it projected for the Northeast: "125 new doctors would be needed [50 to cover 1908-09 population increase, 75 to replace half of those who had died]. To produce this number two new schools, one of moderate size and one smaller, readily suffice. Fortunately they can be developed without sacrificing any of our criteria. The medical schools of Harvard and Yale are university departments, situated in the midst of ample clinical material, with considerable financial backing now and every prospect of more. It is unwise to divide the Boston field; it is unnecessary to prolong the life of the clinical departments of Dartmouth, Bowdoin, and Vermont."[30] In the overall reconstruction, 120 medical schools were, in Flexner's words, to be "wiped off the map."[31]

Justified, on the one hand, by the argument with which Flexner began, this plan was further supported, on the other, by his description of the actual colleges. A few colleges had shown themselves to be exemplary: Western Reserve, Yale, Johns Hopkins, and Harvard, among others. A good number (and almost all of those with sectarian associations of any kind) appeared to be scandalously bad. For example, Kansas Medical College in Topeka, Kansas, had only one dissecting room and it was "indescribably filthy; it contained, in addition to necessary tables, a single, badly hacked cadaver, and was simultaneously used as a chicken yard."[32] Most were second-rate. The University and Bellevue Hospital Medical College in New York City had laboratories that "are developed unevenly, as the resources of the school are not equal to uniform promotion of all the medical sciences."[33] The Tennessee Medical College in Knoxville, Tennessee, had a building that "is externally attractive; within, dirty....The dissecting room is ordinary."[34] The Denver and Gross College of Medicine in Denver, Colorado, had a new and "exceedingly attractive dispensary building," but "its equipment consists of a chemical laboratory of the ordinary medical school type, a dissecting room, containing a few subjects as dry as leather, a physiological laboratory with slight equipment, and the usual pathology and bacteriology laboratories."[35]

The report indicted most medical schools, while offering a clear, specific, and forcefully argued program for change. As everyone involved in planning the report wanted it to do, it documented a discrepancy between the "ideal" and the "real." Indeed, Flexner made this point directly when he said: "Society reaps at this moment but a small fraction of the advantage which current knowledge has the power to confer. That sick man is relatively rare for whom actually all is done that is at this day humanly feasible....We have indeed in America medical practitioners not inferior to the best elsewhere; but there is probably no other country in the world in which there is so great a distance and so fatal a difference between the best, the average, and the worst."[36] The Council on Medical Education had wanted a report like Flexner's to make this discrepancy more widely known. Through a Carnegie Foundation publication it had hoped to persuade those outside the profession that higher and more uniform educational standards, and, in consequence, restricted access to the profession, should be not only a professional, but also a public goal. Flexner had said in the report that "when public interest, professional ideals, and sound educational procedure concur in the recommendation of the same policy, the time is surely ripe for decisive action."[37] And in this instance, as was expected, that certainly proved to be true.

THE OUTCOMES OF THE FLEXNER REPORT

Medical schools had already begun to close and to merge before the Flexner report appeared in 1910. Between 1906, when the

Council on Medical Education was founded, and the year of the report's publication, 31 schools went out of existence. But that number increased steadily after 1910. In that year, there were 155 medical schools; by 1920, there were 85; and by 1930, there were 76 (Flexner had recommended 31.[38] More important by far, huge financial investments in medical education had provided the resources necessary for the laboratories, libraries, professors, and hospital affiliations that made the curricular model suggested by Flexner the norm throughout virtually all of the medical schools in the United States.[39]

In some instances, the report helped to win local interest and support for the move toward a new national paradigm. This was true, for example, at Washington University in St. Louis, where a post-report endowment of several millions of dollars realized changes that faculty members had been urging and working toward for some time. The school had been proprietary until 1906, although, as Kenneth Ludmerer has shown, "Flexner's description of proprietary schools as 'essentially private ventures, moneymaking in spirit and object' did not fit the school."[40] As early as 1872, a Medical Fund Society had been formed with faculty profits to develop the facilities that modern scientific medicine required. It was only after the Flexner report, however, that funds beyond those could be raised. In this instance, as in others, the report quite literally excited public outrage and then interest on the part of the merchant Robert Brookings and other wealthy local businessmen and, as a result, secured for medical reform the levels of financial assistance needed.[41]

In other instances, the capital for medical reform came from philanthropic foundations. The already superior schools were the principal beneficiaries of this aid. For example, between 1911 and 1936, Johns Hopkins received ten million dollars from the Rockefeller's General Education Board (where Abraham Flexner went to work soon after his medical report appeared) and an additional two million from the Carnegie Corporation. One hundred fifty-four million dollars of foundation grants went to medical education between 1910 and the onset of the Depression.[42] Whatever the source, however, the infusion of huge amounts of money clearly made a difference and the result was surely an improvement in the overall quality of American medical education.

Still, not all interests were well served by the changes that came with this new financing. This is particularly evident if one considers the access of black Americans to the medical profession. At the time of the Flexner report there were eight medical schools for blacks; fifteen years after the report's appearance, there were two—Howard Medical School in Washington, D.C., and Meharry Medical College in Nashville, Tennessee. Blacks were of course admitted to some predominantly white institutions, but with medical school-hospital affiliations that too was more difficult, for the hospitals tended to be even more discriminatory than the colleges themselves were. After 1910, it was more difficult for black males to secure medical training than it was even for white females, whose low representation in the profession cannot be attributed to the Flexner report or to the medical reform movement of which it was a part. At the time of the Second World War there were still fewer than one hundred black students at non-black American medical schools. If only because what had been an increasing number of black physicians (between 1890 and 1910 the number of black doctors had tripled) became after 1910 a decreasing number, one may argue that the Flexner report was in effect, if not intent, discriminatory in some of its outcomes. What is more, though one cannot measure the loss, with longer and more expensive training required for all doctors, financially poor aspirants to the profession were also most likely excluded. In some very important ways, therefore, the Flexner report improved American medicine, while making the profession as well as its services less accessible to many.[43]

Finally, and most important here, the Flexner report provided demonstrable support for an argument for standards in other professions, especially law, which Henry Pritchett had made in 1908 while discussing the Carnegie Foundation's projected professional surveys. In calling attention to what he described as the necessity for doctors to be trained in the sciences fundamental to "regular" medicine, even if they wanted to be homeopaths, osteopaths, Christian Scientists, or faith healers (and in his report, Flexner agreed), he had said:

The only possible protection and assurance which the public can have is to insist upon this fundamental training as a preliminary to any practice, and it may rightly suspect the motives of any set of would-be practitioners who undertake to evade these reasonable requirements—necessary alike in the interests of the public and of the profession of medicine. With respect to the practice of law, the public interest is dependent likewise on the enforcement of high professional standards. The practitioner of law does not deal so directly with the personal well-being of every citizen as does the physician but no other profession is so closely related to the development of justice and to the progress of sound public policy. There is no way by which the public can tell whether the practitioner of law will develop into a wise advocate or into a sharp attorney. The only criterion it can impose for its own protection is to require such training for entrance to the profession as will fit the ordinary man for good work in it and will at the same time serve as a means to exclude the unfit.[44]

Deeply convinced of these points, Pritchett was calling on the legal profession to invite a study such as the Council on Medical Education had wanted.

THE CARNEGIE FOUNDATION AND
LEGAL EDUCATION

Although Pritchett had suggested to the trustees that a Foundation inquiry would be welcomed by professional associations in *both* medicine and law, it was not until three years after the publication of the Flexner report that the Foundation was asked to investigate "the conditions under which the work of legal education is carried on in this country."[45] Many things made it more difficult to gain the kind of professional authorization the Foundation wished for a survey of legal education. But the Flexner report gave a sufficient boost to both the profession of medicine and to professionalism in general to enable the Foundation finally to surmount the complications and "opposition" that had delayed its entry into the legal arena.[46] It demonstrated what Pritchett had said in 1908: that "the public interest is dependent...on the enforcement of high professional standards"; and that electrified some groups within the legal profession. Hence, an important outcome of the Flexner report for the Carnegie Foundation as well as for ever-increasing public support of professionalism was that it led the American Bar Association (ABA) Committee on Legal Education and Admission to the Bar specifically to ask for a "similar investigation" to the one Flexner had just completed. Having been "greatly impressed" with the way a Carnegie Foundation bulletin had empowered their fellows in medicine, advocates of higher standards in legal education felt confident that a Carnegie Foundation study would be of similar benefit to them.[47]

To promote this new alliance, Pritchett commissioned two studies: one by Joseph Redlich, an Austrian scholar, and one by Alfred Z. Reed, a Columbia Ph.D. recommended to Pritchett by Charles Beard and several others. The Redlich study was published in 1914 as *The Common Law and the Case Method in American University Law Schools*. It received polite notice in legal circles, but caused relatively little stir. The Reed study was published in 1921 as *Training for the Public Profession of the Law,* and was followed by eight issues of a *Review of Legal Education in the United States and Canada* and another bulletin, *Present-Day Law Schools in the United States and Canada* (1928), all written by Reed. The Reed study was far more controversial than the Redlich report had been. The key points of *Training for the Public Profession of the Law* were rejected by the bar, but the report was nevertheless an important spur to ABA support for high minimum educational standards for legal certification. In law, a strategy similar to the one used to reform medical education, a strategy based on the publication of invited but independent studies, achieved the result advocates of professionalism wished, although it did so in a very different way.

THE CIRCUMSTANCES IN LAW AT THE TIME OF THE CARNEGIE FOUNDATION SURVEYS

Writing to Pritchett in August of 1913, Alfred Reed had cautioned that standardizing legal education would be "a more difficult job than our only precedent (Flexner's survey of the medical schools)."[48] He was right, partly because circumstances within the legal profession were somewhat different from those within the medical profession.

To be sure, just as there had been a proliferation of doctors early in the twentieth century, so had there been a proliferation of lawyers. In 1900, there were 102 law schools with 12,516 students; in 1910, there were 124 law schools with 19,567 students; and by 1920, there were 146 law schools with 24,503 students.[49] More important by far, growth among law schools was greatest among the proprietary night schools. Through these schools "foreigners" were entering the law. Between 1900 and 1910, the number of foreign-born lawyers in New York City increased 66 percent and those of foreign parentage increased 84 percent; the comparable figures for Boston were 77 percent and 75 percent.[50] In this growth and ethnic diversification, organized lawyers, no less than organized doctors, found increasing cause to consider raising educational standards as a means for restricting access to the profession.

As was also the case in medicine, efforts to achieve educational reform were led by legal scholars. Prior to the development of the case method at Harvard and its fairly rapid adoption elsewhere, most law school teachers had been part-time practitioners of the law, not full-time scholars. By 1893, however, there were sufficient numbers of academic lawyers to support the organization of a distinct subdivision within the organized bar. By the turn of the century, they had formed the American Association of Law Schools and had become active in the ABA's education committee (the committee that invited Carnegie Foundation assistance). As was not the case in medicine, however, these academic lawyers had not, did not, and perhaps could not develop as effective a reform campaign as their medical equivalents. This was true for at least three reasons.[51]

First, the ABA was a prestigious but very small organization. Whereas almost 50 percent of the nation's doctors belonged to the AMA in 1910, only 3 percent of the nation's lawyers belonged to the ABA in that year. Hence, the ABA was an elite association that could not support an effective reform lobby like the AMA's Council on Medical Education. Far more than in medicine, standards in law were still set by state legislatures.[52]

Second, in contrast to academic physicians, academic lawyers had less success in convincing even (perhaps especially) their brethren who were practitioners that professional restriction through higher and more uniform educational standards was in their own and the public's interest. They tried to make that case, but they tended to justify their calls for reform as William Draper

Lewis of the University of Pennsylvania did when he said: "If, as a profession, we are awake to our failure to perform our public duties, it is the small class of men who are devoting their lives to legal teaching who must point the way." [53] They asserted that "in our law schools should be found a body of men, competent, trained, impartial and honorable, ready and willing to give their aid and counsel in the formation and settlement of public questions having a legal aspect." [54] With Felix Frankfurter, who professed "'a quasi-religious feeling' about the Harvard Law School," they tended to insist that an academic career was the highest calling, being the best available means to modernize jurisprudence. [55] In championing the reform of legal education, therefore, academic lawyers were rather transparently seeking to make themselves an elite within the legal elite, and trying also to make the university law school, as opposed to the law firm office, the center for the development of the law. Not surprisingly, therefore, their claims were resented by practitioners. [56]

Interestingly, in 1922, when the Carnegie Corporation supported the academic lawyers' claims to be the law's leading "scientists," by establishing the American Law Institute to "re-state" the common law, assistance to the project was constantly criticized and finally terminated largely as a result of resistance to it from an ABA member who was a practitioner, Carnegie Corporation trustee Russell Leffingwell. His assertions that legal "science" was out of touch with the real world exemplified the elite practitioners' disrespect for the elite scholars' presumption of superiority. [57]

Finally, in claiming the Harvard case method as an appropriate national paradigm for all lawyers, legal reformers did not have an educational model as potentially strong as medical reformers had in the Hopkins laboratory-cum-clinic model. As the law had grown, so had "the principles" that the case method had been designed to impart through deduction. That meant that the case method had to be justified primarily as a superior way to teach legal reasoning. But was it superior to the skills of reasoning one might acquire through the kind of apprenticeship in a law office that the case method and the "scientific" law school had been designed primarily to replace? One could certainly debate the point. The case method was for these reasons at least a weaker educational paradigm to try to universalize, especially for would-be practitioners.[58]

THE REED REPORT

One of the interesting and ironic aspects about the most important of the Carnegie Foundation legal surveys, Alfred Reed's *The Public Profession of the Law*, was that, having been invited to strengthen the position of academic lawyers, it described instead all of the weaknesses in their plans. Rather than urging the elimination of the weaker, usually proprietary schools, the so-called night schools, it argued that they be given support and improved. Rather than insisting that at least some college work be required for entrance to all law schools, it argued that entrance standards should vary according to the program a student would pursue.

The Reed report was dense, detailed, and closely reasoned. It cannot be summarized in the schematic way the Flexner report can be. It took eight years to complete, which annoyed Henry Pritchett, who kept urging Reed to stop "going off after details to the practical eclipse of the main point" and to attend less to his "own psychology."[59] It did indeed reflect the complexity of the issues involved in legal or other professional education reform.

In *The Public Profession of the Law*, it was acknowledged that no categorization of law schools could be really valid since the variety of schools was tremendous. Nevertheless, as Reed saw it, there were essentially four basic types, and three of these, he argued, were worthy of support. The "short-course" schools (10 percent of the total) that claimed to teach the technical law in three years or less seemed to Reed indefensible and he said that they should be allowed to "disappear." The schools that maintained high standards for entrance and were full-time and "acknowledged the leadership of Harvard, and teach the national law by the case method" (20 percent of the total) were obviously excellent, but were not the only or necessarily the best model for all legal education. Reed argued that they should be supplemented by two additional types: full-time schools with low entrance standards (then 30 percent of all schools) and part-time night schools (then 40 percent of all schools).[60]

Reed justified the first of these two supplementary types in the following way:

> ...in addition to that class in the community which is able to take the long course of training demanded by the leading law school, and that class which can study law (at the night schools) only while earning its livelihood, there is also an intermediate class, which is not able to go to college, but is able to devote its entire time to studying law. There is no good reason for delaying the education of such students by requiring them to take the protracted course of study that is, or should be, given by the night law schools.[61]

Having, thus, already urged diversity over standardization, Reed chastened the leaders of the bar for not having recognized and helped to raise the caliber of the training offered at the part-time night schools. He was not suggesting by this that the night schools be acknowledged and helped so that they might be able to copy the Harvard style. He believed different kinds of training, to prepare different kinds of lawyers, should be allowed. The night schools, as well as the low-entrance, full-time schools, in his opinion, offered training that would be of special value to local practitioners. More important, however, they provided access to the bar for different classes of people than the national schools tended to do, and this Reed argued was a necessity in a democratic society.

Reed, unlike Flexner, was concerned with "the poor boy's" access to the profession. He said of his suggestion that the night schools be continued and encouraged to lengthen their course of study:

...this extension of the night school course is consistent with the principle, based on political and humanitarian considerations, of not permanently debarring young men of average ability from access into our governing class, simply because they possess modest means. To go farther, and assert that it is not legitimate to delay their admission to the bar beyond the age when more fortunate students have completed their preparation, would be to attempt to reduce the inherent handicap of poverty farther than can be justified, if any account at all is to be taken of educational considerations.[62]

Obviously, the Reed report did not agree with the position of the legal scholars and university consolidators, who believed that all lawyers should have to meet high and uniform entrance requirements (at least some time in college) and should then have to undergo a uniformly long, full-time, and nationally oriented course of professional study in a university-affiliated law school. Beyond that, however, *The Public Profession of the Law* contradicted the wistful and inaccurate claim that law was a classless profession, insisting rather that, if it was now unfortunately stratified by both class and trained competence, it should remain in the future at least diversified by function and open to all. Not surprisingly, this position turned out to be the dynamite. By urging recognition of a diversified bar and by recognizing the night schools that were the viaducts for immigrant entrance to law and politics, the Reed report obtained for the academic lawyers what they had not been able to obtain for themselves: strong ABA endorsement of uniformly high academic standards as a prerequisite for admission to the bar. In other words, the Reed report united the two elites that were represented by the profession's major organized public lobby, its major national association, against its conclusions.[63]

Parenthetically, one might query whether Henry Pritchett had a hand in the ABA reorientation. The ABA's move toward standardization was led by Elihu Root, who was closely associated with the Carnegie philanthropies, and, according to Abraham Flexner's biography of Pritchett, "one of Pritchett's warmest and most beloved friends."[64] Oren Root, Elihu Root's older brother, had taught English at the school Pritchett's father ran, and he had had a strong influence on Pritchett as a young man. Assuming, then, that Pritchett did not agree with the conclusions reached in Reed's bulletin, as Reed himself asserted, it is entirely possible that Pritchett encouraged Root to spearhead the movement that co-opted the report.[65]

Knowledge of what had happened in medicine after publication of the Flexner report and fear of what might happen in law were the Reed report not countered by internally directed reform, did in any case bring the ABA as a whole into the academic lawyers' camp. Mounting xenophobia and anti-Semitism within the bar and throughout the country also played a strong role in resistance to Reed's recommendations.

In 1920, Elihu Root took over as chairman of the ABA's Section on Legal Education and Admission to the Bar. And in 1921, after the prepublication version of *Training for the Public Profession of the Law* had been distributed, a resolution emerged from that committee urging that every candidate to the Bar be required to graduate from a law school. The resolution spelled out the standards those law schools should meet: two years of preparatory work in college, a three year course of study for full-time students and a four year course for part-time students; adequate library facilities; full-time teachers; and so on. The Root Committee's resolution, which was subsequently endorsed by the ABA as a whole, established standards that at least technically ruled out schools for "Lincoln's plain people" as they then existed. By 1931, seventeen states had moved to make two years of college prior to law school a requirement of the bar; by 1939, forty-one states had so moved, and in twenty-three of those states, a diploma from an ABA approved law school was also mandatory.[66]

In law, then, as in medicine, a CFAT bulletin had a considerable impact although of a different sort. *Training for the Public Profession of the Law* was an important factor in the profession's slow move toward universally more rigorous educational standards. It did not urge that trend. But in helping to unite the organized bar against diversity and for uniform and high educational standards, it helped to shape the views of the legal profession's institutional representative to state legislatures and to the public at large. Not directly, as the Flexner report had done, but in an important, if indirect and ironic, way, therefore, the Reed report fostered at least one of the goals of the Carnegie Foundation's professionalizing campaign. It supported the structures for and the credence in professionalism that have grown throughout most of this century, although it did not, as an integral part of that, gain support for the Foundation's claim to be a center of private power necessary to the protection of the public good. Significant as the Reed report was within legal circles, and through those circles within wider arenas, the report itself does not appear to have increased public familiarity with the organization that sponsored it.

Did that matter by the 1920s? Probably not, for the legal profession was not the only group that had noticed the Flexner report. Following the publication of *Medical Education in the United States and Canada,* the Carnegie Foundation had many invitations to sponsor studies ranging from one to survey the organization of hospitals to another to investigate the education of the deaf. Although most of these invitations had to be declined as a result of insufficient funds, at least three of the twenty-five surveys commissioned and completed during Pritchett's tenure in office deserve brief discussion to illustrate the extent to which the

Foundation's professionalization campaign was and was not consistently and in a variety of ways able to extend professional ideals and the bureaucratic structures necessary to support them.

ENGINEERING EDUCATION

As was the case in medicine and in law, a Carnegie Foundation survey helped to move engineering toward a more standardized pattern of training. In engineering, as in the two "major" professions, the Foundation was invited to undertake a study on the presumption that its investigations would strengthen the hand of educators, who were working in this instance to unify and to elevate what were still rather vaguely related groups of skilled trades and occupations. Since 1893, when the Society for the Promotion of Engineering Education (SPEE) was founded to bring together representatives from the many sub-specialties within the field, there had been a strong move among engineering educators to develop "a uniform system of educating engineers...[in the hope of thus] raising the status of the engineering profession."[67] The cause of reform had foundered, however, on SPEE's inability to gain official support from the professional associations in engineering—the American Society of Civil Engineers, the American Institute of Mining, Metallurgical and Petroleum Engineers, the American Society of Mechanical Engineers, the American Institute of Electrical Engineers, and so on. To overcome claims that SPEE recommendations represented the interests of engineering educators, who were out of touch with changes in engineering practice, SPEE president Dugold Jackson, not coincidentally a professor of electrical engineering, which was the fastest growing and least school-based field within engineering, appointed a joint committee with representatives from all of the major professional societies and from SPEE. It was the joint committee that turned to the CFAT for assistance.[68]

In response, the CFAT commissioned a bulletin entitled *Engineering Education*. Appearing in 1918, it fulfilled the objective SPEE held. The Foundation's "impartial observer" in this instance was Charles R. Mann, a physicist who admired the close linkages between technical schools and industry he had observed in Germany. As he conducted the field investigations for his report, he became increasingly impressed with the training programs sponsored by General Electric and Westinghouse. The need for academics to become more sensitive to the demands of industry as well as suggestions for how engineering schools could do that became central features of his study. In consequence, *Engineering Education* gave practitioners what they wanted from the educators, and, with that, good reasons to back reform. By unifying engineers behind academic training and profession-wide standards for that training, it also gave the educators what they wanted—control over the portals of entry into the profession. Overshadowed by the First World War, and in any case addressed to a narrow audience, the Mann report was not of great interest to groups outside of the profession, but it did foster professionalization in yet another domain.[69]

Not all groups could be surveyed on the basis of a professional association invitation, and the Foundation did not have invitations from all such groups in any case. In some instances the divisions within an occupation were more complicated than they were even in engineering, where organized unity around specialized functions compounded a separation between the interests and ambitions of scholars and practitioners more than it did in either medicine or law. This was of course true of the teaching profession, not only at the elementary and secondary levels, but also at the higher levels. Not surprisingly, therefore, it was in this area, the area the Carnegie Foundation was especially concerned with, that its professionalizing campaign had both its least successful and its most interesting results.

At the time the Foundation had begun to receive frequent survey invitations, in other words, just after the Flexner report, Pritchett had told his friend Vanderlip that "my five years work in the Foundation has just begun to ripen." He meant that he already had requests from a half-dozen states to survey their entire "educational organization."[70] In the years that followed, these requests continued to arrive. Through the state surveys that resulted, the Foundation both intentionally and not at all intentionally became involved with the professionalization of academics.

THE PROFESSIONAL PREPARATION OF TEACHERS FOR AMERICAN PUBLIC SCHOOLS

The Foundation's intentional effort to professionalize teachers was made possible by an invited survey of the normal schools of Missouri, which led "to an attempt to evaluate the process itself whereby teachers are prepared, and to an effort to formulate trustworthy principles of procedure."[71] In the bulletin that resulted, which was called *The Professional Preparation of Teachers for American Public Schools* (1920), a special "professionalized" curriculum for the training of all teachers was described and strongly urged. Eschewing the value of liberal arts preparation for the professional study of education, the bulletin recommended a teacher training model in which virtually all courses would present subject matter especially tailored to immediate classroom use. That was a quite different approach from the one the Foundation had recommended in its other professional education bulletins. This bulletin urged a form of "trade" or "vocational" as opposed to "professional" training.

Often referred to as the Missouri Study, *The Professional Preparation of Teachers* was the work of Foundation staff members, ad-

vised and assisted by a number of professors from the still relatively new, often university-affiliated, centers of advanced study in
education: William C. Bagley from Teachers College, Columbia
University; Charles A. McMurray from the George Peabody College for Teachers; and Walter F. Dearborn from the Graduate
School of Education at Harvard, among others. They advanced a
model much like the one Paul Mattingly found to be emerging
among what he described in *The Classless Profession* as the second
generation of American public school leaders.[72] That model had
displaced an earlier one in which it was assumed that "professional" training for teachers should follow and rest upon considerable
academic and "character" training. It had arisen as teachers' insti-
tutes gave way (after the Civil War) to normal schools as the main
setting for professional teacher training. It was at least in part an
outcome both of frustration with the increasingly low levels of
preparation of normal school students and interest in developing
a basis for professionalism in teaching as the reflective status of
this once minister-associated calling declined.

The history of teacher education is still so understudied that
one can only venture the point as a hypothesis, but what appears
to have happened at the end of the century, when graduate schools
of education were established alongside the normal schools, is that
the earlier of these two paradigms (the more "professional") became associated with advanced, even doctoral level study, for
would-be teachers of teachers, and the later paradigm, the one
that had emerged for normal schools (the more "vocational"), became associated with the training of actual elementary and secondary school teachers. Whether or not that hypothesis is correct,
that, in essence, is what the Carnegie Foundation recommended
in the Missouri study.

Within Missouri, some of this survey's suggestions were enacted, or so a follow-up study done ten years later found.[73] Outside of
Missouri the survey's recommendations had little effect.[74] A "pro-

fessionalized" curriculum for teacher training was highly controversial within the National Education Association (NEA), a group
established in 1857 to unite "gentlemen" members of state teachers' associations (women were only admitted to full, rather than
honorary membership in 1886). Its hope had been to develop a
national, more respected, and self-governing profession. In the
1920s the NEA included some advocates of "professionalized"
curricula and also some advocates of "sequential" approaches to
the education of teachers (i.e., liberal arts followed by educational theory and methods—the earlier of the two models—rather
than liberal arts combined with educational theory and practice—
the later). Since the division between these camps had long been
a divisive factor in the NEA, and the Carnegie Foundation's Bulletin offered no new rationale to bring proponents of the "sequential" approach into the camp of those who favored the
"professionalized" approach, the Missouri Study did not unify the
NEA or win its support.[75]

Beyond that, as Jurgen Hurbst has discovered, normal schools
had become a rather common form of free, advanced schooling,
especially for women, throughout the Middle West.[76] They were,
in a sense, the predecessor to the community colleges established
after the Second World War. Were their curricula "professionalized," they might lose their many clients who did not plan to
teach or did not plan to teach for a long period, and perhaps, as a
result, their state support as well. Had the Missouri Study been
successful in establishing a uniform teacher training paradigm, it
would have limited access to advanced study for people of limited
means and especially for women, normal schools often having
been the only colleges available to them. However, since the
Carnegie Foundation study was without organized professional
backing (in a profession that was not closely integrated in any
case), and was also in conflict with local traditions and that aspect
of the public interest in educational opportunity that is support-

ed by free access to education, the plan suggested in the study was not adopted as *the* method of preparation for elementary and secondary school teachers. In this realm, the Carnegie Foundation's professionalizing campaign was a failure.

At the time the Foundation's professional studies were originally planned, teacher training institutions had not been included as a possibility for study. Intending to focus on the most elevated callings, the Foundation had planned to survey the medical school, the law school, the school of theology, and the graduate school. For reasons that are unclear, theology and graduate schools were not studied, but, through a state education survey, the Carnegie Foundation did inadvertently encourage professionalism among the college teachers who were the graduates of the graduate school.

EDUCATION IN VERMONT AND THE AMERICAN ASSOCIATION OF UNIVERSITY PROFESSORS

In 1912, the governor of Vermont empanelled a state commission to answer public criticism of the common schools by investigating "the entire educational system and condition of this state."[77] Foundation trustee Nicholas Murray Butler was a member of this commission, and presumably it was he who had the idea of asking the Carnegie Foundation to undertake the study for the commission. In any case, the bulletin that resulted, which was called *Education in Vermont,* advocated reform of the elementary and secondary school curricula in Vermont and the creation of a centralized educational administration, free of local politics and therefore capable of exercising "expert" supervision, and pointed out the need to develop state normal schools. Soon after its publication, Milo B. Hillegas, the Teachers College professor who surveyed the elementary schools for the Carnegie Foundation, was appointed State Commissioner of Education in Vermont. He

found "the people, the press, the State Board, and all officers...
more than generous in their support" of the reforms he was seeking.[78] J. F. Messenger, head of the University of Vermont's department of education, also claimed that "the demand for teachers
who have had some professional training seems to be increasing,"
and that enrollment in his department had doubled within a year
of the study.[79] *Education in Vermont* had quick and tangible effect,
and as these comments show was an effective instrument for fur-
thering the kinds of changes the Foundation supported.

But that was not all. In *Education in Vermont* the Foundation
maintained, itself acting in this instance as the survey's author,
that institutions of higher education not fully "owned and con-
trolled by the state" should be deprived of all state subsidies.[80]
Because none of the three colleges then receiving state money
(the University of Vermont, Middlebury College, and Norwich
University) was, in the opinion of the Foundation, "a state institution in the strict and complete or even in the ordinary sense of
that term," the report suggested that in the future all three
should have to rely exclusively on tuition, endowment, and other
private sources of income.[81] The Carnegie Foundation's recommendations for higher education were hotly contested in Vermont, and the controversy aroused brought Bulletin Number 7
to national attention.

In January 1915, *School and Society* carried an article by Josiah
Royce, the Harvard philosopher, entitled "The Carnegie Foundation for the Advancement of Teaching and the Case of Middlebury
College." The article argued that the principle enunciated in *Education in Vermont,* that "either the state must completely own and
control an institution, or it must leave it wholly to private bene-
faction," contradicted another principle, the principle of "a wise
provincialism in education." Were the principle set forth in *Education in Vermont* accepted, Royce maintained, it would undermine
"the sort of variety and liberty...which are necessary to the high-

est sort of academic development in this country." Thus, according to Royce, the CFAT's Vermont study raised two interrelated questions: first, that of "the limits of standardization"; and second, that of the limits of administrative control in what Royce described as strictly academic matters.[82] Originally presented as a paper to the organizational meeting of the American Association of University Professors, the article linked *Education in Vermont* and the Carnegie Foundation to issues of academic freedom and professorial recognition in university decision making.

Of course, it was no coincidence that the Royce paper to the AAUP appeared in *School and Society,* James McKeen Cattell, the psychologist who owned and edited *School and Society,* had been challenging the Foundation since it had commenced operation. Cattell wrote to Pritchett constantly, raising all sorts of difficult and, from Cattell's point of view, damaging questions. He used his post as editor—Cattell at one time edited *Science, Popular Science Monthly,* and the *American Naturalist,* in addition to *School and Society*—to publish criticisms of the Foundation written by himself and others and, on occasion, to publicize correspondence (some of which was explicitly labeled confidential) that would present the Foundation in an unfavorable light. He even reprinted a number of negative commentaries on the Foundation in a 1919 book called *Carnegie Pensions.* James McKeen Cattell was a brilliant, unflagging opponent, a master of the art of guerilla warfare. And, as was true of the Royce article, Cattell's campaign against the Carnegie Foundation, though in itself entirely serious and sincere, was intended to rally support for a larger fight. *Education in Vermont,* and, also, of course, Royce's criticism of it, played directly into Cattell's hands.[83]

Cattell was deeply committed to professorial independence and believed that the differentiation of administrative from scholarly functions that was occurring as a part of the growth of bureaucracy within the university was antithetical to such freedom. Conceding that universities did need some kind of governance, and wishing to find a middle road between what he called "the Scylla of presidential autocracy and the Charybdis of faculty and trustee incompetence," Carrell called on the professoriate to strengthen itself as a counterweight to increasing presidential power.[84] Although the AAUP grew out of a 1914 call to a meeting sent out by eighteen Johns Hopkins professors, the origins of that association lie in a plea voiced in Cattell's 1913 book, *University Control.* "An association of professors of American universities, based on associations in the different universities," Cattell argued in the book, would do much "to promote the interests of the universities and to advance higher education and research."[85]

From its beginnings to this day, the AAUP has been concerned first and foremost with inquiring into direct infringements upon professorial rights. Although its members, who were in Walter Metzger's phrase "the aristocrats of academic labor," were generally in agreement with the Foundation's concern with fostering the growth of universities and university-based sciences, they deeply resented the use of the pension fund to secure what might otherwise have been seen as admirable changes.[86] Enhanced no doubt by personal and symbolic distrust of the Foundation's college president trustees, AAUP professors saw the Foundation's "aim to influence institutional improvements...with a system of personal pensions to professors" as a potential if not fully actualized threat to professorial freedom.[87] Having already established a committee to oversee matters related to pensions, in the wake of the Foundation's Vermont survey and Royce's criticism of it, the AAUP established a second Carnegie Foundation watchdog, a committee on the limits of standardization.

Most likely the AAUP would have come into existence without the Carnegie Foundation, but with what Royce described as an administrator-dominated organization that was entirely free of public control to rally against, professorial cohesion was certainly strengthened. Once again, indirectly and ironically, the Foundation helped to rally forces in support of professionalism. It may not have been able to promote clear stratification within teacher education, but even in unplanned ways, it was a profoundly effective booster of professional values as well as of the institutions that helped to establish, extend, and solidify the functional organization of American society.

Systematizing Educational Measurements

In 1938 the Carnegie Foundation published its 29th Bulletin, *The Student and His Knowledge.* The bulletin presented the results of "the Pennsylvania Study," a survey based on an extensive testing program of students in that state. It advocated the use of standardized tests of aptitude and achievement for matching students to educational careers. According to Henry Pritchett's first announcement of the study in 1928, the Foundation was eager for the opportunity to move from the kind of state surveys and studies of professional education it had already sponsored to focus instead on "the experience of the student" and his competence for "vertical" progress through a school system.[1]

The shift of focus from institutional to individual characteristics that was evident in this statement did not mark a basic shift in the Carnegie Foundation's orientation toward educational reform. As had been true from the very beginning of its history, the Foundation was still primarily concerned with developing and supporting hierarchical relationships among all of the educational institutions of the United States. From the first, it had acted to organize the nation's schools and colleges in ways that would support the assumption that "the highest function of a university is to furnish standards for a democracy," and that assumption continued to shape its policies.[2] The new tack the Foundation took in the mid-1920s derived from changing circumstances and not from changing ideals.

To promote a pyramid-like organizational structure for American education, the Carnegie Foundation had initially set standards for "the college." Of necessity, that had also involved setting standards for the institution to which the college always related—"the high school." In that realm, the Foundation initially had relied on standards developed within the NEA. During the 1890s the NEA had appointed two committees to study college-high school relationships, first, the Committee of Ten on Secondary School Studies, and then, the Committee on College Entrance Requirements. The second of these committees had advocated that all colleges formulate admission standards by "units" of instruction time. Following that suggestion, the Carnegie Foundation had mandated that colleges require fourteen "units" for entrance to the freshman year if they wished to be eligible for acceptance to the Foundation's pension fund.[3] That requirement marked the origin of the so-called "Carnegie Unit."

An available and convenient measurement device at the time the Foundation commenced operation, the "unit" remained associated with the Foundation's name even though it quickly became evident to the Foundation that there were potentially more effective ways to foster the kind of college-high school relationship it favored. As early as 1910 Pritchett argued in the *5th Annual Report* that selectivity based on "a few simple examinations which shall demand a high order of efficiency in the fundamental studies" would be the best way to pass students on from school to college.[4] To standardize educational measurements in ways that would support its vision of the college and the college's place in the scheme of things, the Foundation became an early advocate of uniformity in college entrance requirements primarily on the basis of tests.

The Foundation's success as an ombudsman for this position grew over the years in direct proportion to the growth of the science and technology of testing, the use of testing, and college interest in testing. When the Foundation's suggestion of a consolidated testing service was finally achieved with the establishment of the Educational Testing Service (ETS) of Princeton, New Jersey, it did not act alone. As was the case with its professionalizing campaign, the Carnegie Foundation's activities in the field of educational measurement were constrained and empowered by external circumstances and its ability to establish alliances at least as much as they were by its own internally formulated aims.

THE GROWTH OF THE HIGH SCHOOL

When the Carnegie Foundation was established in 1905, the public high school was just becoming the predominant mode of postelementary schooling in this country. It merged two traditions, that of the classically oriented Latin school and that of the more practically oriented academies. Its growth was rapid. Between 1890 and 1900, the percentage of fourteen- to seventeen-year-olds attending high school almost doubled. Within this context, as Theodore Sizer has observed, the 1893 report of the NEA's Committee of Ten was perfectly timed to promote wide discussion of high school purposes and curricula.[5]

The report presented four rigorous and streamlined academic curricula for the high school, the purpose being to promote the teaching of relatively fewer (classical and new) subjects for longer periods of time. Its author was Charles W. Eliot. Carefully publicized and disseminated by Eliot with the assistance of Nicholas Murray Butler and Commissioner of Education William Torrey Harris, the report found a mixed if lively reception. As a publicist for the report, Butler took the lead in praising it in *The Educational Record, Harper's Weekly,* and elsewhere. But others were equally strong in condemning it. The report supported the extension of the elective principle Eliot had inaugurated at Harvard, and the idea of course election in the high school alarmed many.[6]

In addition to that criticism and others having to do with the report's contents, it was attacked because the Committee that endorsed it did not represent all constituencies. Notably absent were women teachers and parents. One rather populist commentator claimed that the report was for this reason "out of sympathy with the steady movement of the American Educational Public." It represented, he charged, "the attempt of its authors and such as that agree with them [sic] to capture the common school system of the country in the vital region [sic] of its upper grammar and high school and reconstruct it, in the interest of the university methods and aims of the present time."[7]

Despite this commentator's fears, the Committee of Ten, while perhaps moving high schools toward greater general similarities in program, did not fully reconstruct them to suit college and university ideals. The very circumstances that made this report so timely as a stimulus for controversy doomed its chances for full implementation. After 1900, public high school enrollment continued to grow at phenomenal rates: by 1910, more than 15 percent of the population between fourteen and seventeen years of age was enrolled and by 1920 more than 32 percent, with the numbers continuing to rise thereafter. In the face of this kind of expansion and diversification of clientele, it was simply impossible to standardize the high school curriculum in a rigorous, academic mold. Once referred to as "the people's college," the high school became ever more popular, rather than uniformly elite and academic, and moved rapidly in the direction of course proliferation. A 1906 study of the curricula of eighty-five schools in 1895 and 1904 concluded that "the report of the Committee of Ten seems not to have influenced directly to a marked degree the curriculum of the public high schools....In fact, more of the specific recommendations of the committee have been actually violated by the trend of highschool organization, or have proved inert, than have been followed."[8] By 1918 a diversity of function and course proliferation was sanctioned by the same group that had sponsored the Committee of Ten's report just fifteen years earlier.

In that year, the NEA's Commission on the Reorganization of Secondary Education published a report known as *Cardinal Principles of Secondary Education,* describing the high school's purposes as both distinct from and broader than college preparation. Arguing that in a democratic society schools should "develop in each individual the knowledge, interests, ideals, habits, and powers whereby he will find his place and use that place to shape both himself and society toward nobler ends," *Cardinal Principles* recommended that high schools order their offerings so as to promote their students' development in seven different areas: health, command of fundamental processes, worthy home membership, vocation, citizenship, worthy use of leisure time, and ethical character. Henceforth, *Cardinal Principles* maintained, secondary school curricula should be designed to prepare students for the pursuits they would follow in adult life.[9]

To Henry Pritchett and other proponents of selective admission to college, these developments were alarming. Speaking to the College Entrance Examination Board (CEEB) on its twenty-fifth anniversary, Pritchett said: "The swarm of untrained and immature youths [now] admitted to the high school...[has made it] convenient...to have a goodly number of elective rivulets [among others, 'Art, Bookkeeping, Band, Stenography, Journalism, Printing, Red Cross, and Home Economics'] in which these little fishes can swim and from which...they may float safely into college, —sometimes to the slaughter, sometimes to other brooks in which little fishes can find safe water." Unless colleges were careful to employ "fair and yet discriminating" devices to measure student fitness for college work, he warned, all academic standards would have to be abandoned.[10]

Pritchett had realized long before 1925 that, despite the Committee of Ten and the calls of other groups for uniform academic high school standards, in practice, standards varied greatly. It was with this in mind that he had urged the use of college entrance tests and had taken every opportunity to praise and support the CEEB. He often mentioned the CEEB in Carnegie Foundation *Annual Reports* and on at least one occasion claimed that it was "the most effective agency working toward uniformity in [the] administration of entrance requirements."[11]

THE COLLEGE BOARD AND THE SAT®

Established in 1900 at a meeting of the Association of Colleges and Secondary Schools of the Middle States and Maryland, the College Board's purpose was to bring school and college teachers together to write, administer, and score subject matter examinations for college admission. The leading figure behind its establishment, and its president from 1900 to 1925, was the ubiquitous Nicholas Murray Butler. The College Board's growth after 1900 was slow but steady. By 1910, the Board had twenty-nine college members and administered examinations to almost 4,000 students; by 1920, with thirty-three college members, it was examining over 15,000 students. Soon thereafter, it also began to offer a test that differed from all of its prior examinations. This test was the Scholastic Aptitude Test, the SAT.[12]

For some time before the SAT was first administered, the colleges that belonged to the College Board had been eager to enlarge their pools of applicants. Having traditionally selected their students from (a relatively few of) the public high schools and (many of) the private schools of the Northeast, Board colleges, with Harvard and Columbia in the lead, increasingly wished to draw students from farther afield. The CEEB's traditional examinations were appropriate to the kind of secondary school preparation that the traditional clienteles of its member colleges had tended to have, and they were not appropriate to the preparation of the new, national, and enlarged clienteles these colleges were now seeking. Hence, the College Board was urged to consider the possibility of giving an examination that did not rely so heavily on preparation in specific subject areas. Encouraged, on the one hand, the Board was compelled, on the other, to begin using the new technology of "intelligence" testing. Some of its member colleges were already giving "intelligence" tests, and, if the Board did not assume this function, there was a strong possibility of erosion of membership and with that of the gains that had been made toward uniform college testing.[13]

As a result of these pressures the Board appointed a committee in 1920 to investigate the possibility of developing and administering a test of "ability" rather than "achievement." The committee was chaired by Carl C. Brigham, a Princeton psychologist, who had worked under Robert Yerkes in developing the so-called "Army Alpha" that was given to more than a million military recruits during the First World War. By 1925 Brigham had invented a short answer "intelligence" test that was given to 8,040 students in the following year.[14]

It was the possible relevance of this new test to the concerns of school officials in Pennsylvania that provided the Carnegie Foundation with the opportunity to become more actively involved in the development of college entrance testing. A combination of factors stood behind this immediate precipitant. As had been true when the Carnegie Foundation had first had an opportunity to study professional education beginning with medicine, developments in science and technology, a changing demographic situation in education, and a concern with promoting social stratification based on knowledge all were involved in facilitating the Foundation's efforts to promote systematization in the realm of educational measurement.

THE PENNSYLVANIA STUDY

In the late 1920s, the educational authorities in Pennsylvania were facing problems that were evident across the nation. Within the forum made available by meetings of the Association of Colleges and Secondary Schools of the Middle States and Maryland (the same group that had spawned the CEEB in 1900), they discussed these problems with their peers. At the Middle States meeting of 1927, for example, James N. Rule, Pennsylvania's Deputy Superintendent of Public Instruction, talked of the challenge he saw in growing high school enrollments. Comparing "the rising tide of American youth demanding admission into our secondary schools and higher institutions of learning" to "the Yellow Peril," Rule worried that all might be lost, "not only the physical plants of our schools but also the cherished standards and traditions of an honored past."[15]

William S. Learned was also present at the 1927 meeting. Since 1913, Learned had been a prolific Carnegie Foundation staff member. Originally a schoolteacher, he had been hired by Henry Pritchett soon after receiving a doctorate from the Harvard Graduate School of Education. He was a man who had clear and certain opinions about what education ought to be. Whether writing in his doctoral thesis about the professionalization of teaching in Germany or subsequently in Foundation *Annual Reports* and bulletins, Learned viewed education in traditional terms. His perspective has been described as "essentialist," and his constant emphasis on the transmission of knowledge as the *sine qua non* of education certainly warrants that label. At a time when educators were discussing the relationship between education and a broad range and variety of purposes and outcomes, Learned was talking about the ways in which education could be made a more powerful medium for the transfer of information and the development of logical thought.[16]

At the Middle States Association meeting of 1927, one of Learned's recent works was much discussed. This was the Carnegie Foundation's Bulletin Number 20, *The Quality of the Educational Process in the United States and Europe*. The bulletin presented Learned's observations following an extended trip to Europe. It reported his belief that America had allowed "sentimental" notions of democracy to blind them to the "realistic" demands of effective education. According to Learned, the "broad, trunk-line school, where every child of democracy may come and choose the information that most attracts him"—in other words, the comprehensive high school supported by *Cardinal Principles*—bred mediocrity. Because, "the active factor in a person's education depends on the nature of the intellectual problem that confronts him and the effect upon him of its progressive solution," schools could not adequately educate anyone, Learned contended, unless they were willing to match each student to the intellectual tasks appropriate to that student.[17]

In no way opposed to the extension of educational opportunity to increasing numbers of people, Learned in other writings applauded attempts to develop new programs to meet the needs of diverse students. Lotus D. Coffman's effort to develop a General College at the University of Minnesota was one example of what Learned thought should be done. Open to all high school graduates who did not score well enough on an entrance test to be admitted to the university, per se, the General College made it possible to educate all those eligible to continue their studies, without modifying what could be offered to and demanded from those able to meet traditional standards and requirements. Admirable to Learned, less for the curricular experimentation so fascinating to more pedagogically oriented educational reformers than for the attempt to distinguish among students and to plan their studies according to those distinctions, the University of Minnesota had, in Learned's opinion, found the proper way to reconcile equality, on the one hand, and academic excellence, on the other. He believed in a diversified and stratified system of education rather than diversity within each and every classroom and therefore looked to testing to solve the problems associated with an enlarging school population.[18]

Learned's views apparently made sense to James Rule, and at the Middle States Association meeting in 1928 Rule announced that the Carnegie Foundation had recently begun an investigation of the state's schools and colleges. The study had been invited, he said, in order to determine "the validity and value of the College Board examinations as to the best method of selecting superior students for admission to the freshman class of Pennsylvania colleges."[19]

Begun with that specific question, the Foundation's study quickly underwent what seems to have been a rather characteristic broadening of focus. As was so often true, it was felt that "fundamental issues" were involved. In consequence, the study was designed to find out what Pennsylvania students actually "knew," how much their "knowledge" increased during their time in school, and how, according to their relative rankings in terms of those measures, they were distributed among Pennsylvania's institutions of higher education. In that way the Foundation hoped to be able to address some of the major educational questions facing the nation as a whole. " 'Why are these young people in high school and college?' 'What is the responsibility of the high school for orienting its pupils with respect to college aims and purposes?' 'How shall the college develop these young people so that their native talents and previous achievement will be completely utilized in attaining the aims of the individual and of the college?' "[20] Those were the questions the Carnegie Foundation considered in a study that cost several hundred thousand dollars and employed scores of workers between the time the fieldwork was started in 1928 and the resulting bulletin published ten years thereafter.

The direction given to the Pennsylvania Study came, not surprisingly, from William Learned. Because he was not trained in educational psychology, Learned turned to Ben D. Wood for assistance. A former student of Edward L. Thorndike and the director of Columbia University's Bureau of Collegiate Educational Research, Wood, too, had talked with Rule at the 1927 meeting of the Middle States Association.[21] Learned asked him to plan, administer, and interpret the testing program that was to provide the data from which the Carnegie Foundation would develop its answers to the questions posited by this study.

Like Learned, Wood was a traditionalist in his view of education. He believed that thinking was dependent upon knowledge and knowledge dependent upon facts. At least at the time of the Pennsylvania Study, Wood also seems to have believed that the ability to remember and integrate facts—the ability to think as he defined it—was an innate rather than an acquired or developed capacity. Wood clearly took issue with those who agreed with John Dewey's belief that thinking could be nurtured and developed if teachers paid sufficient attention to a child's already accumulated experience and sought to develop curricula that would connect with and extend that experience. He maintained that "if a fact cannot make a pupil think, and if a wealth of facts organized into appropriate systems of remembered knowledge cannot create and sustain thoughtful attitudes and habits, it is extremely doubtful that teachers or anything else can."[22] Because Learned believed that the acquisition of knowledge and the solution of intellectual problems must always be the one aim of schooling, and his partner and technical advisor, Ben Wood, believed that responsiveness to facts signified the ability to think and as such was a necessary precondition for education, the Pennsylvania Study was designed to measure the "knowledge," to judge from the actual tests, the information, of high school and college students throughout that state.

To that end, intelligence tests and a variety of "new-type" (i.e., multiple-choice) achievement tests, including "comprehensive" tests to measure a student's "general culture" rather than his or her grasp of a specific field, were given to Pennsylvania high school and college seniors in May of 1928, to college sophomores in 1930, and again to those same students as seniors in 1932.[23] Beyond their emphasis on factual knowledge, the tests had two additional common characteristics. Like all norm-referenced tests, the Pennsylvania tests measured differences rather than similarities among individuals. As a means of ascertaining general competence, as represented by commonly held knowledge and common gains in knowledge, the tests were worthless. Furthermore, because the tests were meant to measure "available knowledge" rather than mastery of a designated curriculum, they were in no way an accurate indication of the effectiveness of the schooling students had received. What the Pennsylvania tests primarily measured were individual discrepancies in both randomly and systematically acquired information.

The results of the Pennsylvania Study were released from time to time prior to 1938 and in that year published as *The Student and His Knowledge*, written jointly by Learned and Wood. The results of the study revealed considerable variation among students within the same institution and among students in all institutions, even among those who had been exposed to the same amount of study material ("Carnegie Units"); a less than clear and universal upward progression in knowledge from sophomore to senior year of college; no clear discrepancy in knowledge between those who went on to college and those who did not; and consistently lower test scores for students in teacher training programs than for other students. More important, perhaps, the Pennsylvania Study demonstrated that "objective" tests of what was taken as an individual's potential for education and an individual's achieved level of education could be administered on a massive scale. Hence, if one accepted the premise that student potential as both IQ and already accumulated "knowledge" was a vital ingredient in predicting educational success, then, clearly, the Pennsylvania Study proved that constant testing, especially at the crucial juncture points of the educational system, was a feasible and advisable way to improve education.

In addition, if one were not convinced that quantifiably measurable student potential was an important predictor of future educational success before reading the results of the study, one would have had trouble dismissing that argument after reading the study. Prior to the CFAT investigation, testing had not been uniformly or universally used in Pennsylvania. Many of the students tested registered a less than satisfactory performance when the knowledge they could demonstrate on the tests was juxtaposed with the knowledge deemed appropriate for their grade level in school or college. The implication of that finding was clear. Testing of students' potential and readiness for further education would have diminished educational failures—the discrepancies between what college freshmen supposedly should have known and actually, as tested, did know. According to the Pennsylvania Study, therefore, precise measures of student potential would increase the efficiency of education. Through testing, colleges might better identify those who would benefit from the kinds of instruction they offered and both schools and colleges might know when and in what areas to accelerate students. Moreover, precise assessments of student potential would decrease waste in education. Through testing, individuals, no less than schools and colleges, might better judge when a given course, program, or degree should not even be attempted. In a variety of ways, exact ratings of student potential would increase both private and public returns to education.

The findings of the Pennsylvania Study also suggested that tests were a more reliable measure of accumulated knowledge than a high school transcript signifying the completion of particular "units" of study. Transcripts had been the basis for educational promotion in Pennsylvania before the study, and the problems revealed by the tests appeared to be causally related to their use as measures of educational fitness. Consequently, the Carnegie Foundation inquiry presented a case for admission procedures based on testing rather than certification. This was the position Pritchett had begun moving toward in 1910.

Finally, since the tests used in Pennsylvania were multiple-choice, true-false, or otherwise "exact" in the answers they required, they did not involve subjective appraisals in the scoring; with the cooperation of IBM, the tests, in fact, had been scored by machines. For this reason, the tests could and did include more questions and therefore covered a wider range of content than essay examinations could do. Thus, the Pennsylvania Study also proved that tests need not suffer from the limitations so often associated with the kind of traditional examinations the CEEB had given for so long.

In sum, as described in *The Student and His Knowledge,* the Pennsylvania Study proved that "new-type" testing programs were the best means available to match different students to different educational institutions and programs. Though criticized by many commentators for many reasons, the Pennsylvania Study was considered an important document by some educators. It was publicly endorsed by Lewis M. Terman, the developer of the Stanford revision of Alfred Binet's pioneering test of individual differences and a leading figure among the psychologists engaged in test development, and it presented what appeared to be a strong case in favor of using test results as the criteria for standards in American education.[24]

A GENERAL EXAMINATION BOARD

Begun in the early stages of the Great Depression and published at the beginning of the Second World War, *The Student and His Knowledge* was undertaken during a decade when the value of standardized testing for college admission was increasingly accepted. At this time, even the elite colleges of the Northeast needed students, and testing enabled them to cast an ever widening net. College interest in testing combined with decreasing levels of foundation funding to the testing agencies that had proliferated in the late 1920s created a situation in which the Carnegie Foundation's testing experts began to consider how they might help to institutionalize further the approach to educational measurement that they were concerned with in the Pennsylvania Study. They came up with the idea of creating a new, consolidated, multipurpose national testing agency.[25]

In the late summer of 1937, William Learned drafted a memorandum describing a plan he had been developing with Ben Wood for a "General Examination Board" that would coordinate the production, interpretation, dissemination, and refinement of tests. As they sought to demonstrate in Pennsylvania, they believed that testing could improve the efficiency and effectiveness of education by fostering a better match between individuals and educational institutions and programs. By reducing competition and overlapping services among testing agencies, they hoped the national testing service described in this memorandum would lower the cost of tests and, by diminishing the discrepancies between what different agencies claimed for and against their still very varied approaches to testing, would also increase public credence in the testing movement. In their opinion, a national testing service would encourage wider test use. Also concerned with fostering the continuing research necessary for the improvement of tests, Learned and Wood advocated a national testing service because they believed that the efficiencies of such a service, combined with the spur it would provide to test use, would create the profits needed to defray the expenses involved in further test research.[26]

Though Learned and Wood promoted the agency they wished to establish primarily in terms of its anticipated future value, a number of more immediate considerations also influenced their thinking. Three matters were particularly pressing. First, for Wood, there was the continued existence of the Cooperative Test Service (CTS), an organization he had founded in 1930. At that time the completion of the Pennsylvania Study was very much in doubt. Pennsylvania schoolteachers were refusing to cooperate with the Carnegie Foundation survey, according to Wood, "because the tests that are now on the market have been used anywhere from two to three to four times in the same institution and...[the] students have memorized them."[27] To meet the needs of the Pennsylvania Study, therefore, while also making multiple-choice achievement tests available to schools throughout the country (most of whom were using more and more tests), Wood had convinced the American Council on Education to sponsor an agency to bring together schoolteachers and measurement experts to design subject-area multi-form examinations. With Wood as its director and financial support from the Rockefellers' General Education Board, the service had been a success.

By 1933, the CTS had distributed 300,000 tests and its annual sales had been increased by approximately 20 percent each year thereafter. Still, in 1937, the original expectation of financial independence by 1940, when the GEB's $500,000 grant ran out, seemed unrealistic. Converting CTS products to machine scorable forms and instituting other improvements had been expensive and had cut into accrued CTS profits more than had been expected. Thus, as Wood indicated in 1936 to Walter A. Jessup, who had become president of the Carnegie Foundation two years earlier, "if the CTS function is to continue after 1940, some means of financing it must be found. Since the function of constructing and editing achievement tests obviously belongs in such an agency as would result from the proposed merger, it would seem that this function could best be financed as a part of the new organization."[28] Financial concern for the future of the CTS, heightened by the wish to become independent of the American Council on Education, whose leadership had tried (unsuccessfully) to redirect some of the GEB grant to other projects, made the establishment of a General Examination Board a high priority for Ben Wood.

Learned, too, had a direct stake in the merger plan he and Wood supported. In the fall of 1937, the Carnegie Foundation, in cooperation with Harvard, Yale, Princeton, and Columbia, began an experimental testing project for graduate and professional school admission that had been dreamed up by Learned and Wood in the course of their work in Pennsylvania. The possibility of such a program had been an interest of the Foundation's for many years, but no program was seriously considered until the availability of the kind of comprehensive, multiple-choice tests developed for the Pennsylvania Study increased the likelihood of securing wide participation as a result of greater test cost efficiency.

The development of a standardized graduate level examination was important to Learned and to the Foundation. With the highest level of the educational system at last included, testing could be used to plan the entirety of an individual's education. Furthermore, with the high schools and, to a lesser extent, the colleges becoming more comprehensive and less selective institutions, the need for careful screening of graduate school applicants seemed to Learned increasingly important. "While the college may seek to educate all comers," Learned argued, "the graduate or professional school is charged with a duty to select those most likely to render broadly effective intellectual service. Knowledge and ability, therefore, cannot be taken for granted...the graduate school needs proof that a student's resources...exist and are adequate."[29] As the transformation of the high school into an institution of mass education, a transformation that began during the early decades of the twentieth century, gave a boost to college entrance testing, so the beginnings of that kind of transformation in the college in the late 1930s gave a boost to graduate school entrance testing.

The instant problem Learned faced at the time he and Wood proposed the merger was finding a home for this most recent innovation, the Graduate Record Examination (GRE). Neither the American Council on Education nor the College Entrance Examination Board was ready to accept the new program, and the Carnegie Corporation, though willing to support the Foundation's experimentation with the examination, did not want to commit itself to continual funding. Certainly as personally invested in the development of the GRE as Wood was in the CTS, Learned saw in the possibility of a General Examination Board a chance for the survival of his pet project.

Finally, and perhaps most important, Wood and Learned wanted a large central testing agency in order to safeguard the continuing use of testing for the purposes with which they were concerned. For them, the scientific description of individual differences was what the testing movement was all about. To their way of thinking, it was through increasing reliance on quantifiable and comparative measurements of a student's capacities that the standards necessary to improve the quality of American education would be introduced and sustained in an equitable and realistic way. Their understanding of the purposes of testing, of what tests could measure and of how they might best be used in education, was not idiosyncratic. It was widely shared among educators and psychologists at the time. And yet, by the 1930s, testing was beginning to be used for new purposes, ones that were fundamentally different from those to which Learned, and Wood, and the Carnegie Foundation were committed. The interest of the Progressive Education Association (PEA) in developing more varied and more pedagogically oriented means of educational evaluation posed a real and recognized challenge to the further extension of testing as a means of sorting students into clearly differentiated classes, programs, and educational institutions. The PEA's efforts to link the science of measurement to problems other than those of primary significance to the Carnegie Foundation called for response.

Beginning in 1933, the PEA sponsored a program called the Eight-Year Study, in which the graduates of twenty-eight private secondary schools and two public school systems were admitted to college without having to meet formal entrance requirements. Hoping in that way to encourage at the high school level the kind of pedagogical and curricular experimentation that up to that time had been more characteristic of elementary schools, the PEA quickly became involved in a controversy about how it should assess student progress. The participating schools did not want to use formal tests; at least, they wanted to use as few formal tests as possible. Having tried some of the tests developed for the Pennsylvania Study, the PEA schools decided that they were seeking objectives for their students that could not be measured in that way. Because many of the colleges insisted on the SAT, the schools accepted that examination, but as a result of their experience with the Pennsylvania tests, they began to request that the PEA develop new means for assessing student growth.[30]

The Carnegie Foundation soon found itself at odds with the position taken by the PEA schools. Initially, the Foundation had favored the experiment, and, on Learned's advice, had secured Carnegie Corporation funds to support the study.[31] Having hoped that the project would weaken the emphasis many colleges still placed on a predetermined number of prescribed "units" for entrance, Learned was deeply dismayed by the PEA schools' unwillingness to use testing to provide "relief from the rigid mechanical curriculum and credit counting of the present regime."[32] Some of the ideas expressed by the school people, particularly one suggestion concerning the possibility of substituting committee appraisals for the results of achievement tests, also struck Learned as "downright silly." Learned was interested in testing, that is, the measurement of "the true capacity of the pupil," and not in what the PEA liked to call "evaluation," that is the assessment of school methods in relation to self-designated outcomes (or, in the broad terms used within the PEA, the "process by which the values of an enterprise are ascertained").[33] Learned, as it turned out, had not really understood what the Eight-Year Study was all about. To him, the need of the moment was the replacement of an old, no longer viable standard, "the unit," with one that was more objective, precise, and otherwise discerning, "the test"; to the PEA, the need was pedagogical reform. Unable to resolve their disagreements over assessment the PEA and the Carnegie Foundation parted company. Beginning in 1934, the PEA's major source of funding became the General Education Board, and with the help of a committee headed by Ralph W. Tyler, an educational psychologist then at the Ohio State University, the PEA began to experiment with new kinds of tests as well as with other new forms of evaluation.[34]

In this situation there were also elements of an old tug-of-war that dated from at least the 1893 report of the Committee of Ten. That report, as the populist critic had suggested in his claim that the high school was being captured by the university, had presumed that college needs as well as college representatives should play a leading role in defining secondary school curricula. The Carnegie Foundation certainly agreed with that—it was a leading advocate of educational hierarchy and of university standard-setting. The PEA was not primarily a college oriented or college dominated group. Its Eight-Year Study sought to win more control for secondary school people in the designing of their own programs.

Unlike the Pennsylvania Study, which was clearly at odds with the reformist thrust announced in *Cardinal Principles,* the Eight-Year Study can be seen as supporting the premises, if not the substance, of that document. Addressing themselves to matters pertaining to teacher effectiveness and curricular appropriateness, in order to tap and develop the potential of each student and to encourage diversity in schooling, the participants in the Eight-Year Study did not urge more refined methods of student selection on the part of the colleges. If anything, they advocated less emphasis on selection and more emphasis on recognizing the validity and importance of diverse capacities and outcomes. In resisting Learned's insistence on established forms of standardized testing and in refusing to give up what he described as "the subjective rating of personal behavior characteristics," the PEA was resisting continuing secondary school subordination to the college.[35]

The Pennsylvania Study and the Eight-Year Study were not entirely comparable, but the PEA study was suggesting support for a different organizational design in education than the Carnegie Foundation favored. A struggle for power between these two views, as represented by the Carnegie Foundation, on the one hand, and the PEA, on the other, certainly played an unstated but important role in the rupture that occurred between the two groups. Though the motive was never explicitly avowed, the directors of the Carnegie Foundation's Pennsylvania Study probably began working for a national testing service at the moment they did because a consolidation of the resources, research capacities, and promotional energies of established testers would help to prevent the move away from testing and hierarchy as bases for educational organization that the PEA was leading. Without testing, as Learned put it, there would be "a return to confusion."[36]

ESTABLISHING THE EDUCATIONAL
TESTING SERVICE

With these matters in mind, Learned and Wood set out to gain allies for their plan. First, they secured expressions of interest in a General Examination Board from the groups they wished to involve in the new agency. Of particular importance was the CEEB. Not only was this group the oldest of the nation's college testing organizations, but its member colleges were among the nation's most selective and prestigious. Their recognition, through CEEB cooperation, would be vital to the success of the projected General Examination Board. Following discussions with representatives of the CEEB as well as with a number of influential educators, Learned and Wood set out to solidify and enlarge support for their plan by interesting James B. Conant in the idea of a new agency.

In 1933 Conant had succeeded A. Lawrence Lowell as president of Harvard. In stature and concerns probably more of a successor to Charles W. Eliot than to the man he immediately followed in that job, Conant had become interested in testing as a result of the national scholarship program he was sponsoring at Harvard. When asked by Ben Wood to give a speech to a 1937 conference of the Educational Records Bureau, an organization founded in 1927 to encourage and coordinate the use of tests and other new instruments for student evaluation and guidance, Conant agreed. He then queried Wood on a possible topic, and Wood urged, with additional support from Carnegie Foundation president Walter Jessup, that he discuss the future of examining agencies and present the possibility of a new organization to the public. Once again, Conant agreed. With the plan for the coordination of testing organizations sponsored by such a prestigious spokesman as the president of Harvard, the promoters of the General Examination Board hoped to gain quick and wide acceptance for their proposal.[37]

In his speech to the Educational Records Bureau, Conant talked of the value of testing and of the possibility of merging existing examination programs. "We need to continue to have varieties of tests and examinations in school, between school and college, and in college," he noted, "but I suggest that we should have a more intimate association of all those interested in this subject so that we might coordinate the activities, exchange ideas and direct a common program of research and study."[38]

The idea Conant was prevailed upon to sponsor turned out to be far more controversial than he had anticipated it would be. As Conant discovered, some leaders of the CEEB favored a test agency merger. They thought uniform testing for college admission was important, and they were alarmed by the drop in student registration for CEEB examinations that had taken place between 1931 and 1937. The drop was partly attributed to the depression and the decline it precipitated in the private schools of the Northeast, from whom the largest number of CEEB candidates still tended to come, and partly to criticisms of CEEB examinations, which still consisted in large part of written essay tests read by predominantly independent schoolteachers. The falling off of registrants was a clear indication that change was needed if, as one supporter put it, the CEEB was not to die "in its fine, old-fashioned four poster bed."[39]

Within the CEEB at the time, there was explicit discussion of the need, not only to revivify, but also to reassert the value of a cooperative testing agency. Indeed, those discussions may have provided a spur to the Learned and Wood General Examination Board plan in the first place. As it had been to the two representatives of the Carnegie Foundation's interest in testing, the willingness of some member colleges to waive examination requirements for the students involved in the PEA's Eight-Year Study was of serious concern to some people involved with the

CEEB. Although supporters of the Board realized that "to fair minded outsiders the Progressive experiment was well-worth watching," they also knew that "if it succeeded completely the usefulness of the Board…was likely to be terminated."[40] Hoping, therefore, that a consolidation would "give the new agency greater power and prestige and thus…increase whatever educational benefits the development and use of good examination and good tests bring," George W. Mullins, secretary of the CEEB, had welcomed the idea of a General Examination Board when Learned first presented it to him several months before the Conant speech.[41] Nevertheless, plans for a consolidated test agency were quickly scotched in the late 1930s, and the man responsible for blocking the proposal came from within the CEEB.

Since the 1920s when he had invented the SAT, Carl Brigham had been conducting research for the College Board. He had great influence within the Board and generally was well thought of within the testing community. It was Brigham who opposed the idea of a consolidation and it was he who persuaded George Mullins and the rest of the CEEB committee set up to consider the merger to thwart the consolidation plan.[42]

Brigham's position was clearly described in a memorandum to the Board on "The Place of Research in a Testing Organization," which, following Conant's speech, was made available to the public through the columns of *School and Society*. Avowedly written in "a strident tone," the memorandum asserted that "the present testing movement carries the germs of its own destruction." "Unless the proposed organization is set up to develop a cure for these afflictions," the memorandum continued, "it will retard rather than advance education." Brigham was concerned with two problems in particular. The first was "premature standardization," or the tendency to develop norms to give meaning to test results before the full significance of what had been tested was fully explored; and the second was a lack of research into the basic questions that needed to be answered if tests were to be "service-able to education itself." According to Brigham, "the literature of pedagogy is full of words and phrases such as 'reasoning,' 'the power to analyze,' and 'straight thinking'..." none of which are understood. "'Thinking,'" Brigham pointed out, "is one of the most obscure topics in psychology and education." Absent inquiry into that process, he maintained, testing would interfere with ef-forts to develop reasonable outcomes for education and the "appa-ratus" necessary to realize them. Firmly convinced that the demands of the market and the "propaganda" of "educational politicians" had stunted the growth of a true "science of educa-tion," Brigham feared that the sales or service component of a large testing agency would overwhelm its research program. For that reason he did not believe it would improve the existing situ-ation.[43]

Brigham's memorandum did not mention either Learned or Wood directly, although it was obviously designed to tarnish their reputations and to cast severe doubts on the validity of their work. Not only did Brigham's substantive points make Learned and Wood's claims for their tests look naive at best and malicious at worst, Brigham's ironic reference to available tests as a "cheap, ready-made camera with a poor lens" made their constant insis-tence that they were improving on "snap-shot" methods of educa-tional diagnosis seem laughable.[44] To anyone at all familiar with the testing movement, the unidentified targets of Brigham's charges would have been readily apparent. "During the last five years the testing movement has taken a new turn," Brigham ar-gued. "The salesmen, realizing the limitations of more itinerant peddlers, sought the vestments of prestige—and these were not hard to get. Instead of coefficients of correlation, we now have pontifical utterances about tests and what they do, ukases from the highest authorities"—from the Carnegie Foundation and even most recently from the president of Harvard University.[45]

Only subtly veiled in the memorandum, Brigham's antipathy to Learned and Wood, to their work, and to their plan was forthrightly expressed in correspondence with Conant and with Learned himself. To Learned, Brigham expressed his position succinctly. On January 4, 1938, he wrote: "the record of the Foundation in the examining field has been so hostile to the ideals of a liberal education that I cannot sit idly by and let this latest destructive move pass unchallenged."[46] To Conant, Brigham explained his position in more detail. First having framed the problem in general terms, he stated: "one of my complaints against the proposed organization is that although the word *research* will be mentioned many times in its charter, the very creation of powerful machinery to do more widely those things that are now being done badly will stifle research, discourage new developments, and establish existing methods, and even existing tests, as the correct ones."[47]

Within a month of his outburst, Brigham had apologized for what he termed his "Pathological," "extraordinarily ugly and ill mannered" behavior. At the time he was suffering from "hypertension," he explained, and was in need of rest to "collect" his "shattered self."[48] Certainly true—Brigham was not well at the time—the apology was nonetheless unfortunate. Brigham's arguments had sprung from deep conviction. He knew from bitter experience how easy and dangerous it could be to speak too soon about the meaning and significance of a test.

In 1923, Brigham had published a book called *A Study of American Intelligence,* in which he had used data derived from the army's World War I testing program to develop what can only be described as a racist interpretation of alleged differences in the "native intelligence" of ethnic groups, the "nordic race" coming out superior to the "alpine" and "mediterranean." The book gave a great boost to the eugenics movement and helped speed passage of legislation restricting immigration. In 1930, albeit for somewhat technical reasons, Brigham publicly announced that the book's conclusions were invalid. The insight he derived from having accepted test results without subjecting them to careful scrutiny had a profound effect on his work thereafter. Few testers in the 1930s insisted upon constant experimentation to the degree that Carl Brigham did.[49]

Conviction aside, Brigham's apology—even more, his inability to sustain the debate he had begun—was unfortunate for another reason. As James Conant realized many years later, the issues Brigham raised were "fundamental."[50] And, when the consolidation plan first proposed by Learned and Wood was revived after the Second World War and, with the Carnegie Corporation acting as broker, was successfully implemented, there was no Carl Brigham to clarify, however stridently, what was at stake. Brigham died in 1943, and the negotiations that culminated in the launching of the Educational Testing Service (it was incorporated in 1947) dealt primarily with problems that in retrospect seem relatively inconsequential. What should each agency—the CEEB, the Carnegie Foundation (as the sponsor of the GRE), and the American Council on Education (as the sponsor of the CTS)—give up to the new organization by way of resources and established functions? How should the various parties be represented in the management of the new organization? What inducements would secure the consensus necessary to carry the plan into action? Those were the questions upon which the committee organized by the Carnegie Corporation and headed by Conant concentrated.[51] As Frank Bowles, a long-time staff member of the CEEB, observed of the committee's final report, "There is scant mention of who is to be tested and why, and no discussion of the role of testing in American education."[52] With no one stepping in to raise the concerns Brigham had voiced, research was indeed designated as a vital purpose of the new testing service, but the implications of a test agency consolidation were not in themselves an important issue in the discussions.

Even with Brigham present, though, a test agency consolidation might well have been accomplished at this time. As the First World War had done earlier, the Second World War had provided a chance further to demonstrate (and develop) the uses of testing. With huge numbers of veterans returning to civilian life and applications for college entrance sky-rocketing, circumstances once again strengthened the position the Carnegie Foundation had been advocating.

However that may be, with the establishment of ETS, long-standing objectives of the Foundation were certainly advanced. Whatever else ETS has accomplished, that agency has increased the nation's reliance on standardized tests as criteria for selective college admission. In that way it has helped to insure hierarchical institutional relationships in American education as well as to promote a national system of education. Beyond that, ETS has played a part in popularizing the belief in "meritocracy" that was evident in the Carnegie Foundation from the first. It has symbolized and extended, even if in more contemporary parlance, the assumption that Henry Pritchett expressed when he argued that the university should set the standards for a democracy. Through its advocacy of systematization in educational measurements, no less than through its professionalizing campaign, the Carnegie Foundation helped to shape the institutional and intellectual contours of "The Great Society."

– 6 –

Renewing the Foundation

In January of 1967, the Carnegie Foundation announced the formation of a commission to "study the future structure and financing of U.S. higher education."[1] After several changes in name, the group was called the "Carnegie Commission on Higher Education." It was chaired by Clark Kerr and included initially fourteen and later nineteen men and women, almost all of whom were well-known figures in American higher education. It held thirty-three meetings in twenty-five different cities and authored or sponsored over one hundred books and reports. In 1973 it was disbanded, and another similar panel was organized in its stead. This group, the "Carnegie Council on Policy Studies in Higher Education," was also chaired by Clark Kerr and had a total membership of eighteen men and women, most of whom were educators and Carnegie Foundation trustees. Like its predecessor, the Council was a prolific commentator on postsecondary education in the United States and abroad and produced a large and varied library, well over fifty monographs in all. To support, first, the Commission and then, the Council, the Carnegie Foundation and the Carnegie Corporation together spent roughly $12,000,000 between 1967 and 1979. If one considers the work of the two groups as continuous, that investment made possible what may have been the longest and broadest survey of higher education ever undertaken in the United States, or, for that matter, anywhere in the world.[2]

Both the Commission and the Council were concerned with developing standards for American education, and both were instrumental in revitalizing the Carnegie Foundation after more than thirty years of relative quiescence and decline. Indeed, it was hoped that both groups would contribute to this outcome: that their significance in and for American higher education would again enable the Foundation to play an important role in educational organization. Through these groups the Carnegie Foundation once more set out to establish itself as a center of policy review within an educational "system" that has always been more directly and immediately subject to pressures for expansion, diversification, and disarticulation than to pressures for consolidation, standardization, and purposefully planned coherence in institutional design and relationship.

These two new ventures of the Carnegie Foundation followed an essentially fallow period in its history, when no new organizing efforts were begun. Pension commitments taken on before TIAA was established in 1918, combined with financial losses at the time of the Great Depression, had left the Foundation virtually bankrupt. Had it not been for loans from the Carnegie Corporation it almost surely would have gone out of existence at that time. A Carnegie Corporation decision to give back to the Foundation money paid on these loans, as well as improving prospects for Foundation financial independence, as calls for pension payments declined with time, were therefore important factors in restoring the Foundation to a function and a place it had held for a relatively brief period once before.[3] Interestingly, though, the recurrence in the late 1960s of circumstances in education and within the Foundation much like those that had originally helped make it possible to turn Andrew Carnegie's pension fund into "one of the Great Agencies for standardizing American education" suggests that more than finances was involved.[4]

In addition to the necessary precondition of financial solvency, three familiar factors helped to bring the Foundation back to life: dramatic growth and change in American higher education and American society; the emergence (or re-emergence) of a "public" that shared a concern with rational governance and clearly defined patterns of institutional relationships in education; and a collaborative effort especially on the part of two men, one a Foundation officer and the other a social scientist and educator. Together these factors made it possible to identify a new "need" for educational consolidation through systematization. In working to fulfill that need, the Foundation renewed itself. The vitality of the Carnegie Foundation has been related to recurrent interest in fostering new levels of integration as a means for building and maintaining a national community in the United States.

GROWTH AND CHANGE IN AMERICAN HIGHER EDUCATION IN THE 1950S AND 1960S

Between the time the Carnegie Foundation was established in 1905 and the time the Carnegie Commission was announced in 1967, American higher education was fundamentally transformed. At the beginning of the century, approximately 4 percent of American young people between the ages of eighteen and twenty-one were enrolled in higher education. Seventy years later, approximately 40 percent of that age group were enrolled. Although higher education enrollments increased steadily throughout the century, it was during the decade between 1950 and 1960 that the first sure signs of really dramatic change occurred. In that ten-year period, for the first time in world history, fully one-third of the age group eighteen- to twenty-one-years-old registered in institutions of higher education.[5]

This unprecedented phenomenon could be attributed to many things, including a great spurt in attendance at two-year junior colleges. Sometimes organized as the first rung in a state's higher education system, such as the one developed in California during the 1940s and 1950s, these two-year institutions made higher education more geographically and financially available to more people. Their popular and often vocationally oriented programs drew large student bodies. Between the middle 1950s and middle 1960s, junior colleges were the fastest growing type of postsecondary institution in the United States, and the enrollment gains of these new institutions outstripped their increasing numbers. Whereas some 250 thousand students were enrolled in 591 junior colleges in 1944–45, well over 600 thousand were enrolled in 598 junior colleges in 1953–54, with the number of junior colleges doubling and their enrollments tripling during the next fourteen years.[6]

This growth in junior colleges and junior college enrollments was, of course, only one aspect of a more general expansion of higher education that was made possible in large measure by increasing, and again unprecedented, levels of local, state, and federal funding. By 1959–60, 45 percent of the income of (all) American institutions of higher education came from some form of tax revenue.[7] Supporting expansion, but not in any way meeting the full cost of educational growth, these new government outlays further blurred the never precise lines between "public" and "private" institutions. By 1959–60, for example, federal funds made up an even larger percentage of the income of private institutions than of public institutions (the figures were 19.6 percent of private institution budgets from federal sources, as compared to 17.3 percent for public institution budgets). Most of this money went to research, especially in the sciences and engineering, although increasing amounts also went for student aid.[8]

Statistics abound to describe the nature and sources of change in American higher education, as the colleges and universities, like the high schools in the 1920s and 1930s, were transformed from elite to mass institutions. But even the few figures given

here should suggest that during the decade prior to the establishment of the Carnegie Commission, there was in American higher
education a situation that once again lent relevance to the kinds
of questions that had been asked at the time the Foundation was
founded in 1905. At that time, there also had been new growth
in higher education, an infusion of new funds to higher education
combined with a need for even more funds, and great disparities
between the variety of institutions that were called colleges.
Whether *the* "academic revolution" took place between 1870 and
1910, as Laurence Veysey has argued, rather than later, as David
Riesman and Christopher Jencks have suggested, there were
major shifts in the structures, roles, and social expectations for
higher education in both periods.[9]

AN EMERGING "PUBLIC"

Alike in this sense, the years during which the Carnegie Foundation was reactivated were also like the early years of its history
in that growth and change were again provoking an articulate
community of concern—a "public" that was beginning to address
the need to study and define what was going on. To an extent, the
Carnegie Foundation may have helped to bring that "public" into
being. From 1955 to 1965, due to the Foundation's inability to
support its own officers, John Gardner served as president of the
Foundation as well as of the Carnegie Corporation. At this point,
the overwhelming majority of Foundation trustees were still
prominent college and university presidents, and throughout his
term Gardner used the Foundation's annual trustee meetings as
colloquia for the debate of educational policy issues. Following
these sessions, he would write up his impressions of the questions
discussed and then publish these as essays in the Foundation's annual reports. The essays on topics such as "Liberal Education,"
"Federal Programs in Higher Education," "The Role of the Col-

lege and University Trustee," and "The Flight from Teaching"
were both lucid and timely and increased annual report circula-
tion from 12,000 in 1956 to 24,250 by 1964.[10] Whether Gardner's writings educated public opinion to the need for rational
planning and standards, which the Carnegie Commission and
Council would later seek to fulfill, is difficult to know. But it does
seem likely that his essays along with his 1961 book, *Excellence,*
helped to frame and encourage interest in the general problem of
balancing excellence and equality, which became the fundamental
issue for the Commission and the Council.[11]

In any case, two matters were bringing educators together at
this time. The first was the so-called "federal presence" in higher
education. Federal assistance to higher education was badly needed and actively solicited and welcomed. Yet, with additional federal money going to those (private) institutions that traditionally
had received little state support, and with the subsequent inevitable increase in the potential for government regulation, there
was a growing conviction that the "independence" considered so
essential to academic freedom and to university self-definition
could be jeopardized. Furthermore, there was also mounting
worry that federal funding could change the relative status, size,
and perhaps quality of different institutions.[12]

Harvard president and Carnegie Foundation trustee Nathan
Pusey had suggested to John Gardner in 1959 that the Foundation
seek Corporation funding to support an investigation of higher ed-
ucation-federal government relationships.[13] Like medical education
reformers before him, Pusey apparently thought Foundation sponsorship of such a study would enhance its "objectivity." His urging
of an apparently disinterested survey showed a concern for educator regulation of education.

Like other earlier Foundation trustees, Pusey was alert to the
politics of education. As the original Foundation trustees had
demonstrated their wish to insulate some of the nation's colleges

from market and other "external" pressures, by defining "the college" as an institution with high entrance standards, a large endowment, and no ties to the state or to denominational groups, so later trustees displayed their concern with the strength and independence and professional leadership of higher education by seeking to reestablish the Foundation's survey role. Although the Pusey-initiated study did not result in a major publication, as had been hoped, it did reflect one of the concerns that was rallying a constituency for the effort the Foundation would undertake when it set up the Carnegie Commission.[14]

Closely related to this was the challenge college presidents and others faced as a result of the social protests that escalated throughout the 1960s. To be sure, most of the violent disruptions of the decade did not happen until the late 1960s, after the Carnegie Commission was already at work. The riots in Newark, New Jersey, and Detroit, Michigan, occurred in July of 1967; Martin Luther King was assassinated in April of 1968; and the Columbia uprising took place in the spring of that year. In January of 1967, when the Carnegie Commission's establishment was first announced, political tensions had not yet escalated to the tragic levels that, among other things, would result in the National Guard shootings of anti-war student demonstrators at Kent State University in 1970. But even in the early and middle 1960s one could not miss seeing that established patterns of social deference and social authority were being seriously challenged, as the government's right to wage war, the universities' right to define the studies and routines of their students, and the white male's right to priority in education, jobs, and politics were publicly and privately called into question. Men and women from across the country lobbied in Washington, students went to Mississippi in the summers of 1963 and 1964 to challenge those rights through peaceful social action, and similarly moderate but forceful efforts to achieve greater participation in power and increased equality could be seen all around.[15]

These protests posed difficult dilemmas for educators. In some instances, faculty members and college administrators were sympathetic to the positions taken by student protesters as well as to the causes they championed in a variety of ways; but often, too, these very same people felt called upon to resist the demands student demonstrators made, if only because they believed their tactics were wrong. Beyond that, protests on and off campus called into question established lines of separation between the academy and the outside world. And this, too, raised new and difficult questions, not only about the appropriateness of student behavior and state police action on campus, but also about the standards of conscience and relevance that should guide teaching and research as well as the governance of a college. Because the stability of American society and American education were inextricably intertwined, social protest broadened and strengthened educator interest in rethinking and reestablishing conventions of conduct that might save American education, and with it American society, from further politicization and turmoil. This concern also stood behind growing interest in "objective" policy review.

A NEW COLLABORATION

Amidst these disquieting developments, John Gardner became Secretary of Health, Education, and Welfare in August of 1965. He passed on to Alan Pifer, who became acting president and then (in 1967) president of the Corporation and Foundation, the problem of deciding what to do with the Foundation as it began to regain a modicum of financial strength. A rather gentle man of medium stature, thoughtful deliberateness, even temperament, and strong convictions, Pifer had had long training for the planning he would lead. Born in Massachusetts in 1921, the son of a well-to-do paper manufacturer, he was educated at Groton School, Harvard College, and Emmanuel College, Cambridge. He had spent most of his career at the Carnegie Corporation. He had worked in the Corporation's Commonwealth Program, primarily on projects having to do with African affairs, and also had served as the Corporation's vice-president since 1963.[16] He brought to his consideration of prospects for the Carnegie Foundation a firm belief in the significance of philanthropy for continuing social experimentation and especially for the maintenance of diverse centers of public and private power in the United States.[17]

Given Pifer's strong conviction concerning the benefit to be had from institutions that could support significant social programs not otherwise supported by the government or the public at large, the problem he faced in studying the Carnegie Foundation's future became a variant of the problem he also faced at the Carnegie Corporation. As government spending for education as well as for other social welfare programs expanded, the philanthropic dollar, in comparative terms, shrank. For example, although the total amount of foundation giving to higher education increased from the first to the middle decades of the twentieth century, the proportionate share of college and university income from foundation sources diminished from roughly 10 percent by 1920 to less than 1 percent by 1970.[18] If foundations were to continue to fulfill unaccounted-for social needs, they were obviously going to have to target more carefully and to maximize the impact of their funds.

As many of Pifer's speeches showed, he was certainly aware of this problem from the time he assumed office. In a very early press interview, he was even able to describe a strategy that would become one of the most characteristic features of his years as Corporation president. Following a discussion of a lack of "quality leadership," especially in government programs, Pifer suggested that foundations sponsor "objective appraisals in the best possible manner by the best possible people."[19] By organizing "experts" to serve as referees and unofficial consultants to what the Pusey recommended study of higher education–government relations had referred to as the "new giant...fund-provider," Pifer believed foundations could supply a reviewing service that would not compete with the government's expanding role, but rather would enhance government effectiveness while also insuring the participation in government policy making of "the best possible people."[20]

During his presidency Pifer's logic was institutionalized in a variety of studies, a number of which were conducted by large panels supported by the Corporation. These included the Carnegie Commission on Educational Television, the Carnegie Commission on the Future of Public Broadcasting, the Carnegie Council on Children, and, of course, the Carnegie Commission on Higher Education as well as the Carnegie Council on Policy Studies in Higher Education. Some of the initial ground work that led to the establishment of the last two groups (which were Foundation sponsored though largely Corporation supported) may have been done before Pifer's presidency. For example, while still at Carnegie, John Gardner, in addition to articulating common concerns for members of the higher education community, had wondered if "we may need a continuing, monitoring study...a radar eye looking things over and seeing what university people need to know."[21] Furthermore, the passage of an "omnibus" (federal) Higher Education Act in 1965, which dwarfed all previous levels and types of federal spending, solidified already mounting interest in nongovernmental higher education review. Still, the establishment of the Carnegie Commission derived largely from Pifer's vision for philanthropy. It bespoke his determination to find ways to organize a new "philanthropic presence" alongside and in constructive but critical tension with the new "federal presence" that was nowhere more evident or needed than in higher education.

Having taken office in August of 1965, Pifer secured trustee approval of a Foundation study of higher education's structure and financing by November of the following year. While seeking advice concerning a possible director for the project, he discovered that Clark Kerr, then president of the University of California, would consider leading the inquiry on a part-time, non-salaried basis.[22] An admirer of Kerr's and of the three-tiered system of higher education he presided over in California, Pifer considered Kerr one of "the best possible people."[23] He was outraged when the California Board of Regents peremptorily dismissed Kerr as president of the University of California on January 20, 1967. Four days later, much sooner than would otherwise have been the case, a "Carnegie study of higher education," to be led by Kerr, was announced to the press. The speed with which Pifer moved indicated his wish to throw public and personal support to Kerr and to protest the way in which the Regents had acted.[24]

As Pifer saw it, Kerr's dismissal resulted from an ugly and dangerous intrusion of politics into academic affairs. During his successful campaign for the governorship of California, Ronald Reagan had promised to restore order to the University of California. Playing on public anxieties aroused by the 1964–65 student protests at Berkeley, Reagan had been able to mobilize sufficient opinion against Kerr to make possible what was to Pifer Kerr's wholly unjustifiable dismissal. The issue as Pifer understood it had nothing to do with the Berkeley protests. The issue had to do with Kerr's long-standing liberal record, with Reagan's opposition to all that it represented, and with larger questions of university governance and independence. Were an action of this kind allowed to pass unprotested, higher education would be further politicized, and the chances for "quality leadership" in education and elsewhere would further decline. From Pifer's point of view, however, there was one fortunate aspect to the Regents' ac-

tions. As trouble at MIT had led Henry Pritchett to turn what he
had expected to be a part-time job into a full-time occupation, so
trouble in California led Kerr to similarly transform what first had
been planned as an honorary, adjunct assignment.[25]

By the time he became chairman of the Carnegie Commission,
Clark Kerr was fifty-six years old, trim, and balding. One writer
said of him at about this time: "With his mild face, his unosten-
tatious suits, and rimless glasses, he at first strikes the observer as
a typical organization man who melts into the background." But
Kerr's personality was far more definite and forceful than his appearance suggested. A rather serious person of wry wit, he had an
extraordinary capacity for concentration and an intensity that be-
lied first impressions.[26]

Reared on a farm in Pennsylvania, Kerr had attended Swarthmore College, where the rigorous academic curriculum sparked
his interest in political theory and the issues taken up by Quaker
faculty members turned his preexisting preference for au-
tonomous action into a lifelong allegiance to Quaker ideals. Grad-
uating from Swarthmore in 1932, at the age of twenty-one, Kerr
had been educated further by involvement in worker cooperatives
in California, by formal studies in economics at Stanford University, the London School of Economics, and the University of California at Berkeley, and by travel in Scandinavia and Eastern
Europe. The beliefs thus nurtured, in the sanctity of individual
conscience, in the value of pragmatic approaches to social problems, and in the necessity of achieving peaceful resolutions in situations of conflict, had remained with him throughout his career
as a scholar, a labor mediator, an academic administrator, and a
government consultant.[27]

Those beliefs were evident in *Industrialism and Industrial Man,*
Kerr's major scholarly work, published in 1960 in collaboration
with John Dunlop, Frederick Harbison, and Charles Myers. There
he and his colleagues studied the ways in which the purposes and

strategies of elite groups influenced the structuring of a country's labor market and through that determined how much and what kind of freedoms individuals would enjoy. The underlying questions of their book were where, when, and how freedom and industrial development had co-existed and could continue to co-exist. Clearly reformist in purpose and explicitly addressed to "the intellectuals, the managers, the government officials, and the labor leaders who today or tomorrow will run their countries," *Industrialism and Industrial Man* tried to demonstrate the consequences of the choices elites would make, and particularly the benefits to be had from increased freedom.[28]

Kerr's beliefs were also evident in the incident that had led, as he described it, to his appointment as the first chancellor of the University of California at Berkeley, a post he had held for six years before becoming president of the entire University. As Kerr told the story, the Regents appointed him to that office because they knew from having observed his behavior during the loyalty oath controversy of 1949 that he could and would stand up under pressure for what he believed. Kerr had himself signed the oath the Regents had demanded of the faculty, but had spoken out forcefully against the dismissal of faculty members who had not signed the oath.[29] Whether or not he was correct in his explanation of the Regents' action, there can be no doubt that in all he had done, Kerr had been guided by a concern for individual freedom and by the command he felt to pursue peaceful and practical ways of extending opportunities for personal development to greater numbers of people. A liberal of deep-seated and considered convictions, a practical-minded man of action, and a utilitarian in his attitudes toward education, Kerr had a clear sense of purpose to bring to the Carnegie Commission.

Beyond that, like Pifer in philanthropy, Kerr had a definite reform strategy to offer. His work in California, combined with his study of the role of elites in the modernization process, had led him to believe that deliberate leadership and planning were needed if American society were to be re-stabilized, before challenges to established authority culminated either in chaos or repression. In the year following his appointment as chairman of the Carnegie Commission, Kerr described what he believed the American situation in the 1960s demanded of him and of other responsible and socially concerned leaders in government, education, and business. He did this in the Marshall Lectures he delivered at Cambridge (England), which were subsequently published as *Marshall, Marx and Modern Times: The Multi-Dimensional Society.*

Stating at the outset that he was speaking "from the point of view of an American pluralist and pragmatist in the 1960s," Kerr attempted in those lectures to analyze the nature of American society and what would be needed to ensure progress. Essential to Kerr's argument was his belief that American society was divided into three groups: an "inner-society," "composed of the managers and leaders, workers and white collar employees, and the independently engaged professional and agricultural and craft personnel that constitute the great productive segment of society"; an "under-class," made up "of the non-integrated and the nonconsulted"; and two "outer elements" which consisted of students and associated intellectuals, on the one hand, and the elderly, on the other. In an ideal society, such divisions might not have existed, Kerr argued, but in the real world there would always be social cleavages and inequities and conflicts. The question, according to Kerr, therefore, was how the consequences of society's inevitable imperfections could be diminished in terms of the costs they extracted from both individuals and the community at large.[30]

In the Marshall Lectures, Kerr offered a number of suggestions as to how that might be done. He suggested, among other things, increased tolerance and planning for greater and more equal access to education. In Kerr's view, education was the process by which people gained entry into "the inner-society" as well as the insight necessary to recognize and exercise the choices available to them. To carry out these suggestions, Kerr also argued that his or anyone else's recommendations for social improvement would only be realized if they were "forced." "Progress no longer just happens," he contended. Progress had become the business of "the invention industry," and was dependent on whether or not the research and development groups, the university scholars, and the corporate, trade-union, and government managers who made up that industry could conduct their business—planning change—in a realistic way. To do that, Kerr said, the leaders of post-industrial society, among whom intellectuals predominated, needed to focus on "small decisions" and "pragmatic solutions." They needed to focus on the immediacies that would promote the effective working of the system, rather than on the larger, theoretical issues that could not be solved in any case, and that could, in consequence, undermine public faith in rational decision making.[31]

The reform strategy Kerr described in the Marshall Lectures guided the work of the group Pifer organized according to his vision of philanthropic design. Kerr was consulted concerning the selection of Commission members, as Pifer was consulted thereafter about many aspects of Commission operation. Sharing a similar commitment to liberal ideals, Pifer and Kerr were able to establish a partnership that helped to ensure continuous Corporation support for the Commission as well as continuous Commission cooperation in efforts to revive the Carnegie Foundation.

THE CARNEGIE COMMISSION ON HIGHER EDUCATION

As originally organized, the Commission was made up of fourteen people in addition to Kerr. The group was put together within four days of Kerr's firing, with help from Lloyd Morrisett, then vice-president of the Carnegie Corporation and Foundation, and E. Alden Dunham, a Corporation program officer for higher education. To insure direct CFAT involvement with the Commission, it included a number of Foundation trustees, and to insure that the Commission could draw on "certain kinds of experience," a recollection of Pifer's that may have been tinged with subsequently developed insight, its members came from somewhat different professional positions.[32] Thus, Carl Kaysen (Director of the Institute for Advanced Study at Princeton) and David Riesman (Professor of Social Sciences at Harvard University) had had "professional experience"; Ralph Besse (Chairman of the Board, Cleveland Electric Illuminating Co.), Clifton Phalen (Chairman of the Executive Committee, Marine Midland Banks), William Scranton (Governor of Pennsylvania), and Norton Simon (Chairman of Hunt Food and Industries Inc.) had had "trustee experience"; Joseph Cosand (President of the Junior College District of St. Louis), William Friday (President of the University of North Carolina), David Henry (President of the University of Illinois), Theodore Hesburgh (President of the University of Notre Dame), Katharine McBride (President of Bryn Mawr College), James Perkins (President of Cornell University), and Nathan Pusey (President of Harvard University), had had "presidential experience"; and Roy Larsen (Chairman of the Executive Committee of Time Inc.), as well as several of the others had had "business experience."[33]

Seeking diversity within a narrow range—most of the Commissioners were middle-aged, white, male influentials—Pifer and his colleagues had drawn from their acquaintance to gather a familiar, well-known, and established group. According to Pifer, the Commission was not intended to be "representative," although after the appearance of its first report, Patricia Harris (Professor of Law at Howard University) and Kenneth Tollet (Dean of the School of Law at Texas Southern University in Houston) were added in recognition of the Commission's need for "black experience"; Kenneth Keniston (Professor of Psychology at the Yale University Medical School) was added in recognition of the Commission's need for "student experience"; Stanley Heywood (President of Eastern Montana State College) was added in recognition of the Commission's need for "state college experience"; and Eric Ashby (Master of Clare College, Cambridge, England) was added in recognition of the Commission's need for "international experience." The Commission was intended to bring together "known ability, experience, judgment, objectivity, and interest in higher education." [34] The authority of rational, responsible, and acknowledged expertise was what Alan Pifer wanted and got.

The decision to include Kenneth Keniston, a scholar who had studied and written with sympathy about the "student experience" more recently than he had lived it, mirrored the thinking that was relied on in putting the Commission together. Those who could most directly *represent* the pressure groups then insistently demanding fuller enfranchisement in American society were not asked to serve on the Commission. Instead, people who might fairly and effectively *interpret* the interests of such groups were called upon.

QUALITY AND EQUALITY

Empanelled in January of 1967, the Commission held its first meeting six months later. Its first report, *Quality and Equality: New Levels of Federal Responsibility for Higher Education*, appeared in December, 1968. [35] Of the twenty-three official reports published by the Commission, this one was the most significant because it established the procedures the Commission would follow, the priorities it would support, and the stature it would gain in the eyes of people both inside and outside of the

Carnegie Corporation and Foundation.

Quality and Equality dealt with one of the issues the Commission had originally been asked to consider—the financing of higher education. It presented a terse, factual description of current levels and types of financial support, and it included fourteen brief but clearly and strongly stated recommendations, all of which had to do with increasing federal aid to higher education. Only fifty-four pages long, and specifically addressed to "those members of the 1969 Congress of the United States and of the executive branch who have key responsibilities in the area of higher education," *Quality and Equality* embodied Clark Kerr's belief that the Commission *should not* produce "mushy reports that didn't say anything," and *should* produce what he called "blueprints for action." [36]

To develop this kind of "usable knowledge," Kerr put together a small staff and a technical advisory committee that gathered and analyzed data for the Commission and then prepared draft reports.[37] In addition, he led the Commission in carefully planned and highly focused talk. At Commission meetings he played a role analogous to what he described in *The Uses of the University* as "the 'clerk of the meeting' who both draws forth and contributes to 'the sense of the meeting' in the Society of Friends." [38] He urged participation by all members in all discussions, where necessary intentionally prompting those who remained silent on any particular issue. He also steered the discussions away from irrelevant and potentially divisive issues. In this way, he was able to elicit a consensus from the Commission, which was then used to guide staff members in preparing the next draft of a report. This may have been a somewhat cumbersome process, but Kerr believed that it was necessary to secure unanimity in a Commission whose members, for all their similarity in age, sex, race, and social location, were people of different and independent mind.[39] In any case, after six full meetings and innumerable conversations supplemented by correspondence, *Quality and Equality* was endorsed by all members of the Commission.

Following this report, all Commission reports were developed and presented in essentially the same fashion. The Commission also remained loyal to the priorities first set forth there. From *Quality and Equality* to *Priorities for Action,* the final report published in 1973, the Commission sought to find and describe and gain support for reforms that might increase equal access to education while also strengthening the quality of education.

In its reports the Carnegie Commission dealt with a great variety of topics:

—the problems of resource allocation and use (for example, the appropriate use of available educational technology, and divisions of responsibility for escalating costs);[40]

—the problem of governance common to most institutions (for example, the respective roles and responsibilities of trustees, presidents, faculties, and students; and the relationships between individual institutions and federal, state, and local authorities);[41]

—the problems of special institutions (for example, those of community colleges and "colleges founded for Negroes");[42]

—and the problems of articulating higher education and work (for example, the relevance of college training to labor market demands, and the questions raised especially for women within academe).[43]

The reports of the Commission are too varied and too numerous to allow adequate, brief summation. But three points were presented as essential to the Commission's basic priorities, the advancement of quality and equality. First, viewing education as a national resource, the Commission urged higher levels of support for higher education (especially from the federal government) combined with greater efficiency in the use of resources (through such means as shortened programs of study, improved counselling with a greater variety of options in education to increase student retention rates, and more careful planning of student-faculty ratios and faculty time). Second, looking at questions of access from the point of view of equality of opportunity apportioned according to merit, the Commission advocated the better targeting of aid for education to those groups that were underrepresented in education, and supported institutional and program diversification so that appropriate and appealing kinds of education might be more available to everyone. Finally, seeing questions of quality as essential to the nation's ability to meet "the challenges of contemporary society," the Commission made suggestions having to do with life on campus (for example, suggesting rules to distinguish between dissent and disruption); it proposed policies that would reduce enrollments in higher education (defined as colleges and universities) but not in postsecondary education (defined as colleges and universities as well as specialty schools, correspondence schools, on-the-job vocational training programs, the armed forces, training in prisons, government programs like the Job Corps, union programs, tutors, education via television, radio, and other cultural resources); it advocated the rethinking and pruning of institutional functions to insure compatibility with resources; and it called for improvements in medical education.[44] Having agreed on its two basic priorities at the start, the Commission was able to survey American postsecondary education and to make recommendations for change according to its assessment of the relationship between those priorities and the subjects it had decided to review. It investigated not just finances and structures, the two subjects originally assigned to it by the Foundation, but "the many vital issues facing higher education in the United States as we approach the year 2000."[45]

Quality and Equality set the Commission's style and basic orientation, and it also established the Commission as a powerful presence among policy making groups.[46] One of its purposes, as Kerr

saw it, had been "to introduce the Commission as a potentially effective influence."[47] Several of the specific recommendations included in the report were enacted through federal legislation in
1972, notably a program of Basic Educational Opportunity Grants
and a Fund for the Improvement of Postsecondary Education.
Whether or not these policy innovations would have been supported without *Quality and Equality* (which was updated and reis-
sued in June of 1970) has been debated.[48] Regardless, the view held
by many members of the Foundation's "public" as well as the view
of the Commission and the Carnegie Foundation was that *Quality
and Equality* provided the spur for these actions. As Alan Pifer indicated, he believed "that the Commission...directly influenced
the spending of...at least $2.4 billion [by 1979] for the BEOGs
program alone." Clark Kerr, among others, agreed.[49]

Generally considered to have been the most effective of the various Commission "blueprints for action," *Quality and Equality* was
followed by a number of other reports that were also thought to
have been influential. This occurred when a report was again
specifically directed at the federal government and timed to coin-
cide with pending legislation. It was believed, for example, that
Higher Education and the Nation's Health (1970) helped shape the
Health Manpower Training Act of 1971.[50] In addition to this,
many of the Commission's sixty sponsored research studies and
twenty-three technical reports were highly regarded, not only in
policy making circles, but in academic quarters as well.[51]

Even if one consulted the Commission's various critics, there
was wide agreement that the group was well known and serving
as a central agency for educational policy review. For this reason,
Donald McDonald of the Center for the Study of Democratic Institutions in Santa Barbara, California, deplored the Commission's focus on what he called "the contours of the educational
process." To McDonald, the Commission was drawing attention
away from "the first principles of education," which he believed

were "the ways of knowing," the ways in which "the human mind moves from knowledge to understanding to wisdom."[52] At least agreeing with McDonald's sense of the Commission's significance, Samuel Bowles and Herbert Gintis, in their 1976 Marxist interpretation of American educational history, claimed that the Commission was "by far the most important effort to restructure U.S. higher education."[53] Obviously, they, too, thought it was important.

The person whose opinion mattered the most, though, was Alan Pifer. Reflecting his own sentiment as well as the opinions he had solicited from the network of educators to whom the Corporation and the Foundation turned for advice, Pifer indicated his appraisal of the Commission in a memorandum to the Foundation's trustees written in 1971. "When the Commission 'completes' its work, it will have in fact produced a vacuum by having demonstrated the continuing value of such an enterprise," he said. On the assumption that no other agency (public or private) was about to establish "a strong, objective center of review, policy studies and policy statements," especially for higher education, Pifer asked the trustees whether there was "a Carnegie responsibility to create some kind of successor to the Commission."[54] Pifer's answer to that question, and the trustees' answer, was "yes," and as a result the Carnegie Council on Policy Studies in Higher Education was established in 1973, when the Commission ended its work.

THE CARNEGIE COUNCIL ON POLICY STUDIES IN HIGHER EDUCATION

Like the Commission, the Council was a prolific source of "usable knowledge." And also like the Commission, the Council considered a great variety of issues:

—the problems of finance in an era of apparent educational "depression" (for example, those having to do with maintaining equality of opportunity as well as academic standards in the face of new competition for students);[55]

—the problems of curriculum (for example, those having to do with sustaining the humanities and the creative and performing arts in the face of greater support for the sciences);[56]

—the problems of movement from school to work and back again (for example, those having to do with the need for more diverse educational career patterns and options);[57]

—the problems of conflict resolution within the university (for example, those having to do with the advisability of college collective bargaining);[58]

—the problems of access especially but not exclusively for minority groups and women (for example, those having to do with affirmative action and resistance to affirmative action);[59]

—and the problems of medical education (for example, those having to do with the strengths and weaknesses of area health education centers).[60]

In the breadth and quality of its publications, in its philosophic orientation, and in its style, the Council was difficult to distinguish from the Commission. But in the aspirations held for it by the Foundation, the Council bore the marks of the Commission's success as well as of changing attitudes toward representation. Having decided that his philanthropic strategy had worked and would work in the realm of higher education, or that what he had once described as expert policy review could advance the public interest in this domain, Pifer designed the Council so that Foundation trustees would assume the role that had been played by members of the Commission. He hoped that if one could move the Commission's function "in-house," Foundation trustees would have a way, through their Foundation affiliation, to help plan the course of American education.[61]

For this reason, the Council was organized as "an integral part of the CFAT and its principal operating arm," with a majority of

Council members serving concurrently as Foundation trustees. As a result of a 1971 change in the Foundation's by-laws that provided for "much wider representation both from within the academic community and outside of it," the Council was a somewhat more diverse group than the Commission had been."[62] At various times it included Ernest Boyer (Chancellor of the State University of New York), Nell Eurich (Senior Consultant for the International Council for Educational Development), Daniel Evans (President of Evergreen State College), Elbert K. Fretwell, Jr. (Chancellor of the University of North Carolina at Charlotte), Margaret MacVicar (Associate Professor at M.I.T.), Frank Newman (President of the University of Rhode Island), Rosemary Park (Professor of Education, Emeritus, at the University of California, Los Angeles), James Perkins (Chairman of the International Council for Educational Development), Alan Pifer (President of the Carnegie Foundation), Joseph Platt (President of the Claremont University Center), Stephen Spurr (Professor at the LBJ School of Public Affairs at the University of Texas at Austin), Pauline Tompkins (President of Cedar Crest College), Clifton Wharton, Jr. (President of Michigan State University), and, of course, Clark Kerr, all of whom were at some time Foundation trustees; and William Bowen (President of Princeton University), Nolen Ellison (President of Cuyahoga Community College), Lois Rice (Vice President of the College Entrance Examination Board), William Roth (a former Regent of the University of California), and William Van Alstyne (Professor of Law at Duke University), who were not trustees.[63]

APPRAISALS OF THE CARNEGIE COUNCIL

Clark Kerr, for one, believed that the Council was somewhat less effective than the Commission had been. The times were different, he stated. There was "a lot more attention being paid to higher education" during the Commission years. "But aside from that," said Kerr, "the membership made a difference." According to Kerr, "The Council was set up in a more representative fashion, if you can call it representing....When the Commission was set up there wasn't all this emphasis upon being representative of the population as a whole. There was more emphasis upon people as individuals, and what they could bring as individuals rather than as men or women or young or old. But this whole idea of representation—it isn't really getting representation, but getting people drawn from a variety of backgrounds—...was an active idea by the time the Council got set up. As a consequence, the Commission tended to have better known people, by and large, than did the Council. That was because when they started working on the Council membership, Dick Sullivan [the Corporation and Foundation treasurer] actually drew up one of those grids for more representation....In terms of carrying weight, because of the people on it, the Commission carried more weight."[64]

Alan Pifer, among others, did not fully agree with Kerr's appraisal. He maintained that, however different in membership and immediate impact, the Council had been, if not as effective as the Commission, certainly as important. He stressed that it too had pointed out the strengths and weaknesses of higher education, had suggested rational, research-based guidelines for institutional and national policies, and had, in this way, helped to promote coherence and system. Pifer's inclination for generosity in praising public service may have influenced his view. More likely, though, his appraisal reflected changes in his sense of philanthropic design.[65]

By the 1970s, Pifer had become deeply convinced of the nation's need for diversity as well as quality in leadership.[66] The concern for "wider representation" that had led him to work for a restructuring of the Foundation's board of trustees also led him to advise "wider representation" on the Corporation's board and more generally in all philanthropic activity. He was convinced by this time that "wider representation" would help to preserve public tolerance for foundations and for the critical appraisals and other policy-making efforts he thought they should provide. By better insuring foundation sensitivity to the variety of "publics" that made up the public at large, "wider representation" would increase the capacity of private foundations to serve "the public good."[67]

Pifer's belief, which had not been evident when he succeeded John Gardner in 1965, was evident in his writings by the time the Carnegie Council was set up. In the 1974 Carnegie Corporation annual report, Pifer included an essay that is worth quoting at length. Called "Foundations and Public Policy Formation," it described his vision for philanthropy in the middle 1970s.

Among the most difficult and important issues facing foundations is the question of the legitimacy and feasibility of their participation in public policy formation. In this function is to be found what is very possibly the most substantial opportunity foundations have today for service to the nation but also, perhaps, their greatest vulnerability...

In these circumstances there are many people involved in the management of foundations, as trustees or administrators, who believe the avoidance of anything even remotely controversial of a public policy nature is the only sensible course to follow....

An alternative and more persuasive view, which some foundation trustees and administrators hold just as strongly as the apostles of low-profile cautiousness hold theirs, is that the only ultimate protection for foundations is to remain relevant, necessary institutions—whatever the risks entailed. The best way for foundations to do this is to be constantly sensitive to public policy issues in the fields in which they operate and not be afraid to initiate or support activities that relate to these issues....

This argument is firmly based because it is rooted in the nature of the American social and political system. In this country we have never thought of the concept of citizen participation in democratic self-government as being confined to the ballot box, essential as that is. We have always recognized a second important element, the right of citizens to advance what they conceive to be the common good through their own initiatives carried out by means of private organizations and associations....

Engaging in activities intended to help shape public policy has its problems for a foundation....

A frequently discussed problem...is one of whether foundations, either consciously or unconsciously, do tend to bring a set of values into play in their program determination and in the making or withholding of grants, and, if so, to what extent the influence of these values is legitimate.

Values of course are of many kinds....What are values to one person are no more than unthinking prejudice and predilection to another. Values also are often in conflict with one another....

There does, however, seem to be one broad set of values which all foundations in this country will probably share, the values embodied in what Gunnar Myrdal, in his brilliant study some years ago of the Negro in American Life, called the American Creed. Briefly, this Creed encompasses a belief in the essential dignity of the individual human being, in the fundamental equality of all men and women, and in certain inalienable rights to freedom, justice and a fair opportunity....If a foundation espouses such a set of values, it will have a broadly humanitarian outlook that is bound to affect the nature of its involvement in public policy issues, turning it instinctively toward those issues which have to do with bettering the condition of the least fortunate members of society. Application of this set of values can be regarded as a departure from "objectivity" so deep and broadly endorsed by the culture as to be inescapable. As a people, we cannot claim neutrality with respect to these values without divesting ourselves of our history, our origins as a nation, and, indeed, our very identity.

No foundation, therefore, any more than any other institution, can be totally "objective."...

Probably the only protection available to a foundation [in insuring reasonable and fair standards for its policies and its efforts to help shape public policies] lies in having a diversified board of trustees and staff in which a reasonably wide variety of *experience* in the nation's life is represented. If there is too much homogeneity in a foundation's management—homogeneity of occupational or professional background, economic status or interest, social perspective, or political persuasion—there is likely to be no one involved at the critical moment of decision to challenge the assumptions underlying a proposed course of action....

Foundations do have a legitimate—indeed essential—role to play in public policy formation, although no one should doubt there are some real risks involved. Nevertheless, if the role is played conscientiously and is informed at every stage by candor, openness and integrity, it seems likely there will be a sufficient degree of overall public tolerance, perhaps even regard, for foundations to ensure their continued independence. Certainly the alternative, which is for them to operate with such cautiousness that they transform themselves gradually into quaint, anachronistic, and ultimately irrelevant, appendages of American society must be regarded both as a clear denial of the public interest that inheres in all foundations and a violation of the public trust which those who manage them have unquestionably accepted.[68]

Now, one should be careful to note in considering the significance of their somewhat different appraisals of the Carnegie Council that Clark Kerr might well have agreed with much if not all that Alan Pifer said here. One should *not* suggest too much of a difference in Kerr's and Pifer's points of view. Both were liberals. Both believed in quality and equality. Both thought the Council as well as the Commission had been worthwhile. Nevertheless, Kerr appeared somewhat more skeptical of the value of constituency representation, even described as "experience" representation, than Pifer did. Perhaps as a result of his long interest and firm belief in the importance of elites in widening opportunities for freedom, Kerr appeared to have been more concerned with the outcomes of elite sponsored reform than with whether or not such efforts, in themselves, offered more people a chance to participate in policy making. Pifer, by contrast, perhaps as a result of his long experience in private philanthropy and his determination to maintain a place for private philanthropy in American society, appeared to have been as concerned with finding new means to allow for wider participation in governance as he was with the outcomes elites could achieve by way of gaining support for reform.

The difference in emphasis between the views of the two men was in part a difference in time-frame; Pifer's views having been more consistent with the belief that greater equality was immediately necessary, Kerr's, with the belief that greater equality was necessary over time. It was also in part a difference concerning the nature of excellence and the proper basis for leadership in a democratic society, Pifer's view suggesting a greater willingness to recognize diversity even in excellence, and Kerr's, a greater disinclination to accept more than one standard (i.e., prominence and recognized achievement) for "the best." By drawing out the implications of the slight differences of belief that existed between the two men, one can see the differences between two of the views of community that predominated in the 1970s: on the one hand, the view that defined community on the basis of equal participation in power, and, on the other, the view that defined community on the basis of equal opportunity to gain access to power.

A RENEWED, REESTABLISHED, AND REORGANIZED FOUNDATION

In the end, what was most important for the Carnegie Foundation about Alan Pifer's and Clark Kerr's convictions was that their thinking was sufficiently compatible to enable them to establish and sustain a long and productive collaboration. As the Council's work neared its end, they agreed that it had demonstrated what the Commission had shown first: that policy studies should be, as

Pifer had put it earlier, a "Carnegie responsibility." General concurrence in that view on the part of the people (mostly educators) outside of the Foundation who were consulted about the Foundation's post-Council future confirmed that determination and in November of 1979 the Foundation was reorganized.[69] At that time Pifer and Kerr both resigned from the posts they held in order to permit a combining of administrative and programmatic responsibilities in the role of a new president. As Alan Pifer explained, when he turned the Foundation over to Ernest Boyer, its seventh president, the Commission and Council had demonstrated to the Foundation "that despite the massive movement of government into areas that were once a private responsibility, there continues to be an important role for private foundations generally, and specifically in higher education for The Carnegie Foundation for the Advancement of Teaching."[70]

By 1979, the Carnegie Foundation had been renewed. As had been true earlier in its history, it had organized surveys of American higher education and also, in this instance, of some aspects of the larger enterprise that was called postsecondary education. Those surveys had been designed to collect data and then to review, classify, categorize, assess, and evaluate, not all, but many of the quantifiable or otherwise comparable aspects of the still motley array of schools, colleges, and universities that made up the nation's "system" of postsecondary education. The Commission and Council approached this task in a fashion that was more inclusive than selective and more consistently intelligent about many issues than searchingly profound about a few. Their approach might be described as more sociological than philosophical, and to the extent that it was philosophical, more pragmatic and utilitarian than idealistic. No less than earlier Carnegie Foundation sponsored surveys, the Commission and Council's approach to education revealed a continuing faith in the value of quantifiable, arithmetic-based and deductive science.

In addition, these Carnegie Foundation sponsored surveys, like earlier Foundation studies tended to support hierarchical patterns of educational organization. The Commission and Council called for greater equality of educational opportunity and for continuing as well as greater quality in education. And they did so, by urging the removal of financial barriers to enrollment in higher education, the maintenance of the selective and elite characteristics of the nation's "best" colleges and universities, and the encouragement of support for and recognition of the necessity for differentiation in higher education and between higher and other forms of postsecondary education according to institutional function, structure, and clientele. In a more equity-oriented, mass society than had existed in 1905, the Carnegie Foundation sponsored a Commission and Council that undertook studies that were in style, consistent accuracy and high caliber, substance, and even outcome not dissimilar from the more noteworthy of the ones the Foundation had supported before.

In the end, therefore, one must at least wonder whether or not the Carnegie Foundation's capacity to develop technologies of influence has depended not only on financial solvency and a recurrence of interest in fostering consolidation, coherence, and integration in American society, but also on still limited capacities to develop, organize, and use knowledge in ways that could advance principles for community organization other than those that presume a correspondence between some form of hierarchy and a stable social order. As the limitations of norm-referenced testing have been recognized, if not yet adequately surmounted, so the limitations of social planning based on even sophisticated—the best available—extensions of "progressive" social science may need also to be acknowledged if different forms of social organization are ever to become seriously imaginable. However that may be, by organizing groups of people, who could gather and appraise educational data, and make themselves heard in influential circles, the Carnegie Foundation once again found a way to revitalize and reestablish itself as an agency of rational standards in American education and American society.

PART III

The Great Society

In *The Public and Its Problems,* John Dewey asked how "The Great Society" could become "The Great Community."[1] He wanted to know how the shared interests, beliefs, and affections that he believed had been a feature of life in earlier, smaller, less industrialized, "face-to-face" communities could be combined with the technological advances that he recognized in the larger, more diverse, more urban, more secular, more impersonal society in which he was living in New York City in 1927. Dewey may have assumed greater harmony in bygone days than actually had existed, and many people have found it unrealistic to hope that a sense of close community can be developed throughout a society such as the one that has emerged during the twentieth century in the United States. Nevertheless, one cannot dismiss the essence of Dewey's concern— the belief that if "society" as a web of formally interconnected institutions must be based in and sustained by the mutual interests and reciprocal regard among people that derive from the sense and experience of "community," then changes in society must be accompanied by changes in the bases for association that create community. One can see this clearly in the history of the Carnegie Foundation.

Henry Pritchett recognized in modern circumstances a need for institutional reform. He was acutely sensitive to the possibilities inherent in a national society and organized the Carnegie Foundation to foster the development of such a society through the organization of institutional systems of education that would insure patterns of social relationship based in education. Perhaps because he was more insistent upon gaining support for his views than upon refining and further developing them, however, Pritchett did not see that his perceptions of social need could conflict with the perceptions of other equally reasonable and patriotic people, and, beyond that, that elite efforts to develop an institutional basis for a more national society could pose serious problems of governance and community. In his certainty that experts could ensure progress by providing responsible direction for the newly emerging, more nationally oriented institutions of "The Great Society," Pritchett failed sufficiently to consider the always important link between the means and ends of governance in a democracy—to wonder if policy making by a few, non-elective custodians of the body politic, an *elite* in Harold Lasswell's sense of the term, was more of an immediate than a sufficient means to democratic ends; and he also failed sufficiently to realize that changes in the institutional structures of a society may require changes in the basis for society in community.

Pritchett's views were grounded in his insistence that governance had been and should remain primarily a matter of voluntary individual and institutional self-regulation and that expert policy review could strengthen governance in that sense. He saw community, as many people in the nineteenth century had, as a sum of separate individuals and therefore held that the preservation of the individual's civil liberties could and should still provide the basis for association in the United States. All of this can be discerned from the position Pritchett took in urging corporate as opposed to social responsibility for pensioning.

During Pritchett's term in office, the Carnegie Foundation had many vociferous critics. Pritchett often misinterpreted and dismissed the issues these critics raised. Their objections to Foundation activities tended to derive from their efforts to grapple with the very problems of governance and community that Pritchett did not see. Whereas Pritchett was convinced that science alone, and therefore expertise, could provide sufficient guidance for governance through voluntary self-regulation, these critics dissented from that view, more or less articulately asserting that in a socially diverse democratic society governance must include processes for legitimating insights derived from science and developed by experts. What is more, whereas Pritchett would have disagreed, these critics would have agreed with a point Jane Addams made three years before the Carnegie Foundation was organized. In a variety of ways, they too would have said that "unless all men and all classes contribute to a good, we cannot even be sure that it is worth having."[2] With Addams they believed that newer and fuller bases for community needed to be found: that public participation in efforts to define and advance "the public good" was vital. The values and the views of community that were held by these critics can be discerned in their opposition to the Carnegie Foundation and its policies.

Finally, during the 1970s, amidst a resurgence of interest in questions of community, the Carnegie Foundation began to address the problems Pritchett had ignored. While pursuing his belief in the necessity for deliberate elite efforts to promote institutional reform, the Foundation also began to recognize the importance of differences in interest and to seek representation of those within the Foundation. Whether or not that would move the Foundation toward full recognition of the value to be had from combining Pritchett's approach to reform with the approaches implicit in the concerns raised by early Foundation critics remained unclear. But the history of this Foundation certainly suggests that only if that happens, only if ways are found to combine the benefits of expert knowledge with the benefits of public participation in policy making, only then will there be a clear and even necessary relationship between "private power" and "the public good."

Corporate vs. State Responsibility: Henry Pritchett and "The Social Philosophy of Pensions"

The final bulletin issued in the term of the Carnegie Foundation's first president was *The Social Philosophy of Pensions,* a brief summary of the principles and technical knowledge derived from the Foundation's twenty-five years of pension administration.[1] There were few Foundation publications in which Henry Pritchett, who was its author, had invested as much time, effort, and thought. For Pritchett, it embodied the fundamental principles that had guided his administration of the Foundation since its organization in 1905.

Throughout the years of his presidency, Pritchett had become increasingly interested in pensioning, in part, because of basic flaws in the original pension plan established in 1905, but even more, because of his growing sense of the significance of pension plan design. Although he remained closely involved with the Foundation's educational studies, he had become convinced that the Foundation's efforts to promote functionally defined hierarchies in and through education were dependent upon the establishment of sound pension systems. As calls for state assumption of responsibility for old age assistance mounted, Pritchett recognized a fundamental challenge to his own principles. Like his friend Herbert Hoover, Pritchett thought individualism and corporate voluntarism should govern a modern democratic society. His campaign to gain support for corporate responsibility in pensioning rested on his belief in individualism and voluntarism as a means of combining the citizen's right to liberty and the society's need for efficiency.

THE FINANCIAL PROBLEMS OF CARNEGIE PENSIONS

When he became president of the Foundation, Pritchett knew relatively little about pensions, annuities, or insurance of any kind, and actuarial and financial information was woefully inadequate. He designed a pension plan that provided relatively large pensions to professors who had accumulated long years of service in a few "accepted" colleges. He hoped in this way to help "accepted colleges" strengthen the caliber of their faculties against the decline of "scholarly influences" by strengthening their capacity to attract and hold the "strong men" who, in turn, would help to strengthen their colleges.[2] Pritchett hoped that the Foundation's pensions would establish the principle of "retiring pay" as an accustomed form of academic compensation.[3]

In 1906 only eight institutions of higher education in the United States and Canada provided faculty pensions.[4] Although Pritchett was certain that good teachers, "the only recognized aristocracy in America," were interested primarily in "the sense of power and the love of study and of the scholar's life," he assumed that even such men of "character" would enter a relatively low-paying profession only with assurances of security in old age.[5] By establishing the principle of the pension, Pritchett sought to make college teaching more competitive with medicine and law in drawing recruits from among the most fit.

Pritchett's logic was reasonable, but the Foundation's pension plan simply did not work as originally intended. From the very first, trustees pushed to extend eligibility for pensions to additional groups of people: Charles W. Eliot wanted pensions for professors' widows; Nicholas Murray Butler wanted them for librarians, registrars, and deans; and many trustees urged that an ever-increasing number of especially "meritorious" individuals outside of the "accepted" institutions be added.[6] Pritchett himself applied for a pension for his father.[7] More and more institutions qualified for entrance to the pension fund; "accepted" institutions sent increasing numbers of applications for pensions; beneficiaries lived for increasingly long periods of time; and, as faculty salaries rose, so did the pensions. As early as 1909, an actuarial study indicated that if the Foundation was to meet the demand, its resources would have to be "very considerably larger"; by 1914, evidence to support that finding was conclusive. The Foundation in 1914 had 2,094 more individuals on its pension list than had been anticipated for that year even in the 1909 actuarial study; and by 1917, estimates indicated that within fifty years, the Foundation would have less than half the income necessary to support the anticipated load.[8]

THE "MORAL" PROBLEMS OF CARNEGIE PENSIONS

Even before it was clear that the Foundation's initial pension arrangement could not be sustained, Pritchett had considered changes in the plan he had devised. Beginning in 1906, he set out to become an expert on pensions. He studied plans in Germany, New Zealand, and England, as well as in the United States. He learned about retirement systems in industry, transportation, civil service, teaching, and the military. And of one key principle he quickly became convinced: contributory pension systems were superior to noncontributory systems from both the financial and social points of view.

Pritchett's understanding of the advantages of pension plans supported jointly by employers and employees was influenced significantly by the studies he read. In 1911, for example, he described a report of the Massachusetts Commission on Old Age Pensions, Annuities, and Insurance as "the most valuable contribution to the subject" yet published in the United States.[9] Having analyzed the relative costs and potential merits of a great variety of foreign and American plans for relief, the Commission had concluded that it was not advisable for the Commonwealth of Massachusetts to establish a general system of old age pensions. Rather, following the approach suggested by Theodore Roosevelt for the federal government, the Commission had urged the state "to promote independent individual savings and strengthen voluntary thrift agencies," partly by requiring that "thrift" be made a compulsory study in the public school, and partly by urging the public to participate in state-guaranteed, voluntary insurance programs. It had also recommended that the state suggest to all "corporations of permanent character" the establishment of their own retirement plans.[10]

The Commonwealth of Massachusetts and its municipalities, as "corporations of permanent character," did have a responsibility to pension their own workers, the report maintained. And because they had a responsibility to establish successful "schemes," all future state and municipal pensions should rest on one "vital and fundamental" premise: the sharing of expense between employers and employees.[11] Contributory pensions were less costly. The Commission's extensive investigations had revealed also that noncontributory plans "must exert a depressing effect on wages, a demoralizing reaction on character and a disintegrating influence on the family."[12]

Appearing at a moment when Pritchett was already doubting the wisdom of his plan, the Massachusetts report helped him make sense of his own observations. As he explained to one of his many professorial correspondents, it was evident to him by 1910 that the pension fund was widely abused. "Undertaken in the interests of the individualists," pensions had in a number of instances been used to subvert individualists. Now able to "lead them gently but firmly up to a Carnegie pension," college presidents were in some cases retiring professors they found troublesome or disagreeable, which meant that "good men were arbitrarily forced to resign." Freeloading professors were also inclined to look to the pension fund as a source of release from academic work—according to Pritchett many were retiring into business—rather than finding in the promise of a pension the kind of freedom from anxiety that would enhance their scholarly productivity. Reflecting on such abuses, Pritchett concluded with chagrin that the "tide of egotism and restlessness and self-deception has risen steadily year by year."[13]

Writing in the *Sixth Annual Report* on the "Moral Influence of a Pension System," he defended Carnegie pensions as having made the "difference between dependence and independence." They had permitted younger men to replace the "worn out," now retired in a "dignified and just" fashion. They had thus helped to "quicken the whole intellectual life of the college."[14] In transforming sleepy colleges into lively centers of teaching and research, pensions were apparently proving as useful as Pritchett had suspected they would during his days at MIT. Yet, as Pritchett also noted, the Carnegie system had had unexpected and undesirable effects, as well. It had made it possible for some professors to mark time until retirement, and therefore to "perform in a perfunctory and machine-like way"; it had encouraged others to argue for special consideration on the claim of "their particular and unusual service"; and it had persuaded some colleges to act as if they had been relieved of all responsibility for faculty welfare. An academic pension system of some kind was indeed desirable, Pritchett concluded, but one protected from "those universal dangers that come from human weakness and human selfishness."[15]

Coming from a man who had thought professors could become the "aristocracy" of a democracy, such a statement was quite a confession. It reflected his disillusionment experienced in a disagreement with Woodrow Wilson, who was in every way Pritchett's peer in moral principles. In the fall of 1910, Wilson had resigned from the presidency of Princeton to become governor of New Jersey. On November 1 of that year, the Carnegie Foundation had received both his letter of resignation from the Foundation's board of trustees and Princeton's application for his pension. Wilson knew that a recent change in Foundation rules made his pension application unsupportable without a special trustee exemption, and the trustees were disinclined to grant such a waiver. Although Pritchett explained that, however admirable Wilson's movement into public office, it was unfortunate that pensions provided encouragement to leave "educational service to undertake other work on salary," Wilson refused to withdraw his request. He had gone into politics because he had counted on a pension, he said, thereby contradicting his earlier claims to have understood the logic for the Foundation's pension rules. Pritchett stood his ground and Wilson was denied a pension.[16] But the incident with Wilson, whom Pritchett had greatly admired, took a heavy toll. The story made its way into the press, bringing criticism to the Foundation and its trustees and deep personal dismay to Pritchett. Writing to Frank A. Vanderlip at the time, Pritchett confessed that he had "seldom been more hurt or more angry."[17]

Pritchett was also under heavy attack from several witty, acerbic, and agile academic critics, who saw him as a symbol of autocracy and administrative authoritarianism.[18] As president of the Carnegie Foundation, Pritchett was a safer, more generally representative, and more visible target than the president of a professor's own institution. Because he stood for and advanced the bureaucratization that helped to change the conditions of academic employment, Pritchett inadvertently forced academics to confront the more painful facts of their situation—their lack of full professional autonomy, their personal subjugation to sometimes arbitrary administration fiat, and, therefore, their need to organize. Expressions of that resentment on occasion left him feeling "chastened."[19]

All of this led Pritchett to conclude that "it is impossible to remove the college teacher from those social and moral influences that affect all men." The arrangements he had established for "Mr. Carnegie's Gift to the Teachers" had been fundamentally misconceived. "It is...a fair question," he wrote in *The Sixth Annual Report,* "whether college pensions ought not, like other pensions, to carry a contributory feature."[20]

THE CHALLENGE OF SOCIAL INSURANCE

In the process of his study of pension questions Pritchett also discovered a troubling social trend. As David Hackett Fischer has put it, "Early in the twentieth century, Americans learned to think of old age in a new way. That stage of life began to be seen as a problem to be solved by the intervention of 'society.'"[21]

In 1850 there had been fewer than one million Americans over sixty years of age. Within twenty years that number had doubled and within forty years it had quadrupled. By 1920 there were eight times as many people sixty or older as there had been in 1850. The total number and proportionate increase has climbed constantly ever since. Less likely to be employed and more likely to live in a city in 1920 than in 1900, and as a result more likely to be dependent, if not on family then on the state, the elderly suffered problems that were "discovered" and publicized by the investigations and writings of settlement workers and journalists. The problems of the aged brought a new orientation to the question of relief.[22]

At approximately the same time that the Carnegie Foundation was established, a small group of social workers and social scientists had begun to discuss what they called "social insurance." Essentially different from private pension plans, generally undertaken by employers to increase worker loyalty and productivity, proposals for old age assistance or social insurance tended to involve an arrangement for a modest equalization of income.[23] As early as 1890, Edward Everett Hale, a widely respected Boston journalist and social reformer, called for "universal life endowments," or non-contributory old age pensions to be supported by the poll tax. Advocates of social insurance tended to urge the use of state powers to provide the necessary relief.[24] Isaac Rubinow, an early and vigorous proponent of government-sponsored old age security, explained in 1913, that social insurance is "the policy of organized society to furnish that protection to one part of the population, which some other part may need less, or, if needing, is able to purchase voluntarily through private insurance."[25]

As Pritchett clearly understood, social insurance was a radical idea. Although its champions recognized the virtue of thrift, they maintained that under existing economic circumstances, personal savings were often impossible to maintain and in any case rarely sufficient as an antidote to poverty in old age. Contradicting traditional arguments for fiscal morality, and for the individual's own responsibility for economic self-sufficiency, supporters of social insurance argued that in modern society state assistance of some kind becomes necessary. Although few described the underlying purpose of social insurance as forthrightly as Rubinow did, and although many who lobbied for old age assistance would have been appalled by his claims, social insurance was, indeed, as Rubinow asserted, an effort to secure "class legislation...to readjust the distribution of the national product more equitably—not in accordance with the ideal demands of equity, but at least with those standards which due consideration for national vitality makes immediately imperative."[26]

To many people of Pritchett's generation, the very idea of social insurance was dangerously un-American, a basic threat to the voluntaristic tradition of American life. That a number of its most articulate backers were Jewish immigrant intellectuals doubtless did not help the cause. But beyond that lay fears of socialism, and the belief that under socialism individual freedom would be lost forever. Social insurance was intended to foster greater equality of condition through state intervention in previously private affairs, and because it was based on the "right to share," its opponents argued, it would undermine "the desire for self-help, self-respect, and independence." [27]

Social insurance nevertheless appealed to many Americans, and the number in favor of state-supported old age relief grew with time. During the first two decades of the century, social insurance was actively supported by the American Association for Labor Legislation, a group composed primarily of liberal academics (Henry Farnum at Yale, J. W. Jenks at Cornell, Henry Seager and Samuel McCune Lindsay at Columbia, and John R. Commons and Richard Ely at Wisconsin). In the 1920s, old age relief was taken up by a little known but widely dispersed and highly influential organization called the Fraternal Order of Eagles. By 1933, some form of legislation mandating minimal government sponsored financial assistance for the elderly had been passed in most states of the union. The proponents of social insurance did their work well. While still governor of New York, Franklin D. Roosevelt was persistently lobbied by Abraham Epstein, a disciple of Isaac Rubinow's who had become a key figure in the movement. [28]

Well before the mid-1920s, by which time the grass roots consensus that would lead to the passage of the federal Social Security Act of 1935 was already evident, Pritchett had sensed the growing popularity of an idea he considered pernicious. He never debated in print with Rubinow, Epstein, or others of their persuasion; and he left no evidence of private contact with them either. But his wish to prevent the establishment of social insurance was a critical factor in encouraging Pritchett to reform the Foundation's pension plan. He wrote in the first public announcement of the Carnegie Foundation's *Comprehensive Plan of Insurance and Annuities for College Teachers:*

Old age pensions for all needy citizens are being asked in many quarters. A widespread sentiment has been created that thru pension legislation something can be had for nothing. The trend of this legislation is paternalistic and undemocratic, and in most cases in disregard of sound economic experience. No greater service can be accomplished at this time, either by the trustees of the Foundation or by the teachers in American colleges, than to set forth in clear and simple terms a conception of pension administration which is just, sound, and feasible, and which appeals to the sense of individual responsibility and personal independence. Lavater's dictum that he who reforms himself does most to reform the public is quite as true of associations of men as of individuals.[29]

THE COMPREHENSIVE PLAN: TIAA

The insurance and retirement system Henry Pritchett developed as an alternative to the Carnegie Foundation's initial plan had three explicit purposes. Like the old plan, it was intended to help professors meet their financial responsibilities when no longer able to work; but it now offered both life insurance and annuities to all teachers in all colleges choosing to participate. The point was no longer to strengthen the faculties of a few colleges or to dignify an entire profession; it was rather to enable all colleges and all professors to dignify themselves.

Through the Foundation's new program, it would be possible for a college professor to "protect himself and those dependent upon him against the two main hazards that lie in the way of one who, lacking independent means, depends upon a modest salary; namely, the risk of premature death during his productive period and the risk of failure of income-earning power when productivity ceases."[30] Both the life insurance policies and the annuity contracts would require contributions from the professor (as well as the college) and, being portable and vested, would resemble savings accumulated in a bank. Drawn in that way, not only to protect academic mobility, but also to inspire thrift, the technical features of the new plan were integrally related to its social purposes.

In the "Moral Influence of a Pension System," Pritchett had argued that "thrift is a fundamental human virtue"; that "the growth of thrift is analogous to the growth of all spiritual and moral faculties"; and that, since "hope, not fear, is the great propulsive power in humanity," an established equity could do more to encourage savings than the fear of destitution.[31] He had had no reason to change his mind since writing that essay in 1911, and obviously assumed that the benefits offered through the new program would act as an incentive. With an established and continuously increasing equity to inspire hope, the teacher might be encouraged to practice the "foresight, self denial, and thrift" required of him in order "to carry his load as the head of a family and as a member of society."[32] Thus led to virtue, the teacher would become an exemplar of individual responsibility.

The Carnegie Foundation's *Comprehensive Plan* was also designed to be "cooperative," that is, to allow colleges and universities to fulfill their responsibilities to their faculties by helping professors fulfill their responsibilities to their families. The policies available through the new system were to be supported jointly by deductions from faculty salaries and by college contributions. The increment now asked of the colleges would, of course, add a new item to their existing budgets. But, since the policies being offered were based on "hazards" spread over a potentially occupation-wide group and since the initial costs of beginning the system as well as the costs of operating it were to be carried by the Foundation (with help from the Carnegie Corporation), that increment would be relatively small. Furthermore, in comparison to the endowment required to establish a sound single institutional plan, the increment would be minimal. Thus, through its "cooperative" features, the plan offered yet another incentive—this one to the colleges—and, once again, a relationship between the system's technical arrangements and its social purposes was clearly intended.[33]

Up to 1916, few American colleges had provided for the pensioning of their faculty members. The number of colleges on the Carnegie list was relatively small and the colleges not on the list in most cases had not undertaken to develop their own plans. According to Pritchett a pension system was advisable, even necessary, in terms of both humanity and business efficiency. It would enable a college to discharge in good conscience those employees who did not earn their keep, particularly the disabled and the aged. Deploring the tendency he perceived in American colleges to increase salaries, build dormitories, promote athletics, and publish glossy catalogues and other advertisements before offering pensions, he argued that "If an obligation rests upon the managers or directors of any form of human organization to face their responsibilities to their employees, that obligation is strongest upon the trustees of colleges and universities. The college corporation stands for something higher than the business corporation. It undertakes to represent an administration devoted to the best ideals of life, the highest purpose of civilization." As teachers were to be led to virtue, so colleges were to be led to a "corporate conscience." To encourage colleges and universities no less than their faculty members to practice "foresight, self-denial, and thrift" was a second goal of the *Comprehensive Plan.*[34]

Finally, the new system was constructed to demonstrate the virtue of a *"pure* insurance and annuity business" (emphasis added).[35] To administer the plan, the Foundation would organize what Pritchett initially envisaged as a "new sub-agency of the Foundation"—the Teachers Insurance and Annuity Association

(TIAA). TIAA would employ actuaries and investment special-
ists, but it would not employ salesmen. Keenly aware, as were
many people at the time, that insurance companies had focused
more intently on gathering policyholders than on taking the pre-
cautions needed to secure those policyholders' investments,
Pritchett wished, through education, to do away with the need for
solicitation, first at TIAA, and then, through the example set by
TIAA, at other insurance companies of responsible intention.
Salesmen should not be necessary, he asserted, to convince "the
citizens of the United States to do that which their own duty
should prompt them to do." Pritchett still assumed that professors were "by their training, of a far higher order of intelligence
than the ordinary individual"; he was confident that when sup-
plied with adequate information concerning insurance, they
would act as all reasonable men ought to do. In turning to TIAA,
unsolicited, he hoped and expected, teachers would educate the
wider public to similar behavior.[36]

To Pritchett, insurance and commerce were not the same; and
he hoped that TIAA would illustrate the difference between an
agency whose business was "pure" expert service and one directed
toward profit in trade. "Unless some of the weaknesses of the present conduct of insurance by the big companies can be overcome,"
he wrote in 1917, "a popular demand will arise for the taking over
of insurance by government."[37] In all of its various features, the
Comprehensive Plan was intended to preserve and to strengthen the
linkage between freedom and responsibility that Pritchett considered so vital.

The plan announced by the Foundation in 1916 was inaugurated with minor changes in 1918, after two years of negotiations
with the Association of American Universities, the National Association of State Universities, and the American Association of
University Professors.[38] Within ten years, TIAA had written almost 12,000 policies. Within twenty years, as the number of par-

ticipating institutions grew, its policies were available to approx-imately one-third of all American college professors.[39] Operated along lines similar to those now mandated through the Employee Retirement Income Security Act for all pension funds, TIAA was actuarially and financially far sounder than the Foundation's earli-er plan had been.[40]

The progress of TIAA was constantly discussed by Pritchett in the Foundation's annual reports. Through consultations with var-ious state agencies, its basic structure was replicated in somewhat modified form in a number of pension plans for elementary and secondary school teachers, and the thinking behind those pro-grams was offered to the public in a variety of Foundation publi-cations.[41] Pritchett and others of the Foundation's staff continued to collect information on retirement systems throughout the world, and using TIAA as a backdrop, often commented upon their strengths and weaknesses. Obviously, Pritchett worked zeal-ously to teach the principles of a sound pension plan and to make TIAA an unquestionable success. For a time, while continuing to serve as president of the Carnegie Foundation, he even served as TIAA's chief executive in full charge of its daily management.

By Pritchett's own estimate, however, TIAA did not fulfill his hopes for it. In discussing pensioning in one of his last expositions as president of the Foundation, Pritchett said: "Important as is the matter of sound actuarial estimate [in the establishment of a re-tirement plan], there are other considerations which precede the actuarial computations and which are fundamental....The prima-ry question that must be settled is the social philosophy upon which the pension system is to rest."[42] For Pritchett, establishing joint employer-employee responsibility for pensions in order to preserve the principle of private as opposed to public responsibil-ity for matters of social welfare was the key question in pension debates. Through the example of TIAA, he had hoped to settle that question directly for academics and indirectly for the nation as a whole, but, as he commented wistfully to Nicholas Murray Butler in 1929, most people had "failed to grasp...the social philosophy underlying the [TIAA] pension system."[43]

By the 1930s many of the principles Pritchett considered necessary for sound pensioning—for example, the need for joint contributions and adequate reserves—were widely accepted by those concerned with retirement questions, and, partly for that reason, were written into the federal government's social security program.[44] Hardly inclusive in its coverage, more regressive than progressive in its taxation arrangements, and directly related to employment in a number of its key sections, the Social Security Act of 1935 was in many ways more compatible with Pritchett's thinking than it was with the thinking of Isaac Rubinow or Abraham Epstein. Rubinow criticized the bill and Epstein condemned it. The bill provided an insurance-like equity. It did not guarantee income adequacy.[45] Still, though insufficient to those eager to introduce fuller measures of income maintenance, the Social Security Act was a major turning point in the history of American social welfare policy. As Roy Lubove has put it in *The Struggle for Social Security*, "It marked a decisive transfer of welfare functions from voluntary to public institutions, and from the local to the federal level."[46] It was that transfer that Pritchett had sought to prevent. The disappointment he expressed to Butler signified his sense of defeat.

LIBERTY AND EFFICIENCY THROUGH VOLUNTARY ASSOCIATIONS

In 1930, the Carnegie Foundation published *The Social Philosophy of Pensions*, setting forth, yet again, the principles in which Pritchett so deeply believed. This bulletin suggests with particular clarity the logic that stood behind Pritchett's position not only on pensions, but also on questions of public and private responsibility in a modern democratic society.

The two central underlying premises of Pritchett's essay were, first, that the nation's prosperity and well-being depended on the initiative, discipline, and integrity of its citizens, and second, that in order to preserve these qualities it was necessary to protect each citizen's liberty and capacity for initiative from virtually all forms of external constraint. He maintained that "no pension system based on charity to the individual can be defended." He seemed to believe that such pensions would diminish the individual's motivation to work and to take care of himself. Pritchett contended that "the primary justification for expenditure of money by a government [acting as a corporation], a university, a church, or a [business] corporation in the inauguration and maintenance of a system of retirement lies in the advancement of the true interests of the service for which the government, the university, the church, or the corporation exists. If that service is not bettered by such a retirement plan, those responsible for the conduct of the institution, whatever it may be, cannot justify the expenditure of funds for a retirement system....Society does not owe any man a pension."[47] Here, Pritchett seemed to have been suggesting that pension plans undertaken to increase productivity would not undermine, but rather add to the individual's motivation to work and to take care of himself.

Over and over again in *The Social Philosophy of Pensions,* Pritchett emphasized the importance of encouraging and supporting "freedom of action," "self-control," "foresight and self-denial," and "thrift."[48] He expressed his full agreement with the basic thesis that Herbert Hoover had developed in his book *American Individualism,* which had appeared in 1922. Like Hoover, Pritchett was of the opinion that: "If we examine the impulses that carry us forward, none is so potent for progress as the yearning for individual self-expression, the desire for creation of something. Perhaps the greatest human happiness flows from personal achievement. Here lies the great urge for the constructive instinct of mankind. But it can only thrive in a society where the individual has liberty and stimulation to achievement. Nor does the community progress except through its participation in these multitude achievements."[49]

How, then, according to Hoover, and also Pritchett, should the community participate "in these multitude achievements"? Not directly in a positive sense, as, for example, through what liberals might have called protective legislation. Instead, Hoover, like Pritchett, maintained that the government should take a more laissez-faire posture in order not to interfere with the individual's "civil liberties." They both recognized a need for social planning and for cooperative social welfare ventures. They did not believe the individual should be expected to act entirely alone. After all, as Pritchett had once put it, the frontier had closed. Nevertheless, to meet the nation's need for planning and cooperative efforts, both men favored private action through voluntary associations as an alternative to direct state action.[50]

Pritchett's view of the proper role for government in a modern, democratic society was forthrightly expressed in the queries he put to his like-minded libertarian friends on those occasions when they appeared to favor what he saw as coercive state limitation of individual liberty. In 1924, for example, he wrote to Charles W. Eliot, who was now retired from the presidency of Harvard, to ask "how so thorough-going a believer in personal liberty as you are could approve the legislation of the Volstead Act."[51] Eliot replied: "I think the fundamental reason is that I have been perceiving for many years, since first New England rum and then whiskey became cheap, that the use of alcohol as a beverage threatens seriously the existence of the white race."[52] Many years later, after he retired from the presidency of the Carnegie Foundation, Pritchett put a similar query to Hoover. Hoover had endorsed legislation limiting child labor and, in this instance, Pritchett wanted to know how he could have gone along with a "socialistic measure" that limited parental liberty and was supported by "that eminent socialist Miss Frances Perkins."[53]

Pritchett seems to have thought the state should encourage community participation in the individual's well-being by allowing and perhaps also, as Hoover did at the Commerce Department and in the presidency, by facilitating the organization of private voluntary associations.[54] Pritchett apparently did not publish or write an exposition of this aspect of his view of the government's role. He did not need to. The government's responsibility to protect the citizen's constitutional and historic right to association was well established; and the topic did not fall within Pritchett's sphere of commentary, which tended to be limited to matters of specific concern to the Foundation, reforms it favored or criticisms it felt called upon to answer.

Pritchett's belief in the value of voluntary associations and in the government's responsibility to allow and even encourage the formation of such associations must be demonstrated in other ways. His actions testify to this belief: his suggestion of a congressional charter for the Carnegie Foundation; his consistently offered congratulations on the founding or enlarging of other educational and philanthropic (voluntary) associations, which began in 1907 with praise for an expansion of the General Education Board; and his varied and repeated efforts to strengthen professional (voluntary) associations, school and college (voluntary) accrediting associations, and other similar groups. Pritchett's conviction that state-imposed limitations on the individual's "civil liberties" were wrong, combined with his recognition of a need for planning and deliberateness in social organization, further supports the contention that voluntary associations were his chosen medium of governance within a modern democratic society. With the possible exception of political parties, which Pritchett thought were selfish and corrupt, there were simply no other organizational models available to insure efficiency without loss of liberty. A voluntary association's lack of coercive power (except perhaps a limited coercive power over its own members) was compatible with what might be called the psychology of social control in which Pritchett believed. He equated strength with individual moral discipline and integrity. He thought effective social control had to come from within the individual and could be called forth most effectively through appeals to altruism, duty, patriotism, and the like. Hence, the persuasive power of institutions that were restricted to educational means of governance was, he believed, an ultimately greater power than the coercive police power that could be exercised by the state. For all these reasons, it is clear that Pritchett favored an essentially voluntary association system of governance in the United States.

The political philosophy that guided Pritchett's leadership of the Carnegie Foundation rested on the belief that liberty was always the single most crucial value in a democratic society. To meet the challenge of changing social and economic circumstances, Pritchett therefore favored voluntaristic institutional change and thought that such reform should be brought about through the educational and promotional efforts of well-trained and responsible leaders and of organizations of experts. In this way, he believed American society could be reorganized to ensure continuing material progress and to meet its citizens' basic needs without jeopardizing established rights and privileges. Pritchett's narrow and inflexible view of democratic priorities made it impossible for him to acknowledge, along with the benefits, the limitations of elite-sponsored, voluntaristic reform. He did not see that there might also be a need for deliberate and even coercive state action to balance liberty with equality; that there might also be a common interest in sacrificing a degree of individual liberty to ensure a modicum of equality, as through state guarantees of at least minimally decent lives for all elderly people; and that political priorities might also need to be reconsidered and redefined as integral parts of any effective reform effort. To promote "the public good" as he understood it, Pritchett looked to "private power." For Henry Pritchett, as for Herbert Hoover, "private power" was by definition for "the public good."

– 8 –

Central vs. Local Control:
The Carnegie Foundation
and Its Critics

If the beliefs Henry Pritchett expressed in his discussions of pensioning are illuminating of the values he believed essential in "The Great Society," the beliefs expressed by some of the Foundation's early critics are similarly enlightening. Pritchett tended to dismiss many of the criticisms made of the Foundation. In a 1915 article he called "Should the Carnegie Foundation Be Suppressed?" he said: "A large proportion of the criticism directed against the Foundation must be left out of discussion on account of the personal element which enters....This sort of criticism can be laid aside. However honest, it is in effect the inevitable reaction against measures which contravene local self-interest....The vision of a foreign corporation sitting in New York, issuing educational edicts manufactured from questionnaires, is well calculated to arouse our latent patriotism for what Professor Royce calls 'provincial independence in education.'"[1]

In his assessment of the purposes of the critics he dismissed in this way, Pritchett was quite correct. Many of the people who opposed the Foundation's activities *were* trying to rally support for "provincialism." But their views were far more principled than Pritchett suggested by his use of this word, and their arguments, as well as Pritchett's failure to engage with those arguments, are important in understanding the problems of policy making that the history of this Foundation illuminates.

Pritchett believed that liberty and individualism were essential values in "The Great Society." On the importance of these values the Foundation's early critics would have agreed. And yet, these critics also cherished other values and believed that the Carnegie Foundation's activities were threatening those as well as liberty and individualism. These critics saw a peril because they believed the Foundation was supporting nationalism at the expense of localism ("provincialism"), universalism in standards at the expense of pluralism, expert participation in standard making at the expense of lay participation, and private authority in policy making at the expense of public authority. While sometimes confusing in the actual conflict of opposing claims, the views of these critics and their differences with Pritchett clarify the limitations of the approach to questions of social reform that Pritchett institutionalized in the Carnegie Foundation.

JOSIAH ROYCE AND "PROVINCIALISM"

Among the critics Pritchett "laid aside" was the Harvard philosopher Josiah Royce. Royce used the word "provincialism" in the article he wrote in 1915 for James McKeen Cattell's *School and Society*. This was the article, read at the organizational meeting of the American Association of University Professors, that was so critical of the Foundation's suggestion in *Education in Vermont* that Middlebury College be denied a state subsidy.[2]

As he made abundantly clear in the essay, Royce, like Pritchett, thought that high standards were needed in education. Beyond that he cherished the importance of individual liberty every bit as much as Pritchett did. And yet, unlike Pritchett, Royce was convinced that the Foundation's "strong tendency to standardize our academic institutions" was fundamentally wrong.[3] Why? This, in part, was what Royce said:

We do not want our institutions reduced to a dead level, or required, by "external pressure," to conform to rules and habits which may not prove to be well adapted to the cultivation of the traditions of any one of the numerous distinct provinces upon whose intellectual and moral prosperity the organized educational life of our country must always depend....

I myself believe that high standards are a blessing. I also believe that standardizing is in general, and especially at the present time in this country, a tendency to something that is evil.

If you tell me as an individual to raise my standards, be those standards intellectual or moral, and if you show me the way by setting me good examples, or by getting me interested in the study of admirable models of mind, of character, or of life, you help me. But if you say: "Go to. Let us standardize our ideals"; that is, "let us all take on the same standard as to our customs, as to our plans, as to our knowledge, as to our investigations, as to our naturally diverse opinions,"—if you say this, you interfere with my due liberty, you tend to make me what the classical Chinese scholar of the old type of Chinese cultivation is said to have been.

We all need standards....we no doubt all need to have certain standards in common. But precisely in those regions of our life where individual judgment and initiative are needed, we do not need the same standards.[4]

Following these general comments, Royce went on to argue that the problem with the Foundation's study of education in Vermont was that it sought to apply to Middlebury College a "universal" standard for determining when an institution should and should not receive state assistance. Because this kind of "universal" standard interfered with local interests and traditions, and thereby violated the principle of a "wise provincialism in education," Royce believed it would limit "variety and liberty" in American life.[5] Royce was not raising a narrow or simple problem of "local self-interest" here. To be sure, he may have left himself open to that charge by using the word "provincialism." But "provincialism" had powerful and positive connotations for Royce. As R. Jackson Wilson has observed, Royce advocated "'provincialism' as a counter to the impersonal alienation of American life."[6]

Royce's philosophy was far too complex to summarize briefly, but his objections to the Carnegie Foundation's attempts to standardize American education cannot be understood apart from two points. As a philosopher, Royce was much concerned with how people know and become "real" to themselves. He believed that in this process the development of "loyalty" was essential, loyalty meaning "the willing and practical and thoroughgoing devotion of a person to a cause."[7] Royce also saw freedom of choice as necessary to the development of loyalty, and hence, personhood. Beyond this, Royce thought the chances for constantly deepening and expanding personal loyalties and common "loyalty to loyalty" itself were diminishing in direct proportion to the growth of centralization in American life. In *The Philosophy of Loyalty,* he wrote: "Further centralization of power in the national government, without a constantly enriched and diversified provincial consciousness, can only increase the estrangement of our national spirit from its own life....The present tendency to the centralization of power in our national government seems to me, then, a distinct danger. It is a substitution of power for loyalty. *To the increase of a wise provincialism in our country, I myself look for the best general social means for training our people in loyalty to loyalty."*[8]

Royce's charge that the Carnegie Foundation's activities would make "mandarins" of the individuals associated with colleges like Middlebury arose from his considered convictions.[9] His criticisms of the Foundation derived from a deep appreciation of the personal and social requirements of individualism. This led Royce to cherish diversity in standards, autonomy for institutions, and respect for local differences, especially as both public and private power was increasingly centralized throughout the United States. For Royce these were necessary antidotes to the impersonal character of life in a large, modern nation state. Lacking Royce's depth of understanding of personhood, as well as Royce's regard for the community institutions and traditions that would help nurture loyalty and personhood, Pritchett did not understand the principles that made Royce as, if not more, concerned with the processes of standard making, more specifically with the chances for voluntary participation in standard making, as he was with the actual substance of standards.

HERBERT CROLY AND "THE NEW NATIONALISM"

Josiah Royce was not one of them, but there were many intellectuals at this time who would have agreed with Henry Pritchett that the centrifugal forces in American society needed to be countered, indeed overpowered, by centripetal ones. Herbert Croly, who provided Theodore Roosevelt with the slogan "the new nationalism" and who became the founding editor of the *New Republic,* was one of these. So far as I am aware, Croly never wrote about the Carnegie Foundation. But he would have been likely to approve of the Foundation's policies far more than Royce did, and for that reason the points upon which he and Pritchett would have agreed and disagreed throw the issues that divided Pritchett and Royce into even bolder relief.[10]

In *The Promise of American Life,* Croly expressed two convictions in which Pritchett would have concurred. First, he made clear his belief in universal standards. While he candidly admitted that he was not sure actually how to identify the quality, Croly argued that "there is only one standard for scientific investigations—the highest standard."[11] He did not see the possibility for diverse forms of excellence that Josiah Royce saw. Second, Croly, like Pritchett and unlike Royce, believed that policy making should be left to experts. He argued that "the disinterested and competent individual is formed for constructive leadership, just as the less competent and independent, but well-intentioned individual is formed more or less faithfully to follow on behind."[12] He thought that "the common citizen can become something of a saint and something of a hero, not by growing to heroic proportions in his own person, but by the sincere and enthusiastic imitations of heroes and saints."[13]

Parenthetically one might note that, while this statement may seem to have been reminiscent of Andrew Carnegie's thinking, it actually appears to have been based on different social aspirations from those Carnegie held. Croly explicitly ridiculed Carnegie's "impassioned and mystical vision of the miraculously constitutive power of first mortgage steel bonds."[14] He believed that Carnegie had wanted to "uplift" everyone, which Carnegie may have wanted to do, although he was less certain than Croly thought about how this feat was to be achieved. That aside, Croly believed that it was "superstitious" even to wish for such equality (equality as likeness). Like Pritchett, he was convinced that the first purpose of education was to train each person to competence for his or her role.[15]

Despite these points of agreement with Pritchett, Croly was deeply concerned with the question Dewey raised in *The Public and Its Problems.* He hoped "the new nationalism" would provide a close sense of community to support the realization of national goals; he argued for a significant enlargement of state powers; he urged more rather than less government regulation.[16] If he read *The Promise of American Life,* Pritchett would have been likely to find it almost as "socialistic" as he later thought the New Deal was. Croly, like Royce in his very different way, was trying to come to terms with the implications for governance and community of turn-of-the-century growth and change. His views and Royce's very different ones suggest that Pritchett's understanding of the reforms needed in the United States was partial at best—one-dimensional.

OTHER PROPONENTS OF "LOCAL SELF-INTEREST"

Other early Carnegie Foundation critics in addition to Josiah Royce challenged what Pritchett saw as the Foundation's effort to advance "the public good," and beneath their various complaints there was a litany of concern with issues of governance and community. For example, in 1910, James R. Day, the chancellor of Syracuse University, wrote to Pritchett to say:

We recognize no right upon the part of your organization or of yourself to make any...official inspections and publish the ex parte statement to the educational world.

We have a Department of Education in this State which acts under the authority of the State in such matters. It is responsible. From any injustice of its acts, we have appeal to the Regents and from them to the legislature. Why should you therefore demand the right or privilege of an inspection for such publication as you have been sending out to the colleges of the country?...

Colleges and Universities are not developed and built up by comparisons. There are varying conditions and elements that must be worked out often under great embarrassments. Men unexpectedly come into the proposition with wise brains and generous gifts and save the little college from the fatal mildew of such unwise and impracticable standardizings as you are attempting.

It has seemed to me an attempt to reduce the colleges of a land which must have more, many more, rather than less colleges as the population increases.

Your whole method in the use of the Carnegie moneys [sic] is aside from the purpose of that marvelously generous man.

The use of the pension fund has been perverted into impertinent meddling with the work of the lawfully constituted educational departments of the States and the chartered autonomy of the institutions which are in no way responsible to you, but may find it necessary to hold you responsible for what you published about them.[17]

The comments made in letters such as this often reflected "local self-interest," though not the mean-spirited selfishness that

Pritchett was most inclined to recognize. In this instance, Abraham Flexner had made criticisms of the University's medical school, actually comparatively mild ones, though Day may not yet have known that.[18] Also, the University had been denied entrance to the Foundation's pension fund which led Day to say: "I showed you that nothing in our Charter requires this University to have a Methodist for its Chancellor or designates any denominational requirement for professors or students....I showed you that the conferences are not required to elect a Methodist for trustee, and that they have absolutely no control or authority in our management and never have assumed to have, and that we do not discriminate even against the Jews or any one from anywhere except in educational requirements, [but] you excluded us on the ground that we are called a Methodist institution! Something that did not embarrass you in the case of several other colleges."[19]

Quite appropriately this man *was* championing the welfare of the university he was associated with. At the same time, although his eloquence and logic fell far short of Josiah Royce's, he was trying to advance principles of local autonomy and of institutional equity. He was concerned with the right of his institution and other institutions to establish and be held accountable for their own distinctive policies and with the right to redress from authority. He believed that private as opposed to public evaluations of colleges was wrong.

Pritchett's brief, polite, and factual response to James R. Day did not indicate any appreciation of these issues.[20] His response presumed that so long as the Carnegie Foundation's facts were accurate, its actions would support "the public interest" in national unity through national educational standards. Perhaps that was true; but, as Day and also Royce suggested, there was also a "public interest" in localism, diversity, and participation in governance. Pritchett's narrow and unchanging belief in governance as voluntary self-regulation and in community as an aggregate of free and distinct individuals precluded the possibility of seeing that.

In other situations, too, Pritchett failed to recognize the issues at stake in criticisms that were made of the Foundation. One can see this again in his reaction to resolutions the Normal Department of the National Education Association (NEA) passed in 1914. To say the least, these resolutions were sweeping and hostile. One held: "We view with alarm the activity of Carnegie and Rockefeller foundation [sic], agencies not in any way responsible to the people, in their effort to control the policies of our state educational institutions; to fashion after their own conceptions and to standardize after their own notion our courses of study; and to surround the institutions with conditions which menace true academic freedom and which defeat the primary purpose of democracy as heretofore preserved inviolate in our common schools, Normal schools, and Universities."[21] Behind the rhetoric of these charges was serious dissatisfaction with central, especially national, educational policy making.

The resolution had been framed in response to a Foundation report on higher education in Iowa issued in conjunction with the Missouri study. The report had been developed by William S. Learned (the Foundation staff member who organized the Pennsylvania Study) and by university professors from outside of Iowa; it had not allowed for the participation of local normal school representatives. It had recommended that normal schools not offer collegiate instruction, arguing that they either should be subordinate to colleges or should meet all college standards. It foreshadowed the recommendations that were made in the 1920 bulletin summarizing the Missouri Study.[22]

Writing to a sympathetic Missouri normal school president about the NEA's condemnation of the Foundation, Pritchett said:

I find it difficult to understand...what you refer to as "The Political Influence of the Carnegie Foundation." I am a little at a loss to know what you mean by this because of all agencies in the country the Carnegie Foundation is one which has no political influence whatsoever. . . .

It would seem to me a little unfair...instead of replying to this argument [about the differences between normal schools and colleges] in the ordinary way to reply to it by what seems to me quite a political action, viz., to put through a committee of the N.E.A. a resolution denouncing the entire work of the Foundation.[23]

Pritchett did not explain why NEA criticism of the Carnegie Foundation *was* "political," while Foundation criticism of educational institutions was *not* "political." But in this instance he does appear to have been trying to understand what had caused all the furor. Still, his letter was characteristic. It dealt primarily with whether the Foundation's "facts" and standards for normal schools were valid, and it expressed his sincere but not entirely logical conviction that it was profoundly unjust to criticize the Foundation for taking "political" positions when it only expressed disinterested concern with the improvement of education. It did not acknowledge the NEA's assertion that public and local, as opposed to private and national authority in education and diverse, as opposed to universal standards in education were inherent to "the public good."

It is certainly important to remember that charges such as those the NEA, James R. Day, and Josiah Royce directed at the Carnegie Foundation came at a time when centralization was becoming an ever more prominent feature of many aspects of American life. As Pritchett was a target for professorial resentment of administrative power in higher education, so the Foundation was a target for teacher resentment of growing bureaucracy and central power in schooling. This does not mean that criticisms of the Foundation were symbolic. They were not. It should only suggest that opposition to the Carnegie Foundation was often related to other broader political contests.

To illustrate further one might note that Margaret Haley was one of the leaders of opposition to the Foundation within the NEA. Haley was a very effective teacher union organizer from Chicago. She fought against William Rainey Harper's efforts to centralize the Chicago public schools, and she defeated a move led by Charles W. Eliot and Nicholas Murray Butler to allow the NEA's president rather than its state delegates to appoint the Association's nominating committee.[24]

As was probably true of all of its critics, Haley had a personal stake in opposing the Carnegie Foundation. She represented the interests of women schoolteachers against the interests of university men, and she believed that those interests had not and would not be heard unless centralized power was resisted in order to assert local participatory rights. There were more women teachers by this time than men, although women were paid less than men and were far less well represented (if they were represented at all) in circles of national educational policy making. Men still held the upper hand in the NEA. Men were the majority in the faculties of university-affiliated schools of education. Men made up the Carnegie Foundation board of trustees. Implicit questions of gender parity were but one of the many, sometimes conflicting and always complicated, bases for dissent from the Carnegie Foundation's efforts to advance its vision of "the public good."

PRITCHETT'S LEGACY

In 1930, when Pritchett left the Carnegie Foundation, it appeared as if many of the social and political questions that had been so in flux as the United States moved into the twentieth century were finally on the way to resolution. Pritchett did not like the growth of government power that became increasingly evident as Franklin D. Roosevelt's triumph over Herbert Hoover began to bring to the federal level what had been an expanding role for state governments. But Croly's vision of a national community appeared to be in the ascendency in the United States in the 1930s and for some time thereafter, and Royce's "provincialism" as well as Pritchett's libertarian voluntarism appeared to have been rather decisively left behind.

Obviously, though, as the political controversies of the 1980s so clearly indicate, the issues that separated Pritchett from the Foundation's early critics and from the proponents of social insurance and social security have not been resolved. Questions of community remain controversial and divisive in the United States and are likely to remain so until more multidimensional approaches to policy making than the one Pritchett institutionalized at the Carnegie Foundation are developed.

If any form of purposive social action must advance the interests of some group and causes at the expense of others, then it was inevitable that Carnegie Foundation efforts to standardize American education would meet with opposition. But Pritchett's approach to defining and advancing "the public good" seems, however inadvertently, to have encouraged opposition. The same qualities that enabled Pritchett to develop effective technologies of influence limited his capacity to consider and explore the value of approaches to social problems that were different from his own.

Pritchett believed in absolute, universal "truth," and could see the significance of consultation as fact gathering but not as interest and need identifying. He was intent upon making change and not upon clarifying the nature of social choices. He preferred schematic, clear, and actionable reports to profound and stimulating investigations and analyses. His approach to reform was based on a conception of leadership that did not allow for reciprocal exchange between leaders and followers. It was essentially autocratic and therefore more likely to call forth deference or resistance than it was to stimulate concern, thoughtful discussion, and cooperative efforts.

Pritchett's approach reflected his very keen interest in assisting what he believed to be the better colleges, the better professionals, and the better high school students; and it also reflected his failure to be concerned with balancing those needs with the different needs of other colleges, other professionals, other high school students, and other less easily identifiable, less organized, and less elite "publics." It was based on his recognition of some aspects of "the public good" and his failure to recognize other aspects. It was effective in accomplishing a number of significant reforms, those reforms being of great benefit to many people. And yet, because Pritchett did not consider the merits of perspectives and priorities that disagreed with his own and did not seek ways to join efficient social action to less efficient processes of community creation, his approach to reform was limited.

Over time, many of the shortcomings of Pritchett's approach were recognized by the Carnegie Foundation, and during Alan Pifer's presidency steps were taken to overcome some of them. When Pifer became president of the Carnegie Corporation and of the Carnegie Foundation he launched a review of Corporation programs that had an important impact on both foundations.

Pifer appointed internal staff task forces to review existing programs and to recommend new directions. One of these, the "Task Force on the Disadvantaged," asked: "How Can the Carnegie Corporation Attack Poverty?" Two points made in answer to that question were: that the Corporation had neglected the "disadvantaged" at least until 1963, when "suddenly...the Corporation awoke to the impact that the desegregation decision and the civil rights movement were having on negro education," and "that poverty [should] become an explicit major focus of the Corporation's program" in the immediate future.[25]

The "Task Force on the Disadvantaged" had a profound effect on the Corporation. According to an internal review done thirteen years after the group reported, one of the "major developments" during Pifer's presidency was a new and central "interest

in social justice as a theme running through all program areas."
Building from its tradition of interest in "individual opportunity," the Corporation developed a "commitment to greater equity
in American life, and to affirmative action to compensate for past
inequities."[26]

That commitment was also evident in the Carnegie Foundation,
partly through Pifer's efforts to introduce "wider representation"
into the Foundation's board of trustees.[27] Not only minority group
members and women were appointed, but also representatives
from a more varied, less elite and homogeneous cross section of
American higher education.

However one describes what was actually "represented" in this
way—background, experience, institutional variety, or all these,
combined with expertise—by beginning to diversify its board,
the Carnegie Foundation made an important statement about the
value of differing voices in philanthropic policy making. Still, the
long-range implications of that statement were not yet fully clear.
Even "wider representation" within the Foundation, though vital,
could not in itself take full account of the problems of governance
and community that had been so troubling to Josiah Royce and
other early Foundation critics.

Some would say that Pritchett's priorities and approach to reform could not be combined with those of the critics. There are
inescapable tensions between views of community as national and
as local; between efforts to assert "the public interest" and "local
self-interest"; between the needs that can be fulfilled by "private
power" and by public participation in power; between the specialized knowledge of experts and the less trained and perhaps less
codified insights of non-experts; between excellence as "*the* best"
and excellence as diverse "bests." Those tensions notwithstanding,
if strong, socially responsive institutions are needed in the United States, efforts to develop such institutions must encompass efforts to develop the many communities of interest, the many

"publics" that are necessary to sustain those institutions through constant and caring criticism and reform. One way that "private power" may be of greater "public" value, then, is by helping to identify ways in which elite and participatory, expert and popular competencies for social planning can be combined, thereby making it possible for more people to work together to make fundamental social renewal a continuous and ubiquitous process.

Comprehensive social reform in that sense was not Henry Pritchett's concern. His legacy was a Foundation that could effectively engage in purposeful social action on behalf of the causes, groups, and interests with which it was in touch. The challenge remained whether the changes in organization and social outlook introduced under Alan Pifer's leadership would result in more encompassing and even more enduringly effective approaches to the use of "private power" for "the public good."

Bibliographic Note

Everyone knows that philanthropic foundations have played an important role in American society during the twentieth century. And yet, until relatively recently, there has been little serious historical scholarship about foundations. Our knowledge of the origins of foundations, of whom and what they have represented, of how they have operated, and of what they have and have not accomplished, and for whom, has come primarily from participants. This book, therefore, is addressed to a still unfortunately large gap in the historical literature, and it may be useful to indicate its relationship to some older and more recent studies. The works that have shaped my thinking on the various specific arguments made in the text are indicated in the notes. Here my concern is briefly to provide an historiographical context for the study as a whole.

Waldemar A. Nielson once said of the literature on foundations: "Any one who has had the unfortunate task—or the curious taste—to read most of the material which has been available about foundations, knows that it is divided roughly into two equally tiresome parts: the self-congratulatory output of foundations themselves; and the ill-informed screeds of the Old Right on the one extreme, the New Left on the other, and the neo-Know Nothings like George Wallace in between" (*The Big Foundations* [New York: Columbia University Press, 1972], p. IX). Nielson's comment came in the preface to a Twentieth Century Fund study, one purpose of which was to stimulate thoughtful but critical talk within foundations and about foundations. His point certainly can be supported. For example, even among recent works there are rather self-congratulatory participant studies, one being Merriman Cuninggim, *Private Money and Public Service: The Role of Foundations in American Society* (New York: McGraw-Hill, 1972); and there are also rather unintelligent and inflammatory outsider accounts, such as William H. McIlhany, II, *The Tax Exempt Foundations* (Westport, Conn.: Arlington House, 1980). Nevertheless, I tend to think Nielson's comment was too sweeping.

As Nielson was aware, there are exceptions to his categories. For example, there are intelligent critical commentaries on foundations by people who have been associated with foundations. I would point to Jane H. Mavety and Paul N. Ylvisaker, "Private Philanthropy and Public Affairs," in *Research Papers Sponsored by the Commission on Private Philanthropy and Public Needs* (Washington, D.C.: Department of the Treasury, 1977), vol. 2, part 1, as one of these. In addition, there are irreverent and popular, but entirely reasonable outsider accounts. Among these, Ben Whitaker, *The Foundations: An Anatomy of Philanthropic Bodies,* rev. ed. (London: Penguin Books, 1979), is exceptionally readable and informative. More important by far, however, for historical purposes, if not for contemporary philanthropic policy purposes, the literature Nielson found unilluminating can be immensely valuable.

This is certainly true of some of the documents written by philanthropists about philanthropy. Generally these fall into one of two very broad categories: lives and institutional studies. In the first category there are many revealing autobiographies. The *Autobiography of Andrew Carnegie* (Garden City, N.Y.: Doubleday, Page, 1909) is useful, as are all of the many autobiographies by participants in Rockefeller philanthropy. Among these are: John D. Rockefeller, *Random Reminiscences of Men and Events* (New York: Doubleday, Page, 1909); Frederick T. Gates, *Chapters in My Life* (New York: Free Press, 1977); Raymond B. Fosdick, *Chronicle of a Generation* (New York: Harper & Brothers, 1958); and Abraham Flexner, *I Remember* (New York: Simon and Schuster, 1940), which deals with the Bamberger endowment for the Institute for Advanced Study in Princeton, New Jersey, as well as with Carnegie and Rockefeller philanthropies.

In addition to these are some biographies philanthropists have written about each other. Of special relevance here are: Abraham Flexner, *Henry S. Pritchett: A Biography* (New York: Columbia University Press, 1943); Raymond B. Fosdick, *John D. Rockefeller, Jr.* (New York: Harper & Brothers, 1956); and John W. Gardner, "Abraham Flexner, Pioneer in Educational Reform," *Science,* 131 (1960): 594–595. I found these works often as illuminating of the authors as of the subjects.

One needs, of course, to supplement the information and interpretations provided in these portraits with more objective accounts. For this, Joseph Frazier Wall's *Andrew Carnegie* (New York: Oxford University Press, 1970) is exceptional in both detail and balance. However, some family commissioned or "approved" biographies are also of value. Burton J. Hendrick, *The Life of Andrew Carnegie*, 2 vols. (Garden City, N.Y.: Doubleday, Doran, 1932) is one; Allan Nevins, *John D. Rockefeller: The Heroic Age of American Enterprise*, 2 vols. (Charles Scribner's Sons, 1940) is another, still better example.

In addition to life histories there are at least three kinds of "insider" foundation institutional histories. First, there are straightforward summations of the kind of program information one would find in annual reports. *The General Education Board: An Account of Its Activities, 1902–1914* (New York: General Education Board, 1915); *Forty Year Report, 1909–1949* (New York: New York Foundation, 1949); and the various Carnegie Corporation Review Series are examples of this type of institutional record.

Second and even more common are full chronicles. Representative examples (in chronological order by publication date) are: John M. Glenn, Lilian Brandt, and F. Emerson Andrews, *Russell Sage Foundation, 1907–1946*, 2 vols. (New York: Russell Sage Foundation, 1947); Edwin R. Embree and Julia Waxman, *Investment in People: The Story of the Julius Rosenwald Fund* (New York: Harper & Brothers, 1949); Raymond B. Fosdick, *The Story of the Rockefeller Foundation* (New York: Harper & Brothers 1952); Howard J. Savage, *Fruit of an Impulse: Forty-Five Years of the Carnegie Foundation 1905–1950* (New York: Harcourt, Brace, 1953); *The First Twenty-Five Years: The Story of a Foundation* (Battle Creek, Mich.: W. K. Kellogg Foundation, 1955); Raymond B. Fosdick, *Adventure in Giving: The Story of the General Education Board* (New York: Harper & Row, 1962); William Greenleaf, *From These Beginnings: The Early Philanthropies of Henry and Edsel Ford, 1911–1936* (Detroit: Wayne State University Press, 1964); George Corner, *A History of the Rockefeller Institute, 1901–1953: Origins and Growth* (New York: Rockefeller Institute Press, 1964); Agnes Lynch Starrett, *The Maurice and Laura Falk Foundation: A Private Fortune—A Public Trust* (Pittsburgh: The Historical Society of Western Pennsylvania, 1966); and Bryan Haislip, *A History of the Z. Smith Reynolds Foundation* (Winston-Salem, N.C.: John F. Blair, 1967)

Finally, there are collective foundation studies, many of which are particularly useful for the comparative program information they provide and for general data on foundation management and organization. F. Emerson Andrews of the Russell Sage Foundation wrote many studies of this kind. Among them are: (with Shelby M. Harrison), *American Foundations for Social Welfare* (New York: Russell Sage Foundation, 1946); *Philanthropic Giving* (New York: Russell Sage Foundation, 1950); and *Philanthropic Foundations* (New York: Russell Sage Foundation, 1956). Two more discursive, less factual studies along the same lines are Abraham Flexner with Esther B. Bailey, *Funds and Foundations: Their Policies Past and Present* (New York: Harper & Brothers, 1952) and Frederick P. Keppel, *The Foundation: Its Place in American Life* (New York: Macmillan, 1930). Warren Weaver, *U.S. Philanthropic Foundations* (New York: Harper & Row, 1967), is also useful. Also, virtually all of.the Carnegie Corporation annual reports during the years of Keppel's presidency (1923–1941) describe and comment upon general developments in "the foundation field."

There are obvious problems with "insider" institutional histories, bias and narrowness of focus among them. Nevertheless, as a non-participant historian recently said of the various Rockefeller institutional histories, works of this kind "will save the serious student...enthusiast, critic, and disinterested scholar alike—much repetitious work in the documents" (John Ettling, *The Germ of Laziness: Rockefeller Philanthropy and Public Health in the New South* [Cambridge, Mass.: Harvard University Press, 1981],p. 257).

As these largely internal documents can provide initial shortcuts to data, so critical commentaries can provide initial entrée to certain issues of relevance to foundation history. For example, Hans Zinsser, "The Perils of Magnanimity: A Problem in American Education," *Atlantic Monthly* (February, 1927), pp. 246–50; and Harold J. Laski, *The Dangers of Obedience and Other Essays* (New York: Harper & Brothers, 1930), ch. 6, raise good questions about the impact of foundations on teaching and research in American colleges. Uncritically hostile and therefore entirely different, but again useful at least as a reflection of attitudes held by some people during the McCarthy period, are articles like: William Fulton, "Let's Look at Our Foundations," *American Legion Magazine* (August, 1952), pp. 22–23, 42–44; and Harold Lord Varney "The Egg-Head Clutch on the Foundations," *American Mercury* (June, 1954), pp. 31–37.

One could cite more literature in all of these categories, although there is no need to repeat the fuller lists of references available in the bibliographies to: *Report of the Princeton Conference on the History of Philanthropy in the United States* (New York: Russell Sage Foundation, 1956); Thomas Reeves, ed., *Foundations Under Fire* (Ithaca, N.Y.: Cornell University Press, 1970); William H. Rudy, *The Foundations: Their Use and Abuse* (Washington, D.C.: Public Affairs Press, 1970); and Ben Whitaker, *The Foundations* (see above), which is especially useful for international references. The point here is simply that older internal accounts as well as external critiques, however biased in both cases, have been essential building-blocks for this book and probably will always be for interpretive foundation studies.

Beginning in the 1920s and 1930s, somewhat more focused and analytical monographs also began to be available. For example, Jesse Brundage Sears, *Philanthropy in the History of American Higher Education* (Washington, D.C.: Government Printing Office, 1922), Harold Coe Coffman, *American Foundations: A Study of Their Role in the Child Welfare Movement* (New York: Y.W.C.A., 1936), and Ernest Victor Hollis, *Philanthropic Foundations and Higher Education* (New York: Columbia University Press, 1938) studied the impact of philanthropy in two special areas. Edward C. Elliot and M. S. Chambers, *Charters of Philanthropies: Studies of the Charters of Twenty-Nine American Philanthropic Foundations* (New York: Carnegie Foundation for the Advancement of Teaching, 1939) provided comparative data on foundation legal arrangements. Edward Christian Lindemann, *Wealth and Culture* (New York: Harcourt, Brace, 1936) dealt with philanthropy in relation to other American institutions. Works like these represented an early effort to place foundations and their activities in a social context, and many of the data they provide can be used to supplement the data available in collective accounts such as the various studies by F. Emerson Andrews.

It was really not until after World War II, however, that non-participant historians began to look at foundation philanthropy. The major catalyst to this new interest may well have been the 1956 Russell Sage conference on the history of American philanthropy (which in turn *may* have been stimulated by the Congressional investigations of the 1950s). The Russell Sage conference was chaired by Merle Curti of the University of Wisconsin. It produced a research agenda with a bibliography (see above). Also, "Dr. Curti was urged to prepare an article" (*Report,* p.

30). Entitled "The History of American Philanthropy as a Field of Research," his essay argued that "the time has come to ask...how important has relatively disinterested benevolence been in giving expression to, and in promoting at home and abroad, a major American value— human welfare? All one can say at the present time, I think, is that the literature of the subject warrants the hypothetical statement, to be tested by investigation, that philanthropy has been one of the major aspects of and keys to American social and cultural development" (*American Historical Review,* 62 [1957]: 352).

To pursue the question he presented here, Curti organized the University of Wisconsin History Project, which was supported by the Ford Foundation. With a number of colleagues, he also produced a fair range of still valuable monographs, among them: "American Philanthropy and the National Character," *American Quarterly,* 10 (1958): 420–37; "Subsidizing Radicalism: The American Fund for Public Service, 1921–1941," *Social Service Review,* 33 (1959): 274–95; (with Judith Green and Roderick Nash), "Anatomy of Giving: Millionaires in the Late 19th Century," *American Quarterly,* 15 (1963): 416–35; *American Philanthropy Abroad: A History* (New Brunswick, N.J.: Rutgers University Press, 1963); (with Roderick Nash), *Philanthropy in the Shaping of American Higher Education* (New Brunswick, N.J.: Rutgers University Press, 1965).

Among the other works by authors in some way associated with this project were: Irvin G. Wyllie, "The Reputation of the American Philanthropist: A Historian's View," *Social Service Review,* 32 (1958): 215–22; Theron F. Schlabach, *Pensions for Professors* (Madison: State Historical Society of Wisconsin, 1963); and John Lankford, *Congress and the Foundations in the Twentieth Century* (River Falls: Wisconsin State University, 1964).

The books and articles that emerged from the Curti project quickly became standard works in the field. Along with Robert H. Bremner, *American Philanthropy* (Chicago: University of Chicago Press, 1960), they provided a basic outline of some of the major contributions foundation philanthropy had made, especially in the areas of education and welfare, and they began to explore relationships between private foundations and their "publics" (Lankford focusing on Congressional attitudes in relation to growing numbers of foundations; Schlabach focusing on state university attitudes toward the Carnegie Foundation).

Curti believed that "philanthropy has been both index and agent" in the development of the "American character" ("American Philanthropy and National Character," p. 424). I would be less inclined to speak of an "American character" than Curti was, but his view of philanthropy has provided a basis for mine. The essential premise of this book—that the Carnegie Foundation has been defined by, has advanced, and has reflected the problems of community definition and community creation that have been so essential to American society throughout the twentieth century—is in many ways a variant of Curti's more general view. One really cannot say that Curti inaugurated a school of historical studies in philanthropy. Too few historians have pursued his "hypothetical" suggestion concerning the significance of philanthropy to justify that claim. But he did develop an approach and perspective that are of continuing value.

Since the late 1950s, a number of developments in American historiography generally have made it possible to ask somewhat different and somewhat more critical questions than were posed as scholars first began to look at the history of philanthropy. Two in particular have shaped my approach and interpretation: first, the better understanding of bureaucracy as a form of social organization that is evident in works as different as Grant McConnell, *Private Power and American Democracy* (New York: Alfred A. Knopf, 1966); Robert H. Wiebe, *The Search for Order, 1877–1920* (New York: Hill and Wang, 1967); and Alfred D. Chandler, Jr., *The Visible Hand: The Managerial Revolution in American Business* (Cambridge, Mass.: Harvard University Press, 1977)—this line of inquiry is discussed in Louis Galambos, "The Emerging Organizational Synthesis in Modern American History," *Business History Review*, 44 (1970): 279–90; and second, the keener realization that ideas about "social reality" cannot be understood apart from the surrounding "social realities" that is evident in works as different as Robert K. Merton, *The Sociology of Science: Theoretical and Empirical Investigations,* edited by Norman W. Storer (Chicago: University of Chicago Press, 1973); Edward A. Purcell, Jr., *The Crisis of Democratic Theory: Scientific Naturalism and the Problem of Value* (Lexington: The University Press of Kentucky, 1973); Charles E. Rosenberg, *No Other Gods: On Science and American Social Thought* (Baltimore: Johns Hopkins University Press, 1976); and Thomas L. Haskell, *The Emergence of Professional Social Science: The American Social Science Association and the Nineteenth-Century Crisis of Authority*

(Urbana: University of Illinois Press, 1977)—this line of inquiry is discussed in Laurence Veysey, "Intellectual History and the New Social History," in *New Directions in American Intellectual History,* edited by John Higham and Paul K. Conkin (Baltimore: Johns Hopkins University Press, 1979).

The insights that have been developed by scholars working on these two problems have helped me ask questions about where the Carnegie Foundation and its activities have fit within established and emerging cultural and social structures. Especially in Part II ("Technologies of Influence"), where the emphasis is on relationships between Carnegie studies and systematization, the kinds of studies cited above were indirectly but profoundly helpful.

I also have been interested in questions having to do with problems of authority in a democratic society, especially as those have been posed recently by Peter Bachrach, a political scientist (see *The Theory of Democratic Elitism: A Critique* [Boston: Little, Brown, 1967] and *Political Elites in a Democracy,* edited by Peter Bachrach [New York: Atherton Press, 1971]); and by John Patrick Diggins (see: "The Socialization of Authority and the Dilemmas of American Liberalism," *Social Research,* 46 [1979]: 454–86 and "The Three Faces of Authority in American History," *Humanities in Society,* 3 [1980]: 127–49). 1 have not drawn directly from the works of these scholars, but especially in chapter eight my questions have been informed by theirs.

Finally, of course, I have been greatly educated by the writings of other historians now working on the history of philanthropy or questions related to it, and the relationship between this study and some of theirs should also be made clear. Some recent studies have been largely descriptive. They have provided careful and detailed accounts of foundation involvement in particular areas, often focusing primarily on developments in the relevant fields. Among these several examples are: Stanley Coben, "Foundation Officials and Fellowships: Innovation in the Patronage of Science," *Minerva,* 14 (1976): 225–40; Robert E. Kohler, "The Management of Science: The Experience of Warren Weaver and the Rockefeller Programme in Molecular Biology," *Minerva,* 14 (1976): 279–306; Martin Bulmer, "The Early Institutional Establishment of Social Science Research: The Local Community Research Committee at the University of Chicago,

1923–30," *Minerva,* 18 (1980): 51–110; and George W. Stocking, Jr., "The Santa Fe Style in American Anthropology: Regional Interest, Academic Initiative, and Philanthropic Policy in the First Two Decades of the Laboratory of Anthropology, Inc.," *Journal of the History of the Behavioral Sciences,* 18 (1982): 3–19.

In sharp contrast to works such as these are studies in which the central questions have to do with relationships between foundation philanthropy and the social class interests of capitalist elites. One article that focuses on this question is Edward H. Berman, "Foundations, United States Foreign Policy, and African Education, 1945–1975," *Harvard Educational Review,* 49 (1979): 145–79. Focusing on Ford, Rockefeller, and Carnegie philanthropy in Africa after World War II, Berman argued, in essence, that. "public rhetoric of disinterested humanitarianism was little more than a facade behind which the economic and strategic interests of the United States have been actively furthered" (p. 146). In revised form, Berman's article has been reprinted in Robert F. Arnove, ed., *Philanthropy and Cultural Imperialism: The Foundations at Home and Abroad* (Boston: G. K. Hall, 1980). Among the other articles in this book are: Barbara Howe, "The Emergence of Scientific Philanthropy, 1900–1920: Origins, Issues, Outcomes," and Sheila Slaughter and Edward T. Silva, "Looking Backwards: How Foundations Formulated Ideology in the Progressive Period."

The interpretation I have tried to develop in this book is, hopefully, both less descriptive and less ideological than the contrasting works cited above. I think one misses a crucial opportunity to explore essential political questions having to do with group interests, especially elite group interests, if one deals with foundation activities apart from the economic, social, and political characteristics, involvements, and views of the people who have established and managed foundations. What is more, as I have tried to show, I believe that in advancing some interests, foundations inevitably have *not* advanced others. Hence, their actions must have political consequences, even when political purposes are not avowed or even intended. To avoid politics in dealing with foundation history is to miss a crucial part of the story.

On the other hand, I also think it is facile and naive to dismiss "the reality" of publicly and privately asserted beliefs having to do with humanitarianism, thereby suggesting that sincerely altruistic convictions have not been actually an important element of philanthropy. I think social class interests are, by themselves, too simple an explanation for any form of human behavior, let alone for such complicated cooperative efforts as are always involved in foundation philanthropy.

Finally, while one realizes the enormous power that foundations have by looking at their histories, one also realizes the very real constraints on their power. As I have suggested, for example, I think one of these (but only one) is existing capacities to imagine order without hierarchy (see p. 152). Ideological arguments often tend, I think, to oversimplify the complexities of "private power."

The kind of critical middle ground I have sought in the interpretation offered in this book is less compatible with the position taken in the articles cited above and more compatible with the position taken in such different works as: James D. Anderson, "Northern Foundations and the Shaping of Southern Black Rural Education, 1902–1935," *History of Education Quarterly,* 18 (1978): 371–96; Stuart D. Brandes, *American Welfare Capitalism, 1880–1940* (Chicago: University of Chicago Press, 1970); Samuel P. Hays, *Conservation and the Gospel of Efficiency: The Progressive Conservation Movement, 1890–1920* (Cambridge: Harvard University Press, 1959); Barry D. Karl, "Philanthropy, Policy Planning, and the Bureaucratization of the Democratic Ideal," *Daedalus,* 105 (1976): 129–49; and Ronald C. Tobey, *The American Ideology of National Science, 1919–1930* (Pittsburgh: University of Pittsburgh Press, 1971). To point out that these works bear similarity to the kind of interpretation I have tried to develop should not suggest, however, that these authors would agree with my interpretation, or that I fully agree with theirs. For example, I am not at all sure that Karl is right in saying "that the conflict between popular democracy and managerial elites is *essential* to the maintenance of a complex democratic system in a technological age" (emphasis added, p. 129). But I do agree with the willingness to raise political problems, without dismissing other issues, that is evident in all of the works cited here.

Within this general historiographical context, I have tried to deal closely with one foundation, without ignoring the economic, political, social, and intellectual circumstances that have shaped it and that it, in turn, has sought to shape. Inevitably, there are limitations in looking at history through a single institutional lens. Nevertheless, the history of philanthropy is still so relatively underdeveloped that I hope this kind of book can be valuable, not only for what is has to say about the Carnegie Foundation, but also for the questions it may raise for continuing work in the field.

Notes

PART I

1. John Higham, "Hanging Together: Divergent Unities in American History," *Journal of American History*, 61 (1974): 7.

2. Two of the best discussions of community as a theme in the social thought of this era are Jean B. Quandt, *From the Small Town to the Great Community: The Social Thought of Progressive Intellectuals* (New Brunswick, N.J.: Rutgers University Press, 1970) and R. Jackson Wilson, *In Quest of Community: Social Philosophy in the United States, 1860–1920* (New York: Oxford University Press, 1968).

3. Robert H. Wiebe, *The Search for Order, 1877–1920* (New York: Hill and Wang, 1967); Graham Wallas, *The Great Society: A Psychological Analysis* (New York: Macmillan, 1914).

4. In addition to the various works cited in the "Bibliographic Note," David Owen, *English Philanthropy 1660–1960* (Cambridge, Mass.: Harvard University Press, 1964) and Robert H. Bremner, *The Public Good: Philanthropy and Welfare in the Civil War Era* (New York: Alfred A. Knopf, 1980) are useful in tracing attitudes about philanthropy.

5. Jean Jacques Rousseau, *The Social Contract and Discourses,* translated by G. D. H. Cole (New York: E. P. Dutton, 1950), especially Book II.

1. Andrew Carnegie and the Gospel of Wealth

1. Quoted in Joseph Frazier Wall, *Andrew Carnegie* (New York: Oxford University Press, 1970), p. 789. This is the fullest and best of the many accounts of Carnegie's life.

2. Robert M. Lester, *Forty Years of Carnegie Giving: A Summary of the Benefactions of Andrew Carnegie and of the Work of the Philanthropic Trusts Which He Created* (New York: Charles Scribner's Sons, 1941).

3. Quoted in an editor's note to the *Autobiography of Andrew Carnegie,* edited by John C. Van Dyke (Garden City, N.Y.: Doubleday, Doran, 1933), p. 328.

4. Ben Whitaker, *The Foundations: An Anatomy of Philanthropic Bodies* (London: Penguin Books, 1974), p. 73.

5. *Autobiography,* p. 223.

6. James Howard Bridge, *Millionaires and Grub Street: Comrades and Contacts in the Last Century* (New York: Brentano's, 1931), p. 35.

Goodness and Richness: A Double-Bind

7. *Dictionary of American Biography,* s.v. "Andrew Carnegie."

8. Reproduced in Wall, *Andrew Carnegie,* p. 225.

The Education of a Philanthropist

9. Burton J. Hendrick, *The Life of Andrew Carnegie,* 2 vols. (Garden City, N.Y.: Doubleday, Doran, 1932), I, 222.

10. "Anne C. L. Botta," in *Miscellaneous Writings of Andrew Carnegie,* edited by Burton J. Hendrick, 2 vols. (Garden City, N.Y.: Doubleday, Doran, 1933), I, 151.

11. *Autobiography,* p. 145.

12. Ibid., p. 327.

13. "A Confession of Religious Faith," in *Miscellaneous Writings,* II, 297.

14. Quoted in *Notable American Women,* s.v. "Anne Charlotte Lynch Botta."

15. *Autobiography,* p. 21.

16. "A Confession of Religious Faith," pp. 305, 316–17, 318–19.

17. Alfred D. Chandler, Jr., *The Visible Hand: The Managerial Revolution in American Business* (Cambridge, Mass.: Harvard University Press, 1977), pp. 258–69. Wall, *Andrew Carnegie,* provides more information on Carnegie's business.

18. Carroll D. Wright, "Are the Rich Growing Richer and the Poor Poorer?" *Atlantic Monthly,* 80 (1897): 302.

19. Morton Keller, *Affairs of State: Public Life in Late Nineteenth Century America* (Cambridge, Mass.: Harvard University Press, 1977), p. 373.

20. Daniel T. Rodgers, *The Work Ethic in Industrial America, 1850–1920* (Chicago: University of Chicago Press, 1974), p. 37.

21. Wright, "Are the Rich Growing Richer," p. 301.

22. Keller, *Affairs of State,* p. 373.

"Wealth"

23. There are many editions of "Wealth." I have used Andrew Carnegie, *The Gospel of Wealth* (Garden City, N.Y.: Doubleday, Doran, 1933), part I—"The Gospel of Wealth: The Problem of the Administration of Wealth," pp. 1–17 and part II— "The Best Fields for Philanthropy," pp. 17–39. All of the various short quotes in the text are from this source with page numbers given in parentheses.

24. The various short quotes are from "A Confession of Religious Faith," pp. 305 and 306, and the *Autobiography,* p. 327.

25. Andrew Carnegie, "The Advantages of Poverty," in *The Gospel of Wealth,* p. 68.

26. William Jewett Tucker, "The Gospel of Wealth," *Andover Review,* 15 (1891): 634 and 637.

27. For a more general discussion of reviews of "Wealth" see Wall, *Andrew Carnegie,* pp. 806–15.

2. Henry Smith Pritchett and the Gospel of Efficiency

1. All the biographical information in this chapter is from Abraham Flexner, *Henry S. Pritchett: A Biography* (New York: Columbia University Press, 1943) and from "Autobiographical Fragments, c. 1876–1939," Henry Smith Pritchett Papers, Library of Congress, Washington D.C. The Flexner volume reproduces much of this schematic autobiography.

2. Flexner, *Pritchett,* pp. 193–94.

The Education of a Scientist

3. Henry S. Pritchett, "The Fiftieth Anniversary of the Founding of the Cosmos Club, 1878–1928, Washington, D.C.," pp. 6–7, 7 pg. ms., CFAT Archive, New York City.

4. Flexner, *Pritchett,* p. 64.

5. Ibid.

6. See Nathan Reingold, "Definitions and Speculations: The Professionalization of Science in America in the Nineteenth Century," in *The Pursuit of Knowledge in the Early American Republic: American Scientific and Learned Societies from Colonial Times to the Civil War,* edited by Alexandra Oleson and Sanborn C. Brown (Baltimore: Johns Hopkins University Press, 1976), pp. 33–69; George H. Daniels, *Science in American Society: A Social History* (New York: Alfred A. Knopf, 1970, chap. 12; and Edward Shils, "The Order of Learning in the United States: The Ascendency of the University," in *The Organization of Knowledge in Modern America, 1860–1920,* edited by Alexandra Oleson and John Voss (Baltimore: Johns Hopkins University Press, 1979), pp. 19–47.

7. Flexner, *Pritchett,* p. 31

8. James Cox, *Old and New St. Louis* (St. Louis: Central Biography Publishing, 1894), p. 119.

9. Flexner, *Pritchett,* p. 47.

10. Ibid., p. 50.

The Politics of "Professional" Science

11. Daniels, *Science in American Society,* chap. 12.

12. Henry S. Pritchett, "The Story of the Establishment of the National Bureau of Standards, " *Science,* n.s. 15 (1902): 281–84.

13. Cited in Daniels, *Science in American Society,* p. 278.

14. Flexner, *Pritchett,* p. 33.

Reforming a College

15. Henry S. Pritchett, "The Educated Man and the State," *Technology Review,* III (1901): 41.

16. Henry S. Pritchett, "The Service of Science to the University, and the Response of the University to the Service," a speech to the Forty-second Quarterly convocation of the University of Chicago, June 17, 1902, pp. 14–15, CFAT Archive.

17. Ibid., p. 6.

18. "Address of President Pritchett," Part II," "Report of the Meeting of M.I.T. Alumni at Huntington Hall, May 4, 1905," *Technology Review,* 7 (1905): 8. See also Samuel C. Prescott, *When M.I.T. Was "Boston Tech,"* *1861–1916* (Cambridge, Mass." Technology Press, 1954), chap. 10 and Samuel Eliot Morison, ed., *The Development of Harvard University* (Cambridge, Mass.: Harvard University Press, 1930), chap. 24.

The Gospel of Efficiency

19. Henry Smith Pritchett, "A Woman's Opportunity in Business and the Industries," An Address Given at the Second Annual Commencement of Simmons College, Boston, June 12, 1907, p. 2, CFAT Archive.

20. Henry Smith Pritchett, "Is There a Place for a Profession in Commerce?" from *Transactions,* no. 70, New England Cotton Manufacturers' Association, Boston, Mass., April 24, 1901, p. 4, CFAT Archive.

21. Henry S. Pritchett, "The Place of Industrial and Technical Training in Popular Education," *Technology Review,* 4 (1902): 24.

22. "A Woman's Opportunity," p. 7.

23. Samuel P. Hays, *Conservation and the Gospel of Efficiency: The Progressive Conservation Movement, 1890–1920* (Cambridge, Mass.: Harvard University Press, 1959), pp. 265–66.

24. Pritchett, "The Service of Science," p. 4. See also *What is Religion? And Other Student Questions: Talks to College Students* (Boston: Houghton, Mifflin, 1906).

25. Henry S. Pritchett, "The Spirit of the State Universities," *University of California Chronicle,* 12 (1910): 22–23.

26. Ibid., p. 21.

27. Henry S, Pritchett, "Modern Culture and the Human Soul," *Phi Beta Kappa Key,* 4 (1920): 70 and 77.

3. Founding the Foundation

1. The other members of the original board were: Hill McClelland Bell, Drake University; T. Morrison Carnegie, New York City; Edwin B. Craighead, Tulane University; William H. Crawford, Allegheny College; George H. Denny, Washington and Lee University; Robert A. Franks, Home Trust Company; William Rainey Harper, University of Chicago; Charles C. Harrison, University of Pennsylvania; Alexander C. Humphreys, Stevens Institute of Technology; Edwin H. Hughes, DePauw University; Henry C. King, Oberlin College; Thomas McClelland, Knox College; Samuel B. McCormick, Western University of Pennsylvania; William Peterson, McGill University; Samuel Plantz, Lawrence University; Henry S. Pritchett, Massachusetts Institute of Technology; L. Clark Secelye, Smith College; Charles F. Thwing, Western Reserve University; Frank A. Vanderlip, National City Bank.

2. Henry S. Pritchett to Frank A. Vanderlip, May 6, 1905, Frank A. Vanderlip Papers, Rare Book and Manuscript Library, Columbia University, New York City.

3. Henry S. Pritchett to Andrew Carnegie, November 16, 1905, CFAT Archive, New York City.

The Administrative Structure of the Carnegie Foundation

4. *Dictionary of American Biography,* s.v. "Edwin Boone Craighead."

5. Pritchett to Vanderlip, May 6, 1905.

6. Memorandum describing the first meeting of the CFAT trustees written by trustee George Hutcheson Denny in Howard J. Savage, *Fruit of an Impulse: Forty-Five Years of the Carnegie Foundation 1905–1950* (New York: Harcourt, Brace, 1953), p. 47.

7. Robert M. Lester, *Forty Years of Carnegie Giving: A Summary of the Benefactions of Andrew Carnegie and of the Work of the Philanthropic Trusts Which He Created* (New York: Charles Scribner's Sons, 1941, pp. 152–53.

8. *CFAT 1st Annual Report* (1906), pp. 15–16.

9. Ibid., p. 38.

10. Ibid., pp. 11, 21–22.

11. Ibid., p. 50.

12. Henry S. Pritchett, "Mr. Carnegie's Gift to the Teachers," *The Outlook,* May 19, 1906, p. 125.

A Break with Tradition

13. Lester, *Forty Years of Carnegie Giving,* pp. 166–71.

14. Alvin Johnson, *Pioneer's Progress: An Autobiography* (New York: Viking Press, 1952), p. 238.

15. Burton J. Hendrick, *The Life of Andrew Carnegie,* 2 vols. (Garden City, N.Y.: Doubleday, Doran, 1932), II, 199; Andrew Carnegie to Daniel Coit Gilman, March 27, 1905, and Henry S. Pritchett to Andrew Carnegie, December 21, 1904, Andrew Carnegie Papers, Library of Congress, Washington, D.C.

16. Quoted in Joseph Frazier Wall, *Andrew Carnegie* (New York: Oxford University Press, 1970), pp. 833–34.

The Personal Politics of Social Change

17. Henry S. Pritchett, "Letter to the Editor," *Science,* n.s. 16 (1902): 587–88; Henry S. Pritchett to Andrew Carnegie, December 13, 1901, Henry Smith Pritchett Papers, Library of Congress, Washington, D.C.

18. Henry S. Pritchett to Andrew Carnegie, January 14, 1902, Pritchett Papers.

19. Howard S. Miller, *Dollars for Research: Science and Its Patrons in Nineteenth Century America* (Seattle: University of Washington Press, 1970), pp. 173–74

20. For more detail on this see Nathan Reingold, "National Science Policy in a Private Foundation: The Carnegie Institution of Washington," in *The Organization of Knowledge in Modern America, 1860–1920,* edited by Alexandra Oleson and John Voss (Baltimore: Johns Hopkins University Press, 1979), pp. 313–41 and David Madsen, "Daniel Coit Gilman at the Carnegie Institution of Washington," *History of Education Quarterly,* 9 (1969): 154–86.

21. Henry S. Pritchett to Andrew Carnegie, March 15, 1902, and March 23, 1903, Pritchett Papers.

22. Henry S. Pritchett, "Beginnings of the Carnegie Foundation," *CFAT 30th Annual Report* (1935), pp. 29–35.

23. Pritchett's efforts to become president of the CIW are discussed in Robert S. Woodward to Thomas C. Chamberlin, July 11, 1904, in *Science in America: A Documentary History, 1900–1939,* edited by Nathan Reingold and Ida H. Reingold (Chicago: University of Chicago Press, 1981), pp. 24–25.

24. Henry S. Pritchett to Andrew Carnegie, December 21, 1904, Carnegie Papers.

25. Massachusetts Institute of Technology, *Annual Report of the President and Treasurer, December 9, 1903* (Boston: Geo. H. Ellis, 1904), pp. 19–20, Institute Archives and Special Collections, Cambridge, Massachusetts.

26. I have not located Carnegie's answer to Pritchett's letter of Decem-

ber 21, 1904, although the substance of his reply is apparent in Henry S. Pritchett to Andrew Carnegie, February 6, 1905, Vanderlip Papers.

27. For general discussions of attitudes toward pensions at this time see Stuart D. Brandes, *American Welfare Capitalism, 1880–1940* (Chicago: University of Chicago Press, 1970) and William Graebner, *A History of Retirement: The Meaning and Function of an American Institution, 1885–1978* (New Haven: Yale University Press, 1980).

28. Andrew Carnegie to Andrew D. White, December 4, 1904, Carnegie Papers.

29. This has been the standard explanation for Carnegie's establishment of the CFAT. See Lester, *Forty Years of Carnegie Giving*, p. 45, and Wall, *Andrew Carnegie*, pp. 870–71.

30. Henry S. Pritchett to Frank A. Vanderlip, January 14, 1904, Vanderlip Papers.

31. Henry S. Pritchett to Frank A. Vanderlip, February 10, 1905, Vanderlip Papers.

32. Pritchett to Carnegie, February 6, 1905.

33. Frank A. Vanderlip, *From Farm Boy to Financier* (New York: D. Appleton-Century, 1935), pp. 76–77. Pritchett's close relationship with Vanderlip is also evident throughout their correspondence.

34. Ibid., esp. pp. 121, 126, 135; *Dictionary of American Biography*, s.v. "Frank Arthur Vanderlip."

35. Vanderlip's ideas are clearly expressed in the articles gathered together in Frank A. Vanderlip, *Business and Education* (New York: Duffield, 1907). Raymond E. Callahan, *Education and the Cult of Efficiency: A Study of the Social Forces that Have Shaped the Administration of the Public Schools* (Chicago: University of Chicago Press, 1962), quotes extensively from a Vanderlip speech to the National Education Association, in which Vanderlip spoke glowingly of Germany, and sets that speech within the milieu it reflected. Vanderlip's compatibility with Pritchett was apparent in his comment that "if I could have lived my life according to a program of desire I would have been engaged in pure science all my days" (Vanderlip, *From Farm Boy to Financier*, p. 23). One of the many places in which Pritchett's admiration for German education was apparent was in Henry S. Pritchett, "How Science Helps Industry in Germany," *Review of Reviews* (1906), reprint, CFAT Archive.

36. Pritchett to Vanderlip, February 6, 1905, Vanderlip Papers.

37. Carnegie's view of pensions is clarified somewhat by the advice he gave one of his wife's correspondents: "The best plan of all is to have a sick relief and superannuation fund to which the employees contribute regularly a small amount and therefore feel that it is their own institution (Andrew Carnegie to Mrs. Craigie, December 2,

1904, Carnegie Papers).

38. Henry S. Pritchett to Frank A. Vanderlip, February 10, 1905, Vanderlip Papers.

39. Andrew Carnegie to Frank A. Vanderlip, May 20, 1914, Vanderlip Papers. Vanderlip's comment that Pritchett called on him because "he needed reinforcements" supports the above argument (Vanderlip, *Farm Boy,* p. 139).

40. "A Plan to Provide a System of Retired Pay to Officers of Instruction in Institutions Which are Not Supported by the State and Which are Non-Sectarian," 14 pg. ms., Vanderlip Papers.

41. Savage, *Fruit of an Impulse,* pp. 3–22.

42. Andrew Carnegie to Henry S. Pritchett, December 11, 1905, CFAT Archive.

43. Andrew Carnegie to Charles W. Eliot, June 16, 1910, CFAT Archive.

44. This is discussed in detail in Theron F. Schlabach, *Pensions for Professors* (Madison: State Historical Society of Wisconsin, 1963) and William Graebner, "The Origins of Retirement in Higher Education: The Carnegie Pension System," *Academe: Bulletin of the AAUP,* 65 (1979): 97–103.

45. Henry S. Pritchett to Frank A. Vanderlip, April 27, 1905, Vanderlip Papers.

46. Henry S. Pritchett to Andrew Carnegie, January 13, 1911, CFAT Archive.

A Pension Fund and a "Great Agency"

47. Andrew Carnegie to Robert H. Thurston, October 16, 1888, quoted in Monte A. Calvert, *The Mechanical Engineer in America, 1830–1910: Professional Cultures in Conflict* (Baltimore: Johns Hopkins University Press, 1967), p. 99.

48. Andrew Carnegie to Henry L. Higginson, November 26, 1904, Carnegie Papers.

49. Savage, *Fruit of an Impulse,* pp. 114–20.

50. Reingold, "National Science Policy in a Private Foundation," especially pp. 318–24.

51. Pritchett to Carnegie, November 16, 1905.

PART II

1. Henry Smith Pritchett, "Shall Engineering Belong to the Liberal Professions," n.d., Address at the Inauguration of Dr. Charles S. Howe as President of the Case School of Applied Science, pp. 4 and 5, CFAT Archive.

2. Henry Smith Pritchett, "Address at the Reunion Banquet, June 8, 1904," *Technology Review,* 6 (1904): 10.

3. Mary Clark Stuart, "Clark Kerr: Biography of an Action Intellectual" (Ph.D. dissertation, University of Michigan, 1980), p. 253.

4. Surveying the Professions

1. Howard J. Savage, *Fruit of an Impulse: Forty-Five Years of the Carnegie Foundation 1905–1950* (New York: Harcourt, Brace, 1953), pp. 56–60 discusses this charter change in greater detail.

2. Pritchett's handwritten draft of the memorandum is in the CFAT Archive, New York City.

The Circumstances in Medicine at the Time of the Flexner Report

3. The figures are from J. Richard Woodworth, "Some Influences on the Reform of Schools of Law and Medicine 1890–1930," *Sociological Quarterly,* 14 (1973): 497.

4. Gerald E. Markowitz and David Karl Rosner, "Doctors in Crisis: A Study of the Use of Medical Education Reform to Establish Modern Professional Elitism in Medicine," *American Quarterly,* 25 (1973): 83–107; Magali Sarfatti Larson, *The Rise of Professionalism: A Sociological Analysis* (Berkeley: University of California Press, 1977), pp. 159–66; and Ellen Condliffe Lagemann, ed., *Nursing History: New Perspectives, New Possibilities* (New York: Teachers College Press, 1983).

5. For a description of early nineteenth-century medical training see Joseph F. Kett, *The Formation of the American Medical Profession: The Role of Institutions 1780–1860* (New Haven: Yale University Press, 1968).

6. Thomas Neville Bonner, *American Doctors and German Universities: A Chapter in International Intellectual Relations, 1870–1914* (Lincoln: University of Nebraska Press, 1963).

7. Donald Fleming, *William H. Welch and the Rise of Modern Medicine* (Boston: Little, Brown, 1954), p. 65. See also Simon Flexner and James Thomas Flexner, *William Henry Welch and the Heroic Age of American Medicine* (New York: Viking Press, 1941).

8. John Field, "Medical Education in the United States: Late Nineteenth and Twentieth Centuries," in *The History of Medical Education,* edited by C. D. O'Malley (Berkeley: University of California Press, 1970), pp. 501–30; Burton J. Bledstein, *The Culture of Professionalism: The Middle Class and the Development of Higher Education in America* (New York: W. W. Norton, 1976), pp. 85–86.

9. Richard H. Shryock, *The Unique Influence of the Johns Hopkins University on American Medicine* (Copenhagen: Ejnar Munksgaard, 1953); and Fleming, *William Henry Welch,* especially chaps. 7–10.

10. The best account of reforms at this time is Rosemary Stevens, *American Medicine and the Public Interest* (New Haven: Yale University Press, 1971), especially chaps. 2 and 3.

11. Ibid., pp. 63–66; James G. Burrow, *AMA: Voice of American Medicine* (Baltimore: Johns Hopkins Press, 1963), esp. chap. 2; James G. Burrows, *Organized Medicine in the Progressive Era* (Baltimore: Johns Hopkins University Press, 1977), chap. 3; and Morris Fishbein, *A History of the American Medical Association, 1847 to 1947* (Philadelphia: W. B. Saunders, 1947), pp. 197–259, 887–922.

12. Kett, *The Formation of the American Medical Profession,* chap. 6; Stevens, *American Medicine,* pp. 26–33, 58–66; and Burrows, *AMA,* chap. 2.

13. A. D. Bevan, "Cooperation in Medical Education and Medical Service," *Journal of the American Medical Association,* 90 (1928): 1173, quoted in Fishbein, *History of the AMA,* p. 897.

14. Savage, *Fruit of an Impulse,* p. 99.

15. Henry S. Pritchett to Alexander C. Humphreys, November 10, 1908, CFAT Archive.

Abraham Flexner and the Flexner Report

16. Abraham Flexner, *I Remember* (New York: Simon and Schuster, 1940), p. 111

17. Ibid., chaps. 8 and 9.

18. Abraham Flexner, *Henry S. Pritchett: A Biography* (New York: Columbia University Press, 1943) pp. 108–09.

19. Fishbein, *History of the AMA,* p. 898.

20. Ibid. The CFAT-Council on Medical Education alliance is clearly described in correspondence between Pritchett and Bevan. Writing to Bevan on November 4, 1909, for example, Pritchett stated: "In all this work of the examination of the medical schools we have been hand in glove with you and your committee. In fact, we have only taken up the matter and gone on with the examination very much as you were doing, except that as an independent agency disconnected from actual practice, we may do certain things you perhaps may not. When our report comes out, it is going to be ammunition in your hands" (CFAT Archive).

21. Flexner, *I Remember,* p. 121.

22. Abraham Flexner, *Medical Education in the United States and Canada,* CFAT Bulletin Number 4 (1910), p. 3.

23. Ibid., p. 5.

24. Ibid., p. 6.

25. Ibid., p. 8.

26. Ibid., p. 12.

27. Ibid., p. 16.

28. Ibid., p. 13.

29. Ibid., chaps. 4-7.

30. Ibid., p. 147.

31. Ibid., p. 151

32. Ibid., p. 227.

33. Ibid., pp. 270.

34. Ibid., p. 303.

35. Ibid., p. 197.

36. Ibid., p. 20.

37. Ibid., p. 19.

The Outcomes of the Flexner Report

38. Biennial Survey of Education 1928–30, 2 vols. (Washington, D.C.: Government Printing Office, 1932), I, 547.

39. Any number of recent commentators on the Flexner report have made these points. In addition to Markowitz and Rosner, "Doctors in Crisis," and Stevens, *American Medicine*, chap. 3, see William C. Rappleye, "Major Changes in Medical Education During the Past Fifty Years," *Journal of Medical Education*, 34 (1959): 683–89; Robert P. Hudson, "Abraham Flexner in Perspective: American Medical Education, 1865–1910," *Bulletin of the History of Medicine*, 46 (1972): 545–61; and Carleton B. Chapman, "The Flexner Report," *Daedalus* (1974): 105–17.

40. Kenneth Ludmerer, "Reform of Medical Education at Washington University," *Journal of the History of Medicine*, 35 (1980): 154.

41. Donna Bingham Munger, "Robert Brookings and the Flexner Report: A Case Study of the Reorganization of Medical Education," *Journal of the History of Medicine*, 23 (1968): 356–71.

42. Ernest V. Hollis, *Philanthropic Foundations and Higher Education* (New York: Columbia University Press, 1938); Stevens, *American Medicine*, pp. 68–69.

43. Stevens, *American Medicine*, pp. 71–73; Leonard W. Johnson, Jr., "History of the Education of Negro Physicians," *Journal of Medical Education*, 42 (1967): 439–46; James L. Curtis, *Blacks, Medical Schools, and Society* (Ann Arbor: University of Michigan Press, 1971), especially, pp. 15–17; C. W. Norris, "The Negro College at Mid-Century," *Quarterly Review of Higher Education Among Negroes*, 19 (1951): 7–11; Mary Roth Walsh, *"Doctors Wanted: No Women Need Apply": Sexual Barriers in the Medical Profession, 1835–1975* (New Haven: Yale University Press, 1977), pp. 236–41, and "The Rediscovery of the Need for a Feminist Medical Education," *Harvard Educational Review*, 49 (1979): 451.

44. *CFAT 3rd Annual Report* (1908), p. 160.

The Carnegie Foundation and Legal Education

45. The letter from the ABA to the CFAT is reproduced in Alfred Zantzinger Reed, *Training for the Public Profession of the Law,* CFAT Bulletin Number 15 (1921), p. xviii.

46. Pritchett told the AMA Council on Medical Education that he was having trouble gaining ABA cooperation at a 1908 meeting, the minutes of which are quoted in Fishbein, *History of the AMA,* p. 898; Pritchett also reported difficulties in the *6th Annual Report* (1911), pp. 87–94.

47. Reed, *Training for the Public Profession of the Law,* p. xviii. The benefit legal reformers expected from a CFAT study is evident in the "Address of the President," *Proceedings of the American Association of Law Schools* (1916), pp. 114–32.

The Circumstances in Law at the Time of the
Carnegie Foundation Surveys

48. Alfred Z. Reed to Henry S. Pritchett, August 28, 1913, CFAT Archive. For a more detailed comparison of professionalization in medicine and law see Michael Schudson, "The Flexner Report and the Reed Report: Notes on the History of Professional Education in the United States," *Social Science Quarterly,* 55 (1974): 347–61.

49. Robert Stevens, "Two Cheers for 1870: The American Law School," *Perspectives in American History,* 5 (1971): 459.

50. Jerold S. Auerbach, "Enmity and Amity: Law Teachers and Practitioners, 1900–1922," *Perspectives in American History,* 5 (1971): 574–75. See also Larson, The Rise of Professionalism, pp. 166–77.

51. Auerbach, "Enmity and Amity," pp. 551–601; Russell N. Sullivan, "The Professional Associations and Legal Education," *Journal of Legal Education,* 4 (1952): 401–26. Arthur E. Sutherland, *The Law at Harvard: A History of Ideas and Men, 1817–1967* (Cambridge, Mass.: Harvard University Press, 1967), chaps. 6 and 7, details the change from part-time to full-time teaching.

52. On the history of the ABA see Brother Norbert and C. Brockman, "The History of the American Bar Association: A Bibliographic Essay," *American Journal of Legal History,* 6 (1962): 269–85; and James Willard Hurst, *The Growth of American Law: The Law Makers* (Boston: Little, Brown, 1950), especially pp. 285–94 .

53. Quoted in Auerbach, "Enmity and Amity," p. 558.

54. Ibid.

55. Ibid., p. 554.

56. Many of the presidential addresses included in the *Proceedings of the Association of American Law Schools* clearly indicate the degree to which academic lawyers saw themselves as a separate and special group, see especially: William Draper Lewis, "Legal Education and the Failure of the Bar to Perform its Public Duties," *Proceedings of the Association of American Law Schools* (1906), pp. 32–49, and Henry M. Bates, "The Strategic Position of the Law Teacher and the Law School," *Proceedings* (1913), pp. 29–46.

57. See for example Russell Leffingwell to Frederick P. Keppel, April 15, 1926, January 7, 1930, and February 2, 1931, Carnegie Corporation Archive, New York City. See also Jerold S. Auerbach, *Unequal Justice: Lawyers and Social Change in Modern America* (New York: Oxford University, 1976).

58. Stevens, "Two Cheers for 1870," pp. 441–49. See also Joseph Redlich, *The Common Law and the Case Method,* CFAT Bulletin Number 8 (1914) and Preble Stolz, "Clinical Experience in American Legal Education: Why Has It Failed?" in *Clinical Education and the Law School of the Future,* edited by Edmund W. Kitch, University of Chicago Law School, Conference Series No. 20, p. 63.

The Reed Report

59. Henry S. Pritchett to Alfred Z. Reed, August 10, 1917, and Reed to Pritchett, October 7, 1921, and July 24, 1922, CFAT Archive.

60. Reed, *Training for the Public Profession of the Law,* p. 415.

61. Ibid.

62. Ibid., p. 416.

63. Stevens, "Two Cheers for 1870," pp. 453–64; Auerbach, "Enmity and Amity," pp. 588–601.

64. Flexner, *Pritchett*, p. 20. See also Philip C. Jessup, *Elihu Root*, 2 vols. (New York: Dodd, Mead, 1938), II, 467–70, and Richard W. Leopold, *Elihu Root and the Conservative Tradition* (Boston: Little, Brown, 1954).

65. Alfred Z. Reed to Henry S. Pritchett, June 27, 1921, CFAT Archive.

66. Sullivan, "Professional Associations and Educators," pp. 411–16.

Engineering Education

67. Matthew Elias Zaret, "An Historical Study of the Development of the American Society for Engineering Education" (Ph.D. dissertation, New York University, 1967, p. 58).

68. In addition to Zaret, chaps. 4 and 5, see David F. Noble, *America By Design: Science, Technology, and the Rise of Corporate Capitalism* (New York: Oxford University Press, 1977), pp. 202–06, and, for the earlier history of the professionalization of engineers, Daniel H. Calhoun, *The*

American Civil Engineer (Cambridge, Mass.: M.I.T. Press, 1960) and Monte A. Calvert, *The Mechanical Engineer in America, 1830–1910: Professional Cultures in Conflict* (Baltimore: Johns Hopkins University Press, 1967).

69. Charles Riborg Mann, *Engineering Education,* CFAT Bulletin 11 (1918); Noble, *America By Design,* pp. 202–06.

70. Henry S. Pritchett to Frank A. Vanderlip, April 10, 1911, Frank A. Vanderlip Papers, Rare Book and Manuscript Library, Columbia University, New York City.

The Professional Preparation of Teachers for American Public Schools

71. William S. Learned, et al., *The Professional Preparation of Teachers for American Public Schools,* CFAT Bulletin 14 (1920), p. xv.

72. Paul H. Mattingly, *The Classless Profession: American Schoolmen in the Nineteenth Century* (New York: New York University Press, 1975), chap. 7.

73. Clyde Milton Hill, *A Decade of Progress in Teacher Training,* Teachers College Contributions to Education, No. 233 (New York: Bureau of Publications, Teachers College, Columbia University, 1927).

74. William C. Bagley, "Twenty Years of Progress in the Professionalization of Subject Matter for Normal Schools and Teachers Colleges," American Association of Teachers Colleges, *Yearbook* (1928), pp. 72–78.

75. Edgar B. Wesley, *N.E.A.: The First Hundred Years, The Building of the Teaching Profession* (New York: Harper & Brothers, 1957), chap. 7; Merle L. Borrowman, *The Liberal and the Technical in Teacher Education: A Historical Survey of American Thought* (New York: Bureau of Publications, Teachers College, Columbia University, 1956), chap. 4; and Lawrence A. Cremin, "The Heritage of American Teacher Education," Part II , *Journal of Teacher Education,* 4 (1953): 246–50.

76. Jurgen Hurbst, "Nineteenth Century Normal Schools in the United States: A Fresh Look," *History of Education,* 9 (1980): 219–27.

Education in Vermont and the American Association of University Professors

77. *Education in Vermont,* CFAT Bulletin Number 7 (1914), p. 3.

78. M. B. Hillegas to Clyde Furst, September 21, 1916, CFAT Archive.

79. J. F. Messenger to Clyde Furst, May 22, 1915, CFAT Archive.

80. *Education in Vermont,* p. 210.

81. Ibid., p. 156.

82. Josiah Royce, "The Carnegie Foundation for the Advancement of Teaching and the Case of Middlebury College," *School and Society,* 1

(1915): 145–50.

83. James McKeen Cattell to Henry S. Pritchett, March 21, 1908, April 17, 1908, May 15, 1909, November 23, 1909, and November 8, 1910, CFAT Archive, illustrate the kinds of questions Cattell raised with Pritchett in a voluminous correspondence that continued for over ten years; examples of published correspondence can be found in *Science,* 32 (1910): 799, and in J. McKeen Cattell, ed., *Carnegie Pensions* (New York: Science Press, 1919). Michael M. Sokal, "The Unpublished Autobiography of James McKeen Cattell," *American Psychologist,* 26 (1971); 626–35 and *Dictionary of American Biography,* s.v. "James McKeen Cattell," suggest the fit between Cattell's battle with Pritchett and his more general fight for academic freedom; and the papers collected in *James McKeen Cattell: Man of Science, 1860–1944,* 2 vols. (Lancaster, Penn.: Science Press, 1947), further illustrate that relationship. Cattell's relationship with Nicholas Murray Butler, his archenemy, which is described in Carol S. Gruber, *Mars and Minerva: World War I and the Uses of the Higher Learning in America* (Baton Rouge: Louisiana State University Press, 1975), pp. 187–212, is also illuminating of the issues with which Cattell was concerned.

84. J. McKeen Cattell, *University Control* (New York: Science Press, 1913), p. 17.

85. Ibid., p. 61. On the formation of the AAUP see Walter P. Metzger, *Academic Freedom in the Age of the University* (New York: Columbia University Press, 1955) and "Origins of the Association: An Anniversary Address," *AAUP Bulletin,* 67 (1965): 229–37.

86. Metzger, *Academic Freedom,* p. 203.

87. *AAUP Bulletin,* 2 (1914): 43.

5. Systematizing Educational Measurements

1. *CFAT 23rd Annual Report* (1928), pp. 52–53.

2. Henry Smith Pritchett, "The Spirit of the State Universities," *University of California Chronicle,* 12 (1910): 17

3. *CFAT 1st Annual Report* (1906), pp. 39–47. On "the Carnegie Unit" see U.S. Department of Health, Education, and Welfare, Bulletin Number 7, *The Carnegie Unit: Its Origin, Status, and Trends* (Washington, D.C.: Government Printing Office, 1954).

4. *CFAT 5th Annual Report* (1910), p. 68.

The Growth of the High School

5. Theodore Sizer, *Secondary Schools at the Turn of the Century* (New Haven: Yale University Press, 1964), chap. 1; Edward A. Krug, *The Shaping of the American High School, 1880–1920* (Madison: University of Wisconsin Press, 1969), chap. 1.

6. Sizer, *Secondary Schools,* chap. 8; Edward A. Krug, ed., *Charles W. Eliot and Popular Education* (New York: Teachers College Press, 1961), chap 4; and Richard F. W. Whittemore, *Nicholas Murray Butler and Public Education, 1862–1911* (New York: Teachers College Press, 1970), pp. 83–88.

7. Quoted in Sizer, *Secondary Schools,* p. 153.

8. Ibid., p. 187 (the quote); p. 199 (enrollment figures).

9. U.S. Bureau of Education, *Cardinal Principles of Secondary Education, A Report of the Commission on the Reorganization of Secondary Education Appointed by the National Education Association* (Washington, D.C.: Government Printing Office, 1918), pp. 9, 11–15.

10. Henry S. Pritchett, "Has the College Board Justified Its Quarter-Century of Life," in *The Work of the College Entrance Examination Board 1901–1925* (Boston: Ginn and Co., 1926), p. 15. See also, Henry S. Pritchett, "Are Our Universities Overpopulated?" *Scribner's Magazine,* 72 (1923): 556–60.

11. *CFAT 3rd Annual Report* (1908), p. 103.

The College Board and the SAT

12. On the College Board see *The Work of the College Entrance Examination Board;* Claude M. Fuess, *The College Board: Its First Fifty Years* (New York: Columbia University Press, 1950); and Michael S. Schudson, "Organizing the 'Meritocracy': A History of the College Entrance Examination Board," *Harvard Educational Review,* 42 (1972): 34–69.

13. Schudson, "Organizing the Meritocracy"; Harold S. Wechsler, *The Qualified Student: A History of Selective College Admission in America* (New York: John Wiley, 1977); and Marcia Graham Synnott, *The Half-Opened Door: Discrimination and Admissions at Harvard, Yale, and Princeton, 1900–1970* (Westport, Conn.: Greenwood Press, 1979).

14. Schudson, "Organizing the Meritocracy"; Fuess, *The College Board,* chap. 5.

The Pennsylvania Study

15. Forty-First Convention of the Association of Colleges and Secondary Schools of the Middle States and Maryland, November, 1927, *Proceedings,* p. 79.

16. Learned's perspective is summarized in Paul Douglas, *Teaching for Self-Education* (New York: Harper & Brothers, 1960). In addition to his writings for the CFAT, the most important Learned monographs are: *The Oberlehrer: A Study of the Social and Professional Evolution of the German Schoolmaster* (Cambridge, Mass.: Harvard University Press, 1914) and *Realism in American Education,* The Inglis Lecture, 1932 (Cambridge, Mass.: Harvard University Press, 1932). Learned's views concerning education are discussed in Krug, *The Shaping of the American*

High School, 1920–1941 (Madison: University of Wisconsin Press, 1972), chap. 11.

17. William S. Learned, *The Quality of the Educational Process in the United States and in Europe,* CFAT Bulletin Number 20 (1927): 5–6, 44.

18. Learned discussed the General College in "The Junior College, the University and the Community," CFAT *29th Annual Report* (1934), pp. 21–35. He also was in favor of "honors' programs," such as the one set up by Frank Aydelotte at Swarthmore, and discussed that program and several others in *The Quality,* pp. 114–25.

19. 1928 Middle States, *Proceedings,* p. 23.

20. William S. Learned and Ben D. Wood, *The Student and His Knowledge,* CFAT Bulletin Number 29 (1938): ix.

21. 1928 Middle States, *Proceedings,* pp. 67–77. Wood's career is summarized in Matthew T. Downey, *Ben D. Wood: Educational Reformer* (Princeton, N.J.: Educational Testing Service, 1965); his best known book, a classic in the testing literature, is *Measurement in Higher Education* (New York: World Book, 1923).

22. Ben D. Wood and F. S. Beers, "Knowledge versus Thinking," *Teachers College Record,* 37 (1936): 496.

23. The Pennsylvania tests are included in the appendices to *The Student and His Knowledge.*

24. On the significance attributed to the Pennsylvania Study see: William S. Learned to Lewis M. Terman, February 10, 1939, CFAT Archive, New York City; I. L. Kandel, *Examinations and Their Substitutes,* CFAT Bulletin Number 28 (1936), pp. 133–40; Albert B. Crawford and Paul S. Burnham, *Forecasting College Achievement: A Survey of Aptitude Tests for Higher Education: Part I—General Considerations in the Measurement of Academic Promise* (New Haven: Yale University Press, 1946); and Max McConn, "How Much Do College Students Learn?" *North American Review* (1932), reprint, CFAT Archive.

A General Examination Board

25. On the increasing use of testing, see David B. Tyack, *The One Best System: A History of American Urban Education* (Cambridge, Mass.: Harvard University Press, 1974), pp. 198–215; Paul Davis Chapman, *Schools As Sorters: Lewis M. Terman and the Intelligence Testing Movement, 1890–1930* (Ph.D. dissertation, Stanford University, 1980); and Rita Joyce Norton, *Private Foundations and the Development of Standardized Tests, 1900–1935* (Ph.D. dissertation, University of Massachusetts, 1980).

26. [William S. Learned], "Main Functions of a 'Board of Educational Appraisal' or a 'General Examination Board,'" [August, 1937] and [Ben D. Wood], "The Establishment of a General Examination Board," December 29, 1936, CFAT Archive.

27. Ben D. Wood, "The Cooperative Test Service," *Educational Record,* 12 (1931): 246.

28. [Wood], "The Establishment of a General Examination Board," p. 22. See also "Confidential Memorandum from W. S. Learned [to Oliver C. Carmichael]," December 4, 1945, pp. 12–14, CFAT Archive; Downey, *Ben D. Wood,* pp. 37–42 and 49–56; and Kandel, *Examinations and Their Substitutes,* pp. 126–29.

29. W. S. Learned, "The Graduate Record Examination: A Memorandum on the General Character and Purpose of the Examination" (1941) CFAT Archives. See also Howard J. Savage, *Fruit of an Impulse: Forty-Five Years of the Carnegie Foundation, 1905–1950* (New York: Harcourt, Brace, 1953), pp. 286–304, and Crawford and Burnham, *Forecasting College Achievement,* pp. 118–23.

30. Wilford M. Aikin, *The Story of the Eight-Year Study* (New York: Harper & Brothers, 1942); Ralph W. Tyler, "Landmarks in the Literature: What Was Learned From the Eight-Year Study," *New York University Education Quarterly,* 11 (1980): 29–32.

31. Carnegie's financial investment in the Eight-Year Study is detailed in memoranda written by Howard J. Savage on March 6 and 7, 1941, CFAT Archive.

32. William S. Learned to Wilford M. Aikin, December 18, 1931, CFAT Archive.

33. William S. Learned to Eugene R. Smith, May 1, 1934, CFAT Archive; Eugene R. Smith, Ralph W. Tyler, and the Evaluation Staff, *Appraising and Recording Student Progress* (New York: Harper and Brothers, 1942), p. 5.

34. The disagreements between the CFAT and PEA were also described in an interview with Ralph W. Tyler, March 21, 1980, Chicago, Illinois.

35. Savage memorandum, March 7, 1941.

36. Ibid.

Establishing the Educational Testing Service

37. The circumstances of Conant's speech are described in James B. Conant, *My Several Lives: Memoirs of a Social Inventor* (New York: Harper & Row, 1970), pp. 424–26 and in the following correspondence: James B. Conant to Walter A. Jessup, September 28, 1937; Walter A. Jessup to James B. Conant, October 1, 1937; and William S. Learned to James B. Conant, October 3, 1937, CFAT Archive. Conant's optimistic views concerning the value of testing are also evident in some of his annual reports as president of Harvard, for example, "President's Report, 1936–1937," *Official Register of Harvard University,* 35 (1938): 5–18. See also Barry James Teicher, "James Bryant Conant and 'The

American High School Today'" (Ph.D. dissertation, University of Wisconsin at Madison, 1977).

38. Conant, *My Several Lives,* pp. 426–27.

39. Fuess, *The College Board,* pp. 120–21, 126.

40. Ibid., p. 122.

41. George W. Mullins to William S. Learned, April 8, 1937, CFAT Archive.

42. Fuess, *The College Board,* pp. 182–84. On Brigham, see Matthew T. Downey, *Carl C. Brigham: Scientist and Educator* (Princeton, N.J.: Educational Testing Service, 1961).

43. Carl C. Brigham, "The Place of Research in a Testing Organization," *School and Society,* 16 (1937): 756–59.

44. Ibid. Wood used the "snap-shot" analogy in many of his writings.

45. Brigham, "Research in a Testing Organization."

46. Carl W. Brigham to William S. Learned, January 4, 1938, CFAT Archive.

47. Carl W. Brigham to James B. Conant, January 3, 1938, CFAT Archive.

48. Brigham to Learned, January 26, 1938.

49. Downey, *Carl C. Brigham,* pp. 26–30; Lee J. Cronbach, "Five Decades of Public Controversy Over Mental Testing," in *Controversies and Decisions: The Social Sciences and Public Policy,* edited by Charles Frankel (New York: Russell Sage Foundation, 1976), pp. 123–47.

50. Conant, *My Several Lives,* p. 428.

51. The concerns of the Conant Committee are evident in the memoranda submitted by the various groups as well as in the participants' statements collected in the Carnegie Corporation's Oral History, Butler Library, Columbia University. See also "Merger of Educational Testing Agencies," Carnegie Corporation board meeting agenda, May 17, 1947, Carnegie Corporation of New York files.

52. Frank Bowles, *The Refounding of the College Board, 1948–1953: An Informal Commentary and Selected Papers* (New York: College Entrance Examination Board, 1967), p. 11. The final report of the Conant Committee is reproduced on pp. 12–17.

6. Renewing the Foundation

1. CFAT press release, January 24, 1967, CFAT Archive, New York City.

2. The history of the two groups is briefly summarized in Alan Pifer, "The Carnegie Commission on Higher Education," An Interim Report reprinted from *CFAT 63rd Annual Report* (1969–70); "The Nature and

Origins of the Carnegie Commission on Higher Education," a speech to
the Pennyvania Association of Colleges and Universities, October 16,
1972; and "A Foundation's Story: The First Seventy-Five Years of The
Carnegie Foundation for the Advancement of Teaching," reprinted from
the *CFAT 62nd Annual Report* (1978–79). A number of funding agencies in addition to the Carnegie Corporation and Foundation, particularly the U.S. Office of Education and the Ford Foundation, also contributed to support the Commission and the Council.

3. The CFAT's financial history is extraordinarily complex. As of June
30, 1965, when Foundation income began to meet pension expenses,
$14,600,000 had been advanced to the Foundation by the Carnegie
Corporation, and, as a result of a 1939 Court Order that allowed the
Foundation to borrow from its own endowment, $6,473,088 of the
Foundation's principal had been spent. Repayments started in 1966,
and, if continued, would have kept the Foundation in bondage until
approximately the year 2000. Corporation trustees therefore voted in
November, 1965, to make grants to the CFAT in the amount of the
repayments for projects within the Corporation's program interests. In
January, 1966, this arrangement was amended at the request of the
CFAT trustees to separate amounts of the annual grants from the
amount of the repayments, realizing that repayments would be small in
the early years. Finally, in 1972, the Corporation voted full forgiveness
of earlier loans and another Court Order was secured, making it unnecessary to further repay the Foundation's endowment. These actions gave
the CFAT free income of its own for the first time in many years. The
early details of the Foundation's financial history are available in
Howard J. Savage, *Fruit of an Impulse: The Carnegie Foundation for the
Advancement of Teaching, 1905–1930* (New York: Harcourt, Brace,
1953).

4. Henry S. Pritchett to Andrew Carnegie, November 16, 1905, CFAT
Archive.

Growth and Change in American Higher Education in the 1950s and 1960s

5. These figures and other statistics for this transformation can be
found in Seymour E. Harris, *A Statistical Portrait of Higher Education*
(New York: McGraw-Hill, 1972), chaps. 2.2 and 5.2.

6. Ibid., chap. 2.4.

7. Ibid., chap. 4.2.

8. Chester E. Finn, Jr., *Scholars, Dollars, and Bureaucrats* (Washington,
D.C.: Brookings Institution, 1978), p. 14. A general account of higher
education in the post-World War II era may be found in John S.
Brubacher and Willis Rudy, *Higher Education in Transition: A History of
American Colleges and Universities, 1636–1976,* third ed. (New York:
Harper & Row, 1976). Seymour E. Harris, *Higher Education: Resources*

and Finance (New York: McGraw-Hill, 1962) and Selma J. Mushkin, ed., *Economics of Higher Education* (U.S. Office of Education, Bulletin No. 5, 1962) are contemporary analyses of major economic trends in higher education.

9. Laurence R. Veysey, "Stability and Experiment in the American Undergraduate Curriculum," in *Content and Context: Essays on College Education,* edited by Carl Kaysen (New York: McGraw-Hill, 1973); Laurence R. Veysey, *The Emergence of the American University* (Chicago: University of Chicago Press, 1965); and Christopher Jencks and David Riesman, *The Academic Revolution* (Garden City, N.Y.: Doubleday, 1969).

An Emerging "Public"

10. *CFAT 49th–59th Annual Reports* (1955–1965); Clara Clapp memorandum to Lonnie A. Sharp, June 24, 1965 CFAT Archive. For more detail on this see Dorothy Eileen Bell, "A Phoenix in Our Midst: The Carnegie Foundation for the Advancement of Teaching and Its Relationship to American Higher Education 1950–1970" (Ph.D. dissertation, University of Illinois at Urbana-Champaign, 1972), pp. 56–68, 181–94

11. John W. Gardner, *Excellence: Can We Be Equal and Excellent Too?* (New York: Harper & Brothers, 1961).

12. One especially relevant, although often misinterpreted, discussion of these matters was Clark Kerr, *The Uses of the University* (New York: Harper & Row, 1963).

13. "Secretary's Informal Minutes" of a CFAT trustee meeting, May 6, 1960, CFAT Archive.

14. "Twenty-Six Campuses and the Federal Government," *Educational Record,* 44 (1963): 95–136, summarized this study's major findings.

15. Mary Clark Stuart, "Clark Kerr: Biography of an Action Intellectual" (Ph.D. dissertation, University of Michigan, 1980), chap. 7, deals especially perceptively with the effects of the 1960s on the Commission.

A New Collaboration

16. "Alan Pifer," *Current Biography* (1965), pp. 334–36.

17. Beginning with an essay called "The Quasi Nongovernmental Organization," Carnegie Corporation of New York, *Annual Report* (1967), Pifer discussed this theme frequently in Corporation *Annual Reports* throughout his presidency.

18. Earl F. Cheit and Theodore E. Lobman, *Foundations and Higher Education: Grant Making from Golden Years through Steady State,* a Technical Report for the Ford Foundation and the Carnegie Council on Policy Studies in Higher Education (San Francisco: Jossey-Bass, 1979), pp. 1–5.

19. *New York Herald Tribune*, August 29, 1965.

20. "Twenty-Six Campuses," *Educational Record,* p. 1.

21. "Secretary's Informal Minutes" of a CFAT trustee meeting, May 6, 1960, CFAT Archive.

22. "Record of Interview: Alan Pifer, Lloyd Morrisett, and Clark Kerr," December 21, 1966; Alan Pifer to Gaylord Harnwell, December 30, 1966, CFAT Archive.

23. "An Interview with Alan Pifer and Alden Dunham, April 4, 1979," *Oral History of the Carnegie Commission on Higher Education,* pp. 9–13, CFAT Archive.

24. CFAT press release, January 24, 1967.

25. "Interview with Pifer and Dunham," *Oral History,* pp. 3–4; Pifer, "A Foundation's Story," pp. 23–24. See also Verne A. Stadtman, *The University of California 1868–1968* (New York: McGraw-Hill, 1970), chaps. 26 and 27, and Stuart, "Clark Kerr," p. 7.

26. "Clark Kerr," *Current Biography* (1961), pp. 245–47.

27. My argument here is based on an interview with Clark Kerr, July 28, 1980, Berkeley, California, as well as on Stuart, "Clark Kerr." Especially for material on Kerr's years at the University of California see also Max Ways, "On the Campus: A Troubled Reflection of the U.S.," *Fortune Magazine* (September, 1965), pp. 131–35, 198, 202, 204, 209, 210, 213, 216, 221, and (October, 1965), pp. 140–46, 170, 178, 180, 182, 186.

28. Clark Kerr, John T. Dunlop, Frederick H. Harbison, and Charles A. Myers, *Industrialism and Industrial Man: The Problems of Labor and Management in Economic Growth* (Cambridge, Mass.: Harvard University Press, 1960), p. 1.

29. Interview with Kerr, July 28, 1980. The loyalty oath controversy and Kerr's involvement in it are described in Stadtman, *The University of California,* pp. 319–39, 377–78.

30. Clark Kerr, *Marshall, Marx and Modern Times: The Multi-Dimensional Society* (London: Cambridge University Press, 1969), pp. 4, 82, 100, 106.

31. Ibid., pp. 94 and 96.

The Carnegie Commission on Higher Education

32. "Interview with Pifer and Dunham," *Oral History,* pp. 21–22.

33. The members of the Commission are identified according to the titles they held when appointed.

34. "Interview with Pifer and Dunham," *Oral History,* pp. 21–22; Pifer "Nature and Origins of the Carnegie Commission," p. 5.

Quality and Equality

35. *Quality and Equality: New Levels of Federal Responsibility for Higher Education* (New York: McGraw-Hill, 1968).

36. Ibid., foreword; "Interview with Kerr," *Oral History*, pp. 5 and 31; and Stuart, "Clark Kerr," chap. 8.

37. I have taken the term "usable knowledge" from Charles E. Lindbloom and David K. Cohen, *Usable Knowledge: Social Science and Social Problem Solving* (New Haven: Yale University Press, 1979).

38. "Postscript—1972," *The Uses of the University* (Cambridge, Mass.: Harvard University Press, 1972), p. 143.

39. Interview with Kerr, July 28, 1980; "Interview with Kerr," *Oral History*, pp. 22–26. Kerr's capacities for leading the Commission to a consensus were repeatedly referred to in "Interview with Pifer and Dunham," and in "Interview with David Riesman, June 30 and July 1, 1979," *Oral History*.

40. *A Chance to Learn: An Action Agenda for Equal Opportunity in Higher Education* (March, 1970); *New Students and New Places: Policies for the Future Growth and Development of American Higher Education* (October, 1971); *Institutional Aid: Federal Support to Colleges and Universities* (February, 1972); *The Fourth Revolution: Instructional Technology in Higher Education* (June, 1972); *The More Effective Use of Resources: An Imperative for Higher Education* (June, 1972); *The Purposes and Performances of Higher Education in the United States: Approaching the Year 2000* (June, 1973); and *Higher Education: Who Pays? Who Benefits? Who Should Pay?* (June, 1973).

41. *The Capital and the Campus: State Responsibility for Postsecondary Education* (April, 1971); *Dissent and Disruption: Proposals for Consideration by the Campus* (June, 1971); and *Governance of Higher Education: Six Priority Problems* (April, 1973).

42. *The Open Door Colleges: Policies for Community Colleges* (June, 1970); *Higher Education and the Nation's Health: Policies for Medical and Dental Education* (October, 1970); *From Isolation to Mainstream: Problems of the Colleges Founded for Negroes* (February, 1971); and *The Campus and the City: Maximizing Assets and Reducing Liabilities* (December, 1972).

43. *Less Time, More Options: Education Beyond the High School* (January, 1971); *College Graduates and Jobs: Adjusting to a New Labor Market Situation* (April, 1973); *Continuity and Discontinuity: Higher Education and Schools* (August, 1973); *Opportunities for Women in Higher Education: Their Current Participation, Prospects for the Future, and Recommendations for Action* (September, 1973), and *Toward a Learning Society: Alternative Channels to Life, Work, and Service* (October, 1973). *Priorities for Action* (1973), a summary volume, touched on matters in all of the four broad categories I have drawn. All Commission reports, as well as its spon-

sored research studies, were published in New York by McGraw-Hill. The Commission also published *A Digest of Reports of the Carnegie Commission on Higher Education* (1974); Stuart, "Clark Kerr," pp. 285–320, treats the reports at length; Lewis B. Mayhew, *The Carnegie Commission on Higher Education* (San Francisco: Jossey-Bass, 1973) provides a thematic summary and review of Commission reports and sponsored research; and Jack Embling, *A Fresh Look at Higher Education: European Implications of the Carnegie Commission Reports* (Amsterdam: Elsevier Scientific Publishing, 1974) considers the Carnegie publications from a European perspective.

44. The quote is from *Quality and Equality,* p. 1; for the Commission's delineation of the differences between higher education and postsecondary education see *Toward A Learning Society.*

45. *Quality and Equality,* foreword.

46. *Quality and Equality* was quickly reviewed in newspapers and journals such as: *Business Week,* December 14, 1968; *Time,* December 20, 1968; *Saturday Review,* December 21, 1968; *The New York Times,* December 13, 14, and 15, 1968; *The Christian Science Monitor,* December 13, 1968; *The Philadelphia Inquirer,* December 13, 1968; and *The Baltimore Sun,* December 13, 1968. *Quality and Equality* was one of the most widely reviewed of the Commission's reports.

47. "Memorandum to Members of the Carnegie Commission from Clark Kerr," December 19, 1968, CFAT Archive.

48. See especially "Carnegie Impact on Pending Education Bills Termed 'Nil,' *College and University Business,* February, 1972, p. 33, and "Kerr Defends Carnegie Impact on Congress," *College and University Business,* May, 1972, p. 4. The position the Commission took on student aid set it in direct opposition to many of the higher education lobby groups in Washington, most of whom favored indirect student aid through lump sum grants to institutions. The Commission had favored direct student aid. To compare the recommendations set forth in *Quality and Equality* with other contemporary policy recommendations see *The Economics and Financing of Higher Education in the United States: A Compendium of Papers Submitted to the Joint Economic Committee, Congress of the United States* (Washington, D.C.: Government Printing Office, 1969).

49. In addition to the commentaries cited above see Pifer, "A Foundation's Story," p. 26, and "A Busy, Nostalgic Week Marks Windup of Carnegie Commission," *The Chronicle of Higher Education,* October 23, 1973, pp. 1 and 3.

50. "A Busy Week," *The Chronicle of Higher Education.*

51. In toto the Commission published 83 research studies. They are summarized in *Sponsored Research of the Carnegie Commission on Higher Education* (1975) as well as in Mayhew, *The Carnegie Commission.*

52. Donald McDonald, "The Carnegie Commission Study of Higher Education: A Six Million Dollar Misunderstanding," *The Center Magazine*, 6 (1973): 32–52 (the quotes are from p. 34). Two other critical views that also stressed the Commission's emphasis on relationships between education and economics are: Wendell V. Harris, "Jencks and the Carnegie Commission: Not So Different Answers to Perhaps the Wrong Question," *Journal of Higher Education*, 46 (1975): 213–25 and Hugh Wayne Jeffers, "A Critical Analysis of the Policy Reports and Recommendations of the Carnegie Commission on the Future of Higher Education" (Ph.D. dissertation, University of Oklahoma, 1974).

53. Samuel Bowles and Herbert Gintis, *Schooling in Capitalist America: Educational Reform and the Contradictions of Economic Life* (New York: Basic Books, 1976), p. 206. See also Alan Wolfe, "Reform without Reform: The Carnegie Commission on Higher Education," *Social Policy*, May/June, 1971, pp. 18–27.

54. Alan Pifer, "Future of the Carnegie Foundation for the Advancement of Teaching," April 5, 1971, p. 5, CFAT Archive.

The Carnegie Council on Policy Studies in Higher Education

55. *More Than Survival: Prospects for Higher Education in a Period of Uncertainty* (1975); *Low or No Tuition: The Feasibility of a National Policy for the First Two Years of College* (1975); *The States and Private Higher Education: Problems and Policies in a New Era* (1977); *Next Steps for the 1980s in Student Financial Aid: A Fourth Alternative* (1979). The phrase "depression" comes from Earl F. Cheit, *The New Depression in Higher Education: A Study of Financial Conditions of Fifty-One Colleges and Universities* (New York: McGraw-Hill, 1975), which was one of the Commission's sponsored research studies.

56. *Missions of the College Curriculum: A Contemporary Review with Suggestions* (1977).

57. *Giving Youth a Better Chance: Options for Education, Work, and Service* (1979).

58. *Faculty Bargaining in Public Higher Education: A Report and Two Essays* (1977).

59. *Making Affirmative Action Work in Higher Education: An Analysis of Institutional and Federal Policies with Recommendations* (1975); *Selective Admission in Higher Education: Comment and Recommendations and Two Reports* (1977); and *Fair Practices in Higher Education: Rights and Responsibilities of Students and Their Colleges in a Period of Intensified Competition for Enrollment* (1979).

60. *Progress and Problems in Medical and Dental Education: Federal Support Versus Federal Control* (1976). The Council's final report was *Three Thousand Futures: The Next Twenty Years for Higher Education* (1980). All Council reports, as well as its sponsored research studies, were pub-

lished in San Francisco by Jossey-Bass.

61. Interview with Alan Pifer, September 11, 1980, New York City.

62. Pifer, "A Foundation's Story," p. 28.

63. The members of the Council are identified according to the titles they held when appointed.

Appraisals of the Carnegie Council

64. "Interview with Kerr," *Oral History,* pp. 11, 10, 7, and 8.

65. Interview with Pifer, September 11, 1980.

66. This is evident in many Pifer essays for Carnegie Corporation Annual Reports. See especially, "Carnegie Corporation in a Changing Society, 1961–1981," Carnegie Corporation of New York, *Annual Report* (1981), which indicates this concern in Corporation programs as well as in Pifer's comments on them.

67. Pifer, "Foundations and Public Policy Formation," Carnegie Corporation of New York, *Annual Report* (1974).

68. Ibid., pp. 3, 5–6, 7–8, 9, 13.

A Renewed, Reestablished, and Reorganized Foundation

69. "Report to the Board of Trustees from the Special Committee on the Future of the CFAT," December 24, 1977, CFAT Archive.

70. Pifer, "A Foundation's Story," p. 26.

PART III

1. John Dewey, *The Public and Its Problems* (1927; Chicago: Swallow Press, 1954).

2. Jane Addams, *Democracy and Social Ethics,* edited by Anne Firor Scott (1902; Cambridge, Mass.: Harvard University Press, 1964), p. 220.

7. Corporate vs. State Responsibility:
Henry Pritchett and "The Social Philosophy of Pensions"

1. Henry S. Pritchett, *The Social Philosophy of Pensions with a Review of Existing Pension Systems for Professional Groups,* CFAT Bulletin Number 25 (1930).

The Financial Problems of Carnegie Pensions

2. All of this can be followed in the CFAT *Annual Reports;* Howard J. Savage, *Fruit of an Impulse: Forty-Five Years of the Carnegie Foundation, 1905–1950* (New York: Harcourt, Brace, 1953) deals extensively with the Foundation's pension rule; the phrase "strong men" is from *CFAT 1st Annual Report* (1906), p. 37.

3. *CFAT 2nd Annual Report* (1907), p. 65

4. Savage, *Fruit of an Impulse,* p. 67.

5. *The Financial Status of the Professor in America and in Germany,* CFAT Bulletin Number 2 (1908), viii.

6. Savage, *Fruit of an Impulse,* pp. 80–81.

7. The application is in the CFAT Archive, New York City.

8. Savage, *Fruit of an Impulse,* pp. 83–85, 113–14.

The "Moral" Problems of Carnegie Pensions

9. *CFAT 6th Annual Report* (1911), p. 23.

10. Commonwealth of Massachusetts, *Report of the Commission on Old Age Pensions, Annuities and Insurance* (Boston: Wright & Potter, 1910), pp. 324–30.

11. Ibid., p. 317.

12. Ibid.

13. Henry S. Pritchett to Professor Shipley, February 24, 1910, CFAT Archive.

14. *CFAT 6th Annual Report,* pp. 30–31.

15. Ibid.

16. Savage, *Fruit of an Impulse,* pp. 85–89.

17. Henry S. Pritchett to Frank A. Vanderlip, January 22, 1912, Frank A. Vanderlip Papers, Rare Book and Manuscript Library, Columbia University, New York City.

18. Typical examples of the criticisms to which Pritchett was subjected can be found in J. McKeen Cattell, *Carnegie Pensions* (New York: Science Press, 1919) and in Claude Charleton Bowman, "The College Professor in America: An Analysis of Articles Published in General Magazines, 1890–1938" (Ph.D. dissertation, University of Pennsylvania, 1938), pp. 57–63.

19. Henry S. Pritchett to Nicholas Murray Butler, February 4, 1919, Nicholas Murray Butler Papers, Rare Book and Manuscript Library, Columbia University, New York City.

20. *CFAT 6th Annual Report,* p. 31.

The Challenge of Social Insurance

21. David Hackett Fischer, *Growing Old in America* (New York: Oxford University Press, 1977), p. 157.

22. W. Andrew Aschenbaum, *Old Age in the New Land: The American Experience Since 1790* (Baltimore: Johns Hopkins University Press, 1978), pp. 58–59, 95–102.

23. Ibid., pp. 47–51, 82–83; Fischer, *Growing Old in America,* pp. 157–87.

24. Sorel Tishler, *Self-Reliance and Social Security, 1870–1917* (Port Washington, N.Y.: Kennikat Press, 1971), pp. 49–50.

25. I. M. Rubinow, *Social Insurance* (New York: Henry Holt, 1913), p. 3.

26. Ibid., p. 491. Arguments similar to Rubinow's may also be found in Lee Welling Squier, *Old Age Dependency in the United States: A Complete Survey of the Pension Movement* (New York: Macmillan, 1912), which summarized a great deal of contemporary literature on the subject.

27. Resistance to social insurance is especially well described in Roy Lubove, *The Struggle for Social Security, 1900–1935* (Cambridge, Mass.: Harvard University Press, 1968). The quotes are on p. 103.

28. Aschenbaum, *Old Age in America,* pp. 120–25, 131–33; Fischer, *Growing Old in America,* pp. 157–87; and Louis Leotta, "Abraham Epstein and the Movement for Old Age Security," *Labor History,* 16 (1975): 359–77.

29. Henry S. Pritchett, *A Comprehensive Plan of Insurance and Annuities for College Teachers,* CFAT Bulletin Number 9 (1916), pp. xviii–xix.

The Comprehensive Plan: TIAA

30. Ibid., pp. 48–49.

31. *CFAT 6th Annual Report,* pp. 30–31.

32. Ibid., pp. 27–28.

33. *Comprehensive Plan,* pp. 37–41, 49.

34. Ibid., p. 21.

35. Ibid., p. 50.

36. *CFAT 22nd Annual Report* (1927), pp. 41–45.

37. Henry S. Pritchett to A. Barton Hepburn, November 12, 1917, CFAT Archive.

38. Savage, *Fruit of an Impulse,* pp. 115–20.

39. *Social Philosophy of Pensions,* p. 24.

40. Alan Pifer, "Fifty Years of TIAA: Its Past and Promise," *Educational Record* (1968), p. 411, reprint, CFAT Archive.

41. Examples of proposals for state pension systems modeled after TIAA are described in Clyde Furst and I. L. Kandel, *Pensions for Public School Teachers,* CFAT Bulletin Number 12 (1918) and Clyde Furst, Raymond L. Mattocks, and Howard J. Savage, *Retiring Allowances for Officers and Teachers in Virginia Public Schools,* CFAT Bulletin Number 17 (1926).

42. *Social Philosophy of Pensions,* pp. 4–5.

43. Henry S. Pritchett to Nicholas Murray Butler, July 22, 1929, Butler Papers.

44. William C. Greenough and Francis P. King, *Pension Plans and Public Policy* (New York: Columbia University Press, 1976), pp. 27–67.

45. A useful contemporary analysis of the Social Security Act by a proponent of social insurance is Paul H. Douglas, *Social Security in the United States: An Analysis and Appraisal of the Social Security Act* (New York: Whittlesey House, 1936); a recent analysis is Martha Derthick, *Policymaking for Social Security* (Washington, D.C.: Brookings Institution, 1979).

46. Lubove, *The Struggle for Social Security,* p. 179.

Liberty and Efficiency through Voluntary Associations

47. *Social Philosophy of Pensions,* p. 8.

48. Ibid., esp. pp. 6–11.

49. Herbert Hoover, *American Individualism* (Garden City, N.Y.: Doubleday, Page, 1923), p. 31.

50. There has been a great deal of new work on Herbert Hoover, much of which is described in the bibliography in Joan Hoff Wilson, *Herbert Hoover: Forgotten Progressive* (Boston: Little, Brown, 1975). My argument is derived especially from Wilson, chaps. 3, 4, and 5.

51. Henry S. Pritchett to Charles W. Eliot, August 22, 1924, Henry S. Pritchett Papers, Library of Congress, Washington, D.C.

52. Charles W. Eliot to Henry S. Pritchett, August 29, 1924, Pritchett Papers.

53. Henry S. Pritchett to Herbert Hoover, January 10, 1937, Pritchett Papers. Frances Perkins was FDR's Secretary of Labor.

54. Wilson, *Herbert Hoover,* chap. 3; Barry D. Karl, "Presidential Planning and Social Science Research: Mr. Hoover's Experts," *Perspectives in American History,* III (1969): 347–409.

8. Central vs. Local Control: The Carnegie Foundation and Its Critics

1. Henry S. Pritchett, "Should the Carnegie Foundation Be Suppressed?" *North American Review* (1915), reprint in CFAT Archive.

Josiah Royce and "Provincialism"

2. Josiah Royce, "The Carnegie Foundation for the Advancement of Teaching and the Case of Middlebury College," *School and Society,* 1 (1915): 145–50.

3. Ibid., p. 145.

4. Ibid., p. 146.

5. Ibid., pp. 148 and 149.

6. R. Jackson Wilson, *In Quest of Community: Social Philosophy in the United States, 1860–1920* (New York: Oxford University Press, 1968), p. 150.

7. Josiah Royce, *The Philosophy of Loyalty* (New York: Macmillan, 1920), pp. 16–17.

8. Ibid., p. 248. See also Bruce Kuklick, *The Rise of American Philosophy: Cambridge, Massachusetts, 1860–1930* (New Haven: Yale University Press, 1977).

9. Royce did not use this word, but it is clearly implied in his *School and Society* article, see the quote above, note 4.

Herbert Croly and "The New Nationalism"

10. Two useful commentaries on Croly's thought are: Charles Forcey, *The Crossroads of Liberalism* (New York: Oxford University Press, 1961) and Samuel Haber, *Efficiency and Uplift: Scientific Management in the Progressive Era 1890–1920* (Chicago: University of Chicago Press, 1964).

11. Herbert Croly, *The Promise of American Life* (1909; New York: E. P. Dutton, 1963), p. 434.

12. Ibid., p. 441.

13. Ibid., p. 454.

14. Ibid., p. 402.

15. Ibid., chap. 13.

16. Ibid., passim.

Other Proponents of "Local Self-Interest"

17. James R. Day to Henry S. Pritchett, February 28, 1910, CFAT Archive, New York City.

18. Abraham Flexner, *Medical Education in the United States and Canada,* CFAT Bulletin Number 4 (1910), pp. 272–73.

19. Day to Pritchett, February 28, 1910.

20. Henry S. Pritchett to James R. Day, April 19, 1910, CFAT Archive.

21. This resolution is quoted and discussed in "Why the Carnegie Resolutions? "*Journal of Education,* 80 (1914): 311–12.

22. Howard J. Savage, *Fruit of an Impulse: Forty-Five Years of the Carnegie Foundation 1905–1950* (New York: Harcourt, Brace, 1953), pp. 136–37.

23. Henry S. Pritchett to W. S. Dearmont, April 25, 1914, CFAT Archive.

24. *Notable American Women,* s.v. "Margaret Angela Haley"; David B. Tyack, *The One Best System: A History of American Urban Education* (Cambridge, Mass.: Harvard University Press, 1974), pp. 169–70.

Pritchett's Legacy

25. "How Can Carnegie Corporation Attack Poverty? A Report from the Task Force on the Disadvantaged," submitted by Stephen H. Stackpole, Margaret E. Mahoney, Frederic A. Mosher, Barbara D. Finberg, Eli Evans, October 16, 1967, Carnegie Corporation of New York files.

26. "Carnegie Corporation's Program: Where We Are and How We Got There," Sara L. Engelhardt and David Z. Robinson, March 11, 1980, Carnegie Corporation of New York files.

27. Alan Pifer, "A Foundation's Story: The First Seventy-Five Years of The Carnegie Foundation for the Advancement of Teaching," reprinted from the *CFAT 62nd Annual Report* (1978–79), p. 28.

Index

A Study of American Intelligence,
119–120
academic freedom, 91–92
Addams, Jane, xvii, 156
American Association for Labor Legislation, 167
American Association of Law Schools, 77
American Association of University Professors (AAUP), 91–92, 171, 180
American Bar Association (ABA), 75, 77, 82–83
American College, The, 66–67
American Council on Education, 109, 110, 111
American Individualism, 174–175
American Institute of Electrical Engineers, 84
American Institute of Mining, Metallurgical and Petroleum Engineers, 84
American Law Institute, 78
American Medical Association (AMA): Council on Medical Education, 64–66, 67–68, 71, 72, 74; membership, 65
American Naturalist, 91
American Society of Civil Engineers, 84
American Society of Mechanical Engineers, 84
Anderson, James D., 204
Andrews, F. Emerson, 197, 198, 199
anti-Semitism, 82, 167
Army Alpha, 100
Arnove, Robert F., 203
Ashby, Eric, 138

Association of American Medical Colleges, 64
Association of American Universities, 171
Association of Colleges and Secondary Schools of the Middle States and Maryland, 99, 101, 102, 103
astronomy, 23–26, 29

Bache, Alexander Dallas, 27
Bachrach, Peter, 202
Bagley, William C., 87
Baker, George F., 49
Basic Educational Opportunity Grants, xii, 142
Beard, Charles, 75
Bellamy, Edward, 14
Berman, Edward H., 203
Bertram, James, 41, 54
Besse, Ralph M., 137
Bevan, Arthur Dean, 64–66
Binet, Alfred, 107
Bodleian Library (Oxford), 42
Botta, Anne Charlotte Lynch, 7–12, 48
Bowdoin College, 70
Bowen, William G., 145
Bowles, Frank, 120
Bowles, Samuel, 143
Boyer, Ernest L., 145, 151
Brandes, Stuart D., 204
Brandt, Lilian, 197
Bremner, Robert H., 200
Brigham, Carl C., 100, 117–120
Brookings, Robert S., 72
Bruce, Robert, 5
Bryant, William Cullen, 8

Bulmer, Martin, 202
Burns, Robert, 5
Butler, Nicholas Murray: and CEEB, 99; and NEA, 96, 189; as CFAT trustee, 37, 38, 89, 160–161, 173

Cardinal Principles of Secondary Education, 98, 102, 114
Carnegie, Andrew: attitude toward experts, 41, 43–44; attitude toward pensions, 17, 42–43, 48, 53–54, 213*n*37; business, 3, 4, 12–13, 48–53; education, 7–12; family, 5, 6, 10; personality, 4–5; philanthropies, 3, 17, 48, 184; relationship with Pritchett, 1–2, 21, 37, 44–55; religious values, 4, 6–12, 19; view of CFAT, 17, 37, 50–55, 66; view of philanthropy, 1–2, 5, 12–20, 41–44, 184; writings, 196
Carnegie Commission on Educational Television, 131
Carnegie Commission on Higher Education, x, 57, 131; appraisals of, 142–143, 150–153; meetings, 122, 138–140; members, 122,136–138; publications, 122, 128–142
Carnegie Commission on the Future of Public Broadcasting, 131
Carnegie Corporation of New York, 3, 41, 52, 73, 78, 197; and poverty, 191–192; and testing, 111, 112, 120; financial support for CFAT, 111, 122, 123, 127, 131, 169, 226*n*3
Carnegie Council on Policy Studies in Higher Education, 57, 131; appraisals of, 150–153; meetings, 122; members, 122, 144–145; publications, 122, 143–144
Carnegie Council on Children, 131
Carnegie Endowment for International Peace, 3
Carnegie Foundation for the Advancement of Teaching (CFAT): alliance with medical reformers, 59–61, 71, 216*n*20; alliance with legal reformers, 74–76; alliance with engineering reformers, 84–85; alliance with testing agencies, 96, 108–121; and politics of knowledge, xii–xiv, 57– 58,

150–153; as agency of policy review, 67, 83, 127–128, 151–153; as proponent of educational systematization, xi, 57–58, 94–96, 113–114, 123–124; as proponent of university, 21–22, 39–41, 59; Bulletins: *see Comprehensive Plan, Education in Vermont, Flexner report, Mann report, Pennsylvania Study, Reed report, Social Philosophy of Pensions, The;* Carnegie's view of, 17, 37, 50–55, 66; charters, ix, 60, 66, 176; critics of, 90–93, 118–119, 156–157,164–165,179–193; election of presidents, 21, 37, 109, 126, 129; pension rules, 39–40, 52, 160–161, 164, 186; Pritchett's view of, xii– xiii, 3 7–44, 60–61; trustees of, xiii, 37–39, 43–44, 60, 66, 137–138, 144–145, 155–157, 211*n*1
Carnegie Institute of Pittsburgh, 3, 43
Carnegie Institution of Washington, 3, 21, 4 2–44, 47, 5 4
Carnegie libraries, 41, 46
Carnegie Pensions, 91
"Carnegie Unit," 57, 95, 105, 107, 113
Cattell, James McKeen, 45, 91–92, 180
Chambers, M. S., 199
Chandler, Alfred D., Jr., 12, 20 1
Channing, William Ellery, 9, 10, 12
Cohen, Stanley, 202
Coffman, Harold Coe, 199
Coffman, Lotus D., 102
College Entrance Examination Board (CEEB), 98–101, 103, 107, 115–117,120
Columbia University, 110, 128
Committee on College Entrance Requirements (NEA), 95
Commission on the Reorganization of Secondary Education (NEA), *see Cardinal Principles of Secondary Education*
Committee of Ten on Secondary School Studies (NEA), 95, 96–98, 113
Common Law and the Case Method in American University Law Schools,

The, 75–76
Commons, John R., 167
community: conceptions of, xiii–xiv, 1–2,150,155–157,190–193; Carnegie's view of, 1–2, 4–5, 14–19; Croly's view of, 183–184; Dewey's view of, 155; Pritchett's view of, 1–2, 156, 174–178, 187; Royce's view of, 181–183
Comprehensive Plan of Insurance and Annuities for College Teachers, 168–172. *See also* Teachers Insurance and Annuity Association (TIAA)
Conant, James B., 115–120
Cooper, Peter, 19
Cooperative Test Service (CTS), 109–111, 120
Conkin, Paul K., 202
Cornell, Mrs. Ezra, 48
Cornell University, 8
Corner, George, 197
Cosand, Joseph P., 137
Cosmos Club, 24, 26, 28
Craighead, Edwin B., 38
Croly, Herbert, 183–184, 189–190
Cuninggim, Merriman, 195
Curti, Merle, 199–201

Daniels, George H., 26
Dartmouth College, 70
Day, James R., 185, 188
Dearborn, Walter F., 87
democratic governance, xi–xiii, 155–157, 159–160, 189–193. *See also* elites; expertise; leadership; representation; voluntary associations
denominational colleges, 40, 42
Denver and Gross College of Medicine, 70
Dewey, John, xvii, 155
Diggins, John Patrick, 202
Dunham, E. Alden, 137
Dunlop, John T., 133

Eastman, John R., 23
Education in Vermont, 89–93, 180
Educational Record, The, 96
Educational Records Bureau, 115–116
educational standards, 57, 107, 123,

190–191; Carnegie's view of, 42; in colleges, 39–41, 94–95, 127–128, 160; in engineering, 84–85; in high schools, 95–99, 102–103; in law, 74–83; in medicine, 62–66, 69–71; in teacher training, 88–89, 93; Pritchett's view of, 29–31, 61, 74–76, 98, 121, 160; universalism vs. pluralism, 180–181, 182, 183
Educational Testing Service (ETS), xi, 96, 115–121
Eight-Year Study (PEA), 112–114, 116
Eliot, Charles W., 175, 189; and Committee of Ten (NEA), 96; as CFAT trustee, 37, 38, 52, 160; as president of Harvard University, 31, 47, 115
elites, xiv; Kerr's view of, 133–136, 149–150, Lasswell's definition of, 156; Pritchett's view of, 163–164. *See also* democratic governance; expertise; leadership
Elliot, Edward C., 199
Ellison, Nolen M., 145
Ely, Richard T., 167
Embree, Edwin R., 197
Emerson, Ralph Waldo, 8, 9, 10, 12
Employee Retirement Income Security Act, 172
engineering education, 84–85. *See also* Mann report; professionalization
Engineering Education, see Mann report
Epstein, Abraham, 167, 173
enrollments: in high schools, 96–99; in higher education, 124–126; in law schools, 76–77; in medical schools, 61, 62
equality: as goal of Carnegie Commission on Higher Education, 127, 141, 152; Carnegie's view of, 4, 6, 14–18, 184
equity, 192
Ettling, John, 198
Eurich, Nell P., 145
Evans, Daniel J., 145
Excellence, 127
expertise, xii, 156; Carnegie's view

of, 41, 43–44; Pifer's view of,
130–131, 149–150; Pritchett's
view of, xvii, 41, 43–44, 55, 156.
See also democratic governance;
elites; leadership; science

Farnum, Henry, 167
Fischer, David Hackett, 165
Fleming, Donald, 63
Flexner, Abraham, 196, 198; biography of Pritchett, 22, 25, 67, 82,
196; career, 66–67, 73. *See also*
Flexner report
Flexner, Simon, 67
Flexner report (on medical education), xi, 57, 61, 186; circumstances at time of, 61–66; compared to Reed report, 76, 81, 83;
outcomes of, 72–73; summary of,
68–71; writing of, 67–68
Fosdick, Raymond B., 196, 197
foundation philanthropy: historiography of, 195–205
Frankfurter, Felix, 78
Fraternal Order of Eagles, 167
Fretwell, Elbert K., Jr., 145
Frick, Henry Clay, 4
Friday, William, 137
Fuller, Margaret, 7
Fulton, William, 198
Fund for the Improvement of Postsecondary Education, 142

Gage, Lyman J., 28, 32, 38
Galambos, Louis W., 201
Gardner, John W., 126–127, 129,
131, 196
Gates, Frederick T., 196
General Education Board (GEB), 72,
109, 113, 197
General Electric, 85
George, Henry, 14
German education, 26, 29; admiration for, 28, 50, 85, 101; in medicine, 62–63, 67
Gilder, Richard Watson, 4
Gilman, Daniel Coit, 42, 47
Gintis, Herbert, 143
Gladstone, William, 42
Glenn, John M., 197
"Gospel of Wealth, The," *see*

"Wealth"
Graduate Record Examination
(GRE), 110–111, 120
"Great Society, The," 1, 35, 55, 121,
155–157, 179, 180
Greeley, Horace, 7
Greenleaf, William, 197

Hague Temple, 48
Haislip, Bryan, 197
Hale, Edward Everett, 166
Haley, Margaret, 188–189
Hall, Asaph, 23
Halstead, William S., 63
Harbison, Frederick H., 133
Harkness, William, 23
Harper, William Rainey, 37, 38, 189
Harper's Weekly, 96
Harris, Patricia Roberts, 137
Harris, William Torrey, 96
Harvard University, 96, 110, 115,
118; Graduate School of Education, 101; Law School, 77, 78, 80;
Medical School, 70. *See also*
Lawrence School of Science
Haskell, Thomas L., 201
Hays, Samuel P., 33, 204
Health Manpower Training Act of
1971, 142
Hendrick, Burton J., 197
Henry, David P., 137
Hesburgh, Theodore M., 137
Heywood, Stanley, 138
high school, 96–99, 101, 102–103
Higham, John, 1, 202
higher education: enrollments, 124
125; financing, 125, 127,
130–131, 139, 140, 142; growth,
124–126
Higher Education Act in 1965, 131
*Higher Education and the Nation's
Health,* 142
Hillegas, Milo B., 89
Hollis, Ernest Victor, 199
Hoover, Herbert, 159, 174–176,
178, 189
Homestead Strike, 4
Howard Medical School, 73
Howe, Barbara, 203
Howe, Julia Ward, 7

IBM, 107
Industrialism and Industrial Man,
   133–134
individualism: Carnegie s view of, 2,
   4–6, 10, 13–19, 35, 48, 53–55;
   Pritchett's view of, 2, 34–35,
   159–160, 174–178, 180, 187;
   Royce's view of, 181–183

Jackson, Dugold, 84
Jencks, Christopher, 126
Jenks, J. W., 167
Jessup, Walter A., 109, 115
Johns Hopkins University, 24, 28,
   42, 66, 92; Medical School, 62,
   63–64, 67–68, 70, 72
Jordan, David Starr, 37, 38
junior colleges, 124–125

Kansas Medical College, 70
Karl, Barry D., 204
Kaysen, Carl, 137
Keller, Morton, 14
Keniston, Kenneth, 138
Kent State University, 128
Keppel, Frederick P., 198
Kerr, Clark, 57, 122; and University
   of California, 132, 134; education
   and thought, 132–136, 145–146,
   149–150; leadership style,
   139–140; view of Carnegie Com-
   mission and Carnegie Council,
   145–146
Kohler, Robert E., 202

Lankford, John, 200
Larsen, Roy E., 137
Laski, Harold J., 198
Lawrence School of Science (Harvard
   University), 31, 38, 47
leadership: Croly's view of, 183–184;
   Kerr's view of, 132–136,
   145–146, 149–150; Pifer's view
   of, 130–131, 132, 146, 149–150;
   Pritchett's view of, 29–30, 35–36,
   156, 190–191
Learned, William S., 101–104, 105,
   108–119, 187
Leffingwell, Russell C., 78
legal education: case method, 78–79;
   enrollments, 76–77; numbers of
   law schools, 76; standards for,

74–76, 79–81, 82–84. *See also* pro-
   fessionalization; Reed report
Lewis, William Draper, 77–78
liberty: Pritchett's view of, 175–178,
   180
Lindemann, Edward Christian, 199
Lindsay, Samuel McCune, 167
Lowell, A. Lawrence, 115
Lubove, Roy, 173
Ludmerer, Kenneth, 72

McBride, Katharine E., 137
McConnell, Grant, 201
McDonald, Donald, 142
McIlhanny, William H., II, 195
McMurray, Charles A., 87
MacVicar, Margaret, 145
Mann, Charles R., 85
Mann report (on engineering educa-
   tion), 85
Marshall, Marx and Modern Times,
   135–136
Massachusetts Commission on Old
   Age Pensions, Annuities and
   Insurance, 162–163
Massachusetts Institute of Technolo-
   gy (MIT): pensions for, 42, 47, 48,
   163; Pritchett as president of, 21,
   28–32, 38, 46, 47
Mattingly, Paul H., 87
Mavety, Jane H., 196
medical education, 38, 141; enroll-
   ments, 61, 62; numbers of medical
   schools, 61, 70, 72, 73; standards
   for, 61–62, 69–71. *See also* Flexner
   report; professionalization
Medical Education in the United States,
   see Flexner report
Meharry Medical College, 73
Mendenhall, Thomas C., 27, 28
Merton, Robert K., 201
Messenger, J. F., 90
Middlebury College, 90, 180–181
Missouri Study, 86–89, 187
Morgan, J. P., 3, 49
Morrisett, Lloyd N., 136–137
Mullins, George W., 117
Myers, Charles A., 133

National Association of State Universities, 171

National Bureau of Standards, 27–28, 32, 46–47, 49–50
National Confederation of State Medical and Licensing Boards, 64
National Education Association (NEA), 88, 95, 187–189
Naval Observatory, 23, 24, 25
New Deal, 184
"New Nationalism, The," 183–184
New Republic, 183
Newcomb, Simon, 23
Nevins, Allan, 197
Newman, Frank, 145
Nielson, Waldemar A., 195
Nineteenth Century Club, 8
normal schools, 86, 87, 88, 187–188
North American Review, 14, 17, 45, 46
Norwich University, 90

Outlook, 40

Park, Rosemary, 145
Peirce, Benjamin, 27
Pennsylvania Railroad, 3, 7
Pennsylvania Study, 108, 109, 112, 114, 187; summary of, 103–107
pensions, 48; CFAT rules for, 39–40, 52, 160–161, 164, 186; corporate responsibility for, 48, 159, 162, 170. *See also Social Philosophy of Pension, The;* TIAA
Perkins, James A., 137, 145
Phalen, Clifton W., 137
Philosophy of Loyalty, The, 182
Pifer, Alan, 129–132; attitude toward experts, 149–150; view of Carnegie Commission, 143; view of Carnegie Council, 144, 146; view of philanthropy, 130–132, 146–150, 151, 191–193
Platt, Joseph B., 145
Poe, Edgar Allan, 7
Popular Science Monthly, 91
postsecondary education, 57, 122, 141, 151
Present–Day Law Schools in the United States and Canada, 76
Princeton University, 110, 164
Pritchett, Henry Smith: advocate of educational hierarchy, 21–22, 29–36, 121; advocate of social efficiency, 2, 27–28, 32–36, 41, 57;

and Flexner report, 60–61, 66, 74; and Reed report, 75–76, 79, 82; as president of TIAA, 172; as trustee of Carnegie Corporation, 41–42; at MIT, 21, 28–32, 38, 46, 47; at University of Munich, 26, 29; at U.S. Coast and Geodetic Survey, 26–28; at Washington University, 25, 26, 62; attitude toward experts, xvii, 41, 43–44, 55, 156; education, 23–26, 82; faith in science, 2, 23, 30, 31, 34–36, 54–55, 156; family, 23, 25, 26, 82, 161; personality, 22–23, 47; relationship with Carnegie, 1–2, 21, 37, 44–55; religious values, 23, 24, 26, 34–35; response to critics, 179–193; view of CFAT, xv, 37–44, 52–53, 60–61; view of national development, 32–36, 50, 55, 57, 155–157; view of pensions, 47–48, 159–173; view of philanthropy, 1–2, 44; view of testing, 95, 98
professional education, 32–33, 57, 61. *See also* Flexner report; Mann report; Missouri study; Reed report
Professional Preparation of Teachers for American Public Schools, The, see Missouri study
professionalization, 47, 59–60; in engineering, 84–86; in law, 75–83; in medicine, 61–73; in science, 24–29, 54; in teaching, 85–89, 91–93
progress: Carnegie's view of, 2, 9, 11–12, 14–20, 53–55; Kerr's view of, 136; Pritchett's view of, 2, 32 36, 54–55, 156
Progressive Education Association (PEA), 111–114, 116. *See also* Eight-Year Study
Promise of American Life, The, 183–184
Prudden, T. Mitchell, 63
Public and its Problems, The, 155, 184
Purcell, Edward A., Jr., 201
Pusey, Nathan M., 127–128, 137

Quality and Equality: New Levels of Federal Responsibility for Higher

Education, 138–142. *See also*
Carnegie Commission on Higher
Education
*Quality of the Educational Process in the
United States and Europe, The,* 102

racism, 119, 175
Redlich, Joseph, 75
Reagan, Ronald, 132
Reed, Alfred Z., 75
Reed report (on legal education) cir-
cumstances prior to, 76–79; com-
pared to Flexner report, 76, 81,
83; outcomes of, 76, 79, 81–84;
summary of, 79–81
Reeves, Thomas, 199
Remsen, Ira, 66
*Report of the Princeton Conference on the
History of Philanthropy in the United
States,* 199
representation, 137–138, 144–145,
157, 192–193; Kerr's view of,
146, 149–150; Pifer's view of,
146–150, 192
*Review of Legal Education in the United
States and Canada,* 76
Riesman, David, 126, 137
Rice, Lois R., 145
Rockefeller Institute for Medical
Research, 67
Rockefeller, John D., 196
Rockefeller, John D., Jr., 49
Rodgers, Daniel T., 13
Roosevelt, Franklin D., 167, 189
Roosevelt, Theodore, 34 , 46, 162,
183
Root, Elihu, 82
Root, Oren, 82
Rosebery, Lord, 5
Rosenberg, Charles E., 201,
Roth, William M., 145
Rousseau, Jean Jacques, 2
Roy, Rob, 5
Royal Institute (London), 45
Royce, Josiah, 90–93, 179,
180–183, 184–186, 188, 192
Rubinow, Isaac, M., 166, 167; 173
Rudy, William H., 199
Rule, James N., 101, 103, 104
Rush Medical College, 64

Scholastic Aptitude Test (SAT),
99–100, 117
School and Society, 90, 91, 117, 180
Schlabach, Theron F., 200
Schurman, Jacob Gould, 36
science, xiv; and law, 78–79; and
medicine, 62–64, 69; and social
planning, 152–153; in Pritchett's
career, 23–29; professionalization
of, 24–29. *See also* Pritchett
Science, 27, 45, 91
Scranton, William W., 137
Seager, Henry, 167
Sears, Jesse Brundage, 199
Silva, Edward T., 203
Simon, Norton, 137
Sizer, Theodore R., 96
Slaughter, Sheila, 203
social Darwinism, *see* Spencer, Herbert
Social Insurance, 165–168, 190
Social Philosophy of Pensions, The, 159,
173–174
Social Security Act of 1935, 167,
173
Society for the Promotion of Engi-
neering Education (SPEE), 84
specialization: in education, 87–89,
91–93; in engineering, 84–86; in
law, 77–79; in medicine, 63
Spencer, Herbert, 8, 9, 12
Spurr, Stephen H., 145
St. Andrew's University, 9, 10
state universities, 39–40, 42, 90,
171
Stanford, Leland, 19
stewardship of wealth, 1–2, 5,
16–20. *See also* Carnegie, view of
philanthropy
Stillman, James, 49
Starrett, Agnes Lynch, 197
Stocking, George W., Jr., 203
Stratton, Samuel S., 28
Struggle for Social Security, The, 173
Student and His Knowledge, The, see
Pennsylvania Study
Swedenborg, 10
Syracuse University, 185–186
systematization of education, *see*
Carnegie Foundation, as proponent
of teacher education, 85–89, 187.
See also Missouri study

Teachers Insurance and Annuity Association (TIAA), xii, 53–54, 123, 168–173
Tennessee Medical College, 70
Terman, Lewis M., 107
testing, 57; agencies for, 98–101, 108–114, 115–117, 120–121; for college admission, 95, 98–100, 108; norm–referenced, 105, 152; views of, 94–96, 105–107, 111–114, 116–121. *See also* Pennsylvania Study
Thorndike, Edward L., 104
Tobey, Ronald C., 204
Tollett, Kenneth, 137
Tompkins, Pauline, 145
Training for the Public Profession of the Law, see Reed report
trusteeship of wealth, *see* stewardship of wealth
Tucker, William Jewett, 18–19
Tulane University, 38
Tyler, Ralph W., xix

University and Bellevue Hospital Medical College, 70
University Control, 92
University of California, 132–133, 134
University of Minnesota, General College, 102–103
University of Vermont, 90
U.S. Coast and Geodetic Survey, 26–28, 33, 38, 49
U.S. Office of Weights and Measures, *see* National Bureau of Standards
Uses of the University, The, 139

Van Alstyne, William, 145
Vanderlip, Frank A., 28, 38, 49–51, 86, 164, 213*n*35

Varney, Harold Lord, 198
Veblen, Thorstein, 22
Veysey, Laurence R., 126, 202
vocational education, 32–33, 86–89, 140–141
Volstead Act, 175
voluntary associations, 176–178, 186–187

Wall, Joseph Frazier, 196
Wallas, Graham, 1
Waxman, Julia, 197
"Wealth," 12, 13, 14–20
Weaver, Warren, 198
Westinghouse, 85
Washington University, 25, 26, 62; Medical School, 72
Welch, William Henry, 62–64
Western Reserve Medical School, 70
Wharton, Clifton R., Jr., 145
White, Andrew D., 8, 48
Wiebe, Robert H., 201
Wilson, R. Jackson, 181–182
Wilson, Woodrow, 37, 164
Whitaker, Ben, 196, 199
women teachers, 88, 97, 189
Wood, Ben D., 104, 105, 108–120
Wright, Carroll D., 14
Wyllie, Irvin G., 200

xenophobia, 76–77, 81–82, 101

Yale University, 110; Medical School, 70
Yerkes, Robert M., 100
Ylvisaker, Paul N., 196

Zinsser, Hans, 198